America Takes Over

1965-67

The Vietnam Experience

America Takes Over

1965-67

by Edward Doyle, Samuel Lipsman,
and the editors of Boston Publishing Company

Boston Publishing Company/Boston, MA

Boston Publishing Company

President and Publisher: Robert J. George
Vice President: Richard S. Perkins, Jr.
Editor-in-Chief: Robert Manning
Managing Editor: Paul Dreyfus

Senior Writers:
  Edward Doyle, Samuel Lipsman, Terrence Maitland, Stephen Weiss
Senior Picture Editor: Julene Fischer

Staff Writers: Clark Dougan, Peter McInerney
Researchers:
  Michael T. Casey, Kerstin Gorham, Scott Kafker, Denis Kennedy, Jane T. Merritt, Richard Schorske, Glenn Wallach

Picture Researchers: Wendy K. Johnson, Kathleen A. Reidy
Picture Staff:
  Martha Davidson, Shirley L. Green (Washington, D.C.), Kate Lewin (Paris), Mira Schachne (New York)
Picture Assistant: Kathryn Steeves

Historical Consultants:
  David P. Chandler, Vincent H. Demma, Lee Ewing, Ernest May
Picture Consultant: Ngo Vinh Long

Assistant Editors: Karen E. English, Jeffrey L. Seglin

Production Coordinator: Douglas B. Rhodes
Production Editor: Patricia Leal Welch
Editorial Production:
  Pamela George, Elizabeth Hamilton, Amy P. Wilson

Design: Designworks, Sally Bindari

Circulation Manager: Jane Colpoys
Business Staff:
  James D. Burrows, Christine E. Geering, Jeanne C. Gibson, Darlene Keefe, Kathleen A. Rushton, Elizabeth Schultz

About the editors and authors

Editor-in-Chief *Robert Manning*, a long-time journalist, has previously been editor-in-chief of the *Atlantic Monthly* magazine and its press. He served as assistant secretary of state for public affairs under Presidents John F. Kennedy and Lyndon B. Johnson. He has also been a fellow at the Institute of Politics at the John F. Kennedy School of Government at Harvard University.

Authors: *Edward Doyle*, an historian, received his masters degree at the University of Notre Dame and his Ph.D. at Harvard University. *Samuel Lipsman*, a former Fulbright Scholar, received his M.A. and M.Phil. in history at Yale. Mr. Doyle and Mr. Lipsman have coauthored other volumes in *The Vietnam Experience*.

Historical Consultants: *David P. Chandler*, a former U.S. foreign service officer, is research director of the Centre of Southeast Asian Studies at Monash University in Melbourne, Australia. His major publications include *In Search of Southeast Asia: A Modern History* (coauthor) and *The Land and People of Cambodia*. *Vincent H. Demma*, an historian with the U.S. Army Center of Military History, is currently working on the center's history of the Vietnam conflict. *Lee Ewing*, editor of *Army Times*, served two years in Vietnam as a combat intelligence officer with the U.S. Military Assistance Command, Vietnam (MACV) and the 101st Airborne Division. *Ernest May* is Charles Warren Professor of History at Harvard University.

Picture Consultant: *Ngo Vinh Long* is a social historian specializing in China and Vietnam. Born in Vietnam, he returned there most recently in 1980. His books include *Before the Revolution: The Vietnamese Peasants Under the French* and *Report From a Vietnamese Village*.

Cover photo:
Men of the 1st Cavalry Division (Airmobile) leave their base at An Khe to conduct a search and destroy mission in the A Shau Valley.

Library of Congress Catalog Card Number: 82-61227

ISBN: 0-939526-03-4

10 9 8 7 6

Contents

War Footing

There were no presidential speeches proclaiming crusades "to make the world safe for democracy" or days which "shall live in infamy." There were no Congressional declarations or United Nations resolutions. There were no banner headlines or home front mobilizations. But in April of 1965, America was at war.

Already, on March 8, two marine battalions totaling 3,500 men had landed at Da Nang. Now, in mid-April, they were joined by two more battalions to augment the marine forces at Da Nang, as well as to establish a new base at Phu Bai, forty-five miles north of Da Nang near Hue. By April 20 the 9th Marine Expeditionary Brigade (MEB), as the marine contingent commanded by Brigadier General Frederick J. Karch was named, totaled 8,607 men, including one full battalion (the 3d Battalion of the 4th Marines, or 3/4) and ten UH-34 helicopters at Phu Bai.

In early May the first U.S. Army ground combat unit arrived in South Vietnam. The 173d

Airborne Brigade landed in Vung Tau, at the mouth of the Saigon River. They would soon establish their headquarters at Bien Hoa, twelve miles north of Saigon, guarding the airfield there. At the same time, the marines were establishing their third tactical area of responsibility (TAOR) at a newly constructed airfield in Chu Lai (see map, page 14). By the end of May approximately 20,000 American combat troops—seven marine battalions and supporting units and two army battalions—had swollen the ranks of American forces in Vietnam to 46,500.

The troops were digging in to fight a war. But the combat troops of the American armed forces represented only the head of a body with a very long tail—the logistical support. The marines had been the first to take on a combat role in Vietnam precisely because their tail was the shortest. They carried what they needed with them. But as the build-up continued throughout 1965 the logistical needs became greater and greater, a massive problem that commanding General William Westmoreland needed more than a year to solve. A few statistics show the immensity of the problem: By December 31, 1965, almost 1.3 million tons of dry cargo had been shipped to Vietnam from the United States, over $35 million worth of construction had been completed, and some seventy-five million barrels of petroleum products—gasoline, oil, and lubricants (POL)—had been consumed along with fifty thousand tons of ammunition. In all, one hundred sixty-five thousand tons of cargo were reaching Vietnamese ports and airfields each month.

Back in the United States these statistics, while unnoticed by many, took on real meaning for some Americans. The workers at the Oscar Mayer plant in Madison, Wisconsin, were turning out 2.6 million canned hams for shipment to the troops. From Chicago the Borg-Warner Company began sending more than seven hundred thousand steel helmets for the army, which had procured no new helmets since 1958. In Huntsville, Alabama, Safety First Shoe was working on an order for 253,907 pairs of nylon-topped jungle boots, while de Rossi & Son was shipping one hundred thousand tropical raincoats from its plant in Vineland, New Jersey. These purchases were insignificant compared to the $58 million order placed with Kaiser Jeep and the two hundred and fifty million dollars in orders the army placed for some sixteen hundred helicopters.

There were other ways in which the new war in Vietnam was impinging on an otherwise quiet American home front. The television networks began the construction of additional telephone lines between Vietnam and Hawaii to facilitate increased coverage. By midsummer all three networks had sent their first full-time correspondents to Vietnam, where they were based in Saigon. Garrick Utley of NBC, Malcolm Browne of ABC, and Morley Safer of CBS formed the first trio of an endless number of television reporters who would make Vietnam the first "living room" war. Other media also picked up the beat. In the four months between April 1 and July 31, 1965, *Time* and *Newsweek* each ran four cover stories on the war in Vietnam.

For a small minority of Americans the increased tempo of the war began another saga. Fifteen thousand students spent this Easter weekend not lying on the beaches of Fort Lauderdale, but marching at the White House in America's first national antiwar protest. Two weeks later college campuses across the nation, hooked up by closed-circuit television, presented a new cultural phenomenon—the Vietnam teach-in. Even Las Vegas felt the impact. Nevada's marriage business experienced a record rush in late August as young men flocked to the state for "quickie" weddings to meet the August 26 deadline for deferment from the draft by reason of marriage.

There were other stories in the news that seemed to have little to do with Vietnam: Three teenagers from the affluent California suburb of Carpinteria were arrested for growing marijuana in their back yards; school officials began preparing to combat a new problem—long hair and other violations of long-standing school dress codes. They were isolated stories expressing uneasiness about the path of the new generation. That they would merge with the news from Vietnam to extend the dimensions of America's Vietnam experience was foreseen by few.

For the American servicemen stationed in Vietnam, long hair, which regulations defined as anything over three inches on top, could still be found only on the base barbershop floor. And they didn't have to watch the six o'clock news to know that a war was going on. Still, they were happy in late April to hear President Johnson officially declare all of Vietnam a combat zone, retroactive to January 1, 1965. It not only meant that they would all receive combat pay but provided certain tax advantages. The entire compensation of enlisted men and the first $6,000 of officers pay were exempted from federal income tax. And if it made any difference to them, Washington told them that they were no longer fighting a "guerrilla war." In Pentagonese the Vietnam War would be classified as "limited conventional" because units larger than 4,000 men were operating in the field.

The enclave strategy

Whether it was called a guerrilla war or a limited conventional war, the marines guarding the air base at Da Nang knew that they were fighting a war. But they had little idea of what their objectives were or how they were to be deployed.

Preceding page. Soldiers from the U.S. Army 101st Airborne Division arrive at Cam Ranh Bay aboard the U.S.N.S. General Le Roy Eltinge in July 1965.

Marine recruits go through processing at Parris Island, South Carolina. As the war in Vietnam widened, even the marines, who had a proud tradition of accepting only volunteers, began to rely on the draft.

When the marines first landed in Da Nang on March 8, 1965, their sole mission was to guard the airfield. The secret National Security Action Memorandum (NSAM 328) of April 6 had broadened their mission "to permit their more active use under conditions to be established and approved by the Secretary of Defense." But NSAM 328 failed to provide any coherent strategy. Maxwell Taylor, the U.S. ambassador to South Vietnam and one of the last opponents to the use of American combat troops, sought to severely restrict their activity. In an embassy cable to Washington, he developed a modified enclave strategy that emphasized security patrols in the immediate environs of the coastal air bases American servicemen were guarding—the enclaves. They were, however, authorized to serve as a reserve strike force but only within a fifty-mile radius of their bases. Care was taken to insure that the

marines would have their backs to the sea to facilitate a constant flow of supplies from the American-controlled sea lanes.

Under General Westmoreland's urging, NSAM 328 also approved the deployment of an additional eighteen to twenty thousand men to "fill out existing units and supply needed logistic personnel." The accent was on the latter. Westmoreland was preparing the ground for the possible deployment of more troops. Taylor reluctantly approved, noting that "these engineers can be very useful in SVN [South Vietnam] whether or not we ever introduce additional divisions."

On April 20, Ambassador Taylor, joined by General Westmoreland, met in Honolulu with Defense Secretary Robert McNamara, William Bundy from the State Department, Joint Chiefs of Staff Chairman General Earle G.

With the war heating up in mid-1965, the McDonald Aircraft plant in St. Louis rushes the construction of Phantom F-4 jet fighters.

Wheeler, and other high officials to plan the next phase of the build-up. A request by Westmoreland for seventeen maneuver (or infantry-type) battalions and the necessary support troops was granted. An additional deployment of 40,000 troops, including 7,000 from "Third Country" allies Korea and Australia, was authorized. Four brigade-sized enclaves were to be established at Chu Lai, Qui Nhon, Quang Ngai, and Bien Hoa. When all had closed in Vietnam total U.S. strength would reach 82,000, although the men from the 173rd Airborne were considered to be only on temporary duty.

The greater flexibility of deployment authorized by NSAM 328 was greeted with joy at Da Nang. Taylor predicted that the worst enemy of American troops would be boredom, calling their air base defense "an inglorious static defensive mission unappealing to them." Experiences during March proved Taylor correct. The marines were restricted to an eight-square-mile TAOR around the air base and failed to engage the Vietcong even once. The enemy inflicted no casualties on American ground troops. The first Americans killed on patrol were shot by another marine. Having lost their way in the dark, two marines came upon their third partner from the rear. He turned and fired.

On April 20, after extensive discussions with the ARVN I Corps commander, Major General Nguyen Chanh Thi, who believed that the marines were "not ready to operate . . . in enemy country," the marines began to patrol beyond the perimeters of the TAORs, as far as six miles in front of their former positions. Finally, on April 22 a patrol from Company D, 3rd Reconnaissance Battalion, 3rd Division found a VC force estimated at one hundred and five men nine miles southwest of Da Nang. A company from the 1st Battalion, 3rd Marines was helilifted into the area to help pursue the enemy. But the Vietcong were not ready to fight the Americans and vanished. One VC was killed and one marine wounded.

A single enemy KIA proved to be a lot in those early spring months of 1965. In mid-May Sergeant Robert Robinson said, "I just can't believe this ain't Camp Pendleton. I keep expecting somebody to come out here any minute and say that maneuvers are over and we can go home." One night the sky lit up with flares. Some of the marines thought that maybe the VC were finally attacking. But Sergeant Robinson knew better. "It's probably those damned monkeys playing around with the trip flares again," he said. Monkeys they were; an otherwise uneventful night passed.

Early lessons

Maybe the marines were lucky. The quiet months of spring gave them an opportunity to learn about the war they were fighting. There were many things to learn and first came names. On May 6 the 9th MEB became the III Ma-

rine Expeditionary Force only to change its name one day later at the request of the U.S. Embassy to the III Marine Amphibious Force (III MAF). The French had called their troops an Expeditionary Force, and the marines wanted to avoid that unfortunate reminder to the Vietnamese population. Less than one month later the marines received a new commander, Major General Lewis W. Walt, who commanded III MAF until 1967 and was then appointed assistant commandant of the Marine Corps in 1968.

The marines also began to learn more about their TAOR. Intelligence revealed that within twenty-five miles of Da Nang seven Vietcong combat units totaling 560 men were operating and that there were 1,480 troops within a fifty-mile radius. But they knew little of their day-to-day movement or their relation to the civilian population. One marine staff officer said simply, "intelligence of what the situation was, was nonexistent." By the end of 1965 they would know more. VC troop strength was low, but the NLF apparatus "permeated the southern portion of the TAOR." The marines estimated that the insurgents controlled one-third of the population in I Corps and influenced another third. The marines found themselves in an exasperating situation—surrounded by VC-controlled territory but confronted by only a small number of enemy soldiers.

Drawing upon this knowledge, the marines quickly learned that it made little sense to sweep through a village, clearing it of VC (if any had remained) and then moving out. The NLF apparatus, nearly invisible because it was civilian, would quickly reestablish control of the village. The lesson was obvious. As General Walt put it, the "marines were into the pacification business."

The earliest marine pacification efforts were ad hoc and sketchy and supplemented the ongoing pacification work of American advisers and ARVN units. Medical officers offered their services to nearby villages; other marines helped coordinate the dispensing of relief from private organizations such as CARE. On June 7, 1965, III MAF issued orders establishing a civic action policy and appointing Major Charles Keever as III MAF civil affairs officer. Civic action was defined as the "term applied to the employment of the military forces of a nation in economic and social activities which are beneficial to the population as a whole." General Walt said that the goal of civic action was to "build up the [South Vietnamese] government by providing it with the respect and loyalty of its citizens."

Marine pacification efforts were not limited to promoting the cooperation and enlisting the good will of the Vietnamese population. A carefully applied measure of force was employed to place the people under marine control. In early June the 2nd Battalion, 3rd Marines, commanded by Lieutenant Colonel David A. Clement, "convinced" the inhabitants of two hamlets to move about five miles, near the village of Le My, where the marines had already established a strong presence. According to

A transport flight out of Da Nang in spring 1965 turns into a rescue mission. Lance Corporal James C. Farley leaves his door gun to help two wounded marines who have barely made it to Farley's helicopter after theirs was downed by Vietcong machine gunfire.

Clement "the people were hesitant to move—reluctant to give up their homes." But Clement persuaded the people to accept his offer by directing artillery fire close to their hamlets night after night. After the villagers finally agreed to his offer, Clement admitted, "I suppose given a free choice, the people would not have left their hamlet. I influenced their decision by honesty, sincerity, and a hell of a lot of H & I [harassment and interdiction] fires." But Clement justified his actions: "This permitted the battalion to conduct a counterinsurgency campaign based upon the situation as it appeared to the [Vietnamese] people on the ground. This privileged position permitted a great deal of person-to-person confidence to develop, and along with it, a personal commitment to the government cause."

Improvising as they went along, the marines were learning fast. In their view, control of the population was the objective of their operations. As Marine Commandant General Wallace Greene, Jr., put it, "My feeling, a very strong one which I voiced to the Joint Chiefs, was that the real targets in Vietnam were not the VC and the North Vietnamese, but the Vietnamese people." The logic of the war in Vietnam was leading the marines, unconsciously, to approach the strategy of the NLF, employing a combination of conciliation and coercion.

The marines had the luxury in April and May to learn these lessons because, on the ground, the war seemed to be going well for the South Vietnamese. The decision on February 13 to institute Rolling Thunder and bomb North

Farley breaks down after returning to Da Nang. He had saved one of the marines but the other later died, and he had been unable to rescue a third.

Vietnam seemed to have the desired effect of improving ARVN morale. More important, on February 19, Westmoreland received authorization to use American air power *openly* in support of South Vietnamese troops, *within* the boundaries of South Vietnam. In April the inspired South Vietnamese military stole the offensive from the seemingly demoralized Vietcong.

ARVN's day

On April 4 the ARVN 21st Division destroyed an insurgent enclave beside the Communist-held U Minh Forest in the Ca Mau Peninsula. Two Ranger battalions, twelve B-57 jet bombers, and twenty A-1 Skyraiders joined the battle.

Three days later 258 Vietcong lay dead from the onslaught, which cost the lives of twenty-one ARVN soldiers and six American army advisers.

The ARVN offensive gathered momentum on April 15 when 230 South Vietnamese and American fighter-bombers, in the biggest air strike of the war, dropped one thousand tons of bombs on a suspected Vietcong forest enclave in Tay Ninh Province. Throughout the day, bunker-like installations went up in flames and Vietnamese and U.S. Air Force and marine and, for the first time, U.S. Navy aircraft bombarded the area.

On April 29 GVN troops killed eighty-four guerrillas and took thirty-one prisoners along the Co Luong River in Kien Hoa Province, while helicopter fire and American

NORTH VIETNAM

LAOS

I CORPS

CAMBODIA

II CORPS

III CORPS

IV CORPS

Hue
Phu Bai (U.S.)
Da Nang (U.S.)
Chu Lai (U.S.)
Quang Ngai (U.S.)
Kontum
Pleiku
Qui Nhon (U.S.)
Darlac
Song Be
Dong Xoai
Nha Trang (Korean)
Cam Ranh
Tay Ninh
Bien Hoa (U.S.)
Saigon
Vung Tau (U.S.)
U Minh Forest
Bac Lieu

Miles
0   100
Kilometers
0   100

N
S

Spring–Summer 1965

⚪ Allied enclaves

✴ ARVN offensive (April–May 1965)

☆ Major VC spring offensive attacks (May–June 1965)

····· Military corps boundaries

B–57 jet bombers killed an estimated seventy more. American analysts later called the last week of April one of ARVN's most successful to that date. Six VC were claimed killed for every dead GVN soldier.

The government offensive continued into May. On the fourteenth and fifteenth, ARVN defeated two VC battalions (about five hundred troops) near Bac Lieu in Ba Xuyen Province. ARVN claimed 178 insurgents killed.

Despite ARVN's improved performance, U.S. officials remained uneasy. Westmoreland credited the relative lack of Vietcong aggression to their desire to build up their forces for an offensive in the late spring when the monsoon winds would bring rain and heavy cloud cover to hamper U.S. air activities. The central highlands showed subtle signs of Vietcong strength and activity.

Most important, however, was the confirmed presence of a North Vietnamese Army battalion, the 2d Battalion of the 101st Regiment, 325th Division, in Kontum Province. American intelligence had followed the infiltration of the battalion down the Ho Chi Minh Trail into Laos but then had lost it. It was presumed to have broken into smaller units and infiltrated into the central highlands, a fact first noted in February and now confirmed. Vietnamese intelligence claimed that four other NVA battalions were also operating in the area, but American confirmation was lacking.

In May the signs became more ominous. Guerrilla attacks on roads near Saigon increased, and the city daily grew more isolated from the surrounding countryside. Six bridges were blown up on Highway 1 north of Saigon in mid–May, and VC roadblocks increased on Highway 4, connecting the capital to the Mekong Delta. In Saigon the police arrested a Vietcong soldier dressed in an ARVN uniform, reportedly part of a similarly disguised VC unit, and a twenty-man platoon of insurgents disguised as GVN troops staged a daylight attack on a textile mill just five miles north of Saigon on May 13. Daylight raids in general were increasing, a sure sign of NLF confidence.

Slowly the insurgents began to step up their attacks. On May 11 a guerrilla regiment of about fifteen hundred men overran Song Be, the small provincial capital of Phuoc Long Province, north of Saigon. One thousand Vietnamese Rangers and militiamen, assisted by forty U.S. Special Forces advisers, were stationed in the town. The VC held Song Be for seven hours before a heavy U.S. air attack at dawn allowed GVN forces to reoccupy the area. Although Song Be had a population of only two thousand, it marked the first time that a town—and a provincial capital at that—had been held by the guerrillas since Kontum was occupied in 1961. Five U.S. Army advisers and forty-two Vietnamese soldiers died in the attack, while about eighty civilians lost their lives. American advisers later protested the meager defense put up by the Vietnamese regular troops in the onslaught.

The opponents of the Rolling Thunder program had been proven at least partially correct. The boost to ARVN morale turned out to be short-lived. In mid–April the 5th ARVN Division had been mistakenly fired upon by its own jets and was now fearful of the American jets overhead.

On May 18 rain stalled a government offensive twenty miles below the demilitarized zone, a reminder that the coming rains would increasingly hinder government operations. On May 24 the anxious Saigon government launched a major offensive in Kontum Province, where North Vietnamese battalions now reinforced the Vietcong. But the insurgents lay low, avoiding the GVN troops and preparing for their own offensive. They struck six days later, on May 29.

The clouds open

A thick layer of clouds, pregnant with the monsoon rains, covered the hills of the central highlands as Main Force Vietcong units emerged from their secret camps and attacked the 1st Battalion of the South Vietnamese 51st Regiment west of Quang Ngai City. The VC quickly dispensed with the 1st Battalion and then moved to surround and ambush additional troops from the 51st Regiment as they—and their three American advisers—came to the rescue. To the Americans, led by First Lieutenant Donald Robison, the only course of action was to attempt a break out.

When the Vietnamese commander refused to heed their advice, the three Americans chose to make a break alone. Under pursuit by the VC, the advisers managed to reach safety through paddy fields and irrigation trenches. They heard one last intense volley at the ARVN encampment and then silence. The three Americans and twenty-six GVN soldiers were the only survivors to tell of the decimation of the ARVN 51st Regiment.

The next day reinforcements from the 39th Vietnamese Rangers attempted a counteroffensive. They were almost immediately ambushed but managed to take a small hill after suffering heavy casualties. Late that night Staff Sergeant Willie D. Tyrone radioed back that "Everything is quiet." "We'll try to get in there at first light and pull you out," headquarters responded. Next morning helicopters found the hill strewn with bodies of Vietcong and government troops. Willie Tyrone's was among them.

The Vietcong, whose numbers were never determined, were finally dislodged from their position when American jet pilots were able to saturate the area with bombs. But other VC units struck in Darlac, Pleiku, and Phu Bon provinces, wiping out another Vietnamese battalion. In the first week of the offensive the government had lost more than one thousand of its best troops. General Nguyen Chanh Thi, GVN commander of I Corps, admitted that only American air power had saved Quang Ngai Province. Defense Department analysts later reported that "the ARVN commanders on the scene had displayed tactical stupidity and cowardice."

Worse was to come. In mid-June two regiments of the Vietcong attacked a Special Forces camp and district headquarters at Dong Xoai. The ARVN command sent reinforcements only piecemeal, and they were chopped up by the guerrillas. The battle raged for four days and almost required the first commitment of an American battalion, one from the U.S. 173d Airborne Brigade, to save the ARVN unit before the VC retreated and government troops reoccupied the city. It was the bitterest fighting yet of the war. In the second week of June ARVN casualties doubled the previous record high. By the end of June MACV considered five ARVN regiments and nine separate battalions "combat ineffective" due to the manpower shortages resulting from the heavy casualties, up from two regiments and three battalions on May 31. And as for ARVN claims that VC casualties had exceeded their own, Defense Department analysts could only respond that if true, they "were a mute testimony to the enemy's regenerative capability."

The scope of Vietcong attacks had surpassed all Ameri-

Accompanied by their American advisers, ARVN ground troops advance on an enemy position in April 1965. That April was one of ARVN's most effective fighting months.

can expectations, and MACV felt obliged to revise its estimate of enemy strength. As late as March 17, 1965, MACV had estimated Vietcong strength at thirty-seven thousand troops and one hundred thousand irregulars. On July 21 MACV increased its estimates by one-third. Even these new figures probably were conservative and did not include the recently infiltrated NVA troops. More important, because the insurgents required less logistical support, they could put 72 fighting battalions into the field to counter 133 infantry-type ARVN battalions. The government's advantage had dipped below two to one in a situation in which ten to one was considered desirable.

Westmoreland: more troops

The devastation of the Vietcong spring offensive put tremendous pressure on Washington to enlarge the role of American servicemen. On June 7 General Westmoreland sent a long, pessimistic cable to Admiral Ulysses S. Grant Sharp, commander in chief of Pacific forces (CINCPAC), and the JCS, detailing the situation on the ground in South Vietnam. Westmoreland's goals were twofold: He wanted more American combat troops committed, and he wanted restrictions lifted on their deployment within South Vietnam.

Westmoreland painted a grim picture of the situation on the ground in South Vietnam. "So far," he said, "the VC have not employed their full capabilities in this campaign. . . . The Vietcong are capable of mounting regimental-size [approximately two-thousand-man] operations in all four ARVN corps areas, and at least battalion-sized attacks in virtually all provinces. . . . ARVN forces on the other hand are already experiencing difficulty in coping with this increased VC capability. Desertion rates are inordinately high. Battle losses have been higher than expected." After pointing out that ARVN had lost the equivalent of four battalions in the offensive, Westmoreland reported that a newly instituted program to expand ARVN would have to be used, at least until November, just to fill the holes in existing units decimated by the offensive. Westmoreland concluded: "I see no course of action open to us except to reinforce our efforts in SVN with additional U.S. or Third Country forces as rapidly as is practical during the critical weeks ahead."

This cable initiated the so-called "forty-four battalion request," in which Westmoreland asked that American troop strength in Vietnam be increased from fifty thousand to over two hundred thousand. The months of June and July would see another soul-searching appraisal of the situation in Vietnam by senior U.S. officials again wondering if there were, indeed, any limits to the escalation.

The American troops in their enclave bases had been spared the brunt of the enemy offensive which was concentrated around Saigon and in the central highlands. But shortly after midnight on July 1 the marines guarding the air base at Da Nang got their first taste of heavy Vietcong firepower. Late on the night before, a heavily armed VC attack force consisting of a special operations company and a mortar company crossed the Cau Do River south of Da Nang. By midnight they reached the southeastern perimeter of the air base, knowing that the outer portion of the southern perimeter was guarded by ARVN troops rather than U.S. Marines. Digging under the outer perimeter fence, a thirteen-man demolition team then crossed an open area and cut a hole in the inner perimeter fence. A single marine sentry, hearing something in the dark, threw an illumination grenade.

At that moment the enemy opened fire and ten demolitions experts raced onto the airfield. They destroyed an F-102 Corvair and two C-130 transport planes and damaged another F-102 and a C-130. Lieutenant Colonel Verle E. Ludwig immediately sent a reinforcing squad from Company C of his 1st Battalion, 9th Marines. But in those few minutes the enemy withdrew from the field. By 7:00 A.M. Company B from the 1/9 was searching the area for the sappers. Fourteen suspects were rounded up, but none was connected to the attack. ARVN soldiers did find a wounded North Vietnamese intelligence officer who told them that the attack had been planned and rehearsed for over a month.

In comparison to the events to come, it was a minor attack. But this first assault on a base supposedly secured by American troops generated world-wide publicity and a call to General Walt early that morning from the White House watch officer (but not from President Johnson himself). It pointed out the need for the marines to expand their operations around the air base to prevent the enemy from building up for future attacks.

On July 2, one day after the attack, General Walt sought authorization from the ARVN I Corps commander, General Thi, to extend the marine TAOR south of the air base to include the area five miles south of the Cau Do River, the direction from which the attack came. On July 20 General Thi reluctantly agreed, acknowledging that his men could not guarantee the security of the air base. But the extension of the TAOR presented the marines with a new problem. The area south of the Cau Do was densely populated and sympathetic to the VC. Contact between marines and Vietnamese civilians was bound to increase as the marines attempted to secure the area. Within two weeks a Zippo cigarette lighter would ignite the tense situation on the ground—and on the American television screen.

Fire at Cam Ne

On August 3, Company D of the 1st Battalion, 9th Marines, entered a complex of villages known as Cam Ne in an operation conducted with the 3d Marines. Cam Ne was a village with long-standing Communist sympathies, having supported the Vietminh throughout the long French Indochina War. Vietcong regulars, as well as local guerrillas, moved with ease among the population. To differentiate between enemy and civilian was difficult if not impossible for American troops, a condition which was to pose both danger and moral dilemmas for American soldiers throughout the war.

As the marines advanced upon the village they took continual small-arms fire, but upon entering the village they could find no enemy soldiers. Instead, snipers seemed to be directing isolated fire from behind civilian huts. One platoon began to burn the huts. By the marine count, fifty-one huts were demolished. Four marines were wounded. But little was seen of the enemy. They were estimated to total from thirty to one hundred soldiers; no one really knew. Seven enemy were believed dead, but there was no evidence. The VC carried off their dead, wounded,

and weapons. One ten-year-old boy was killed in the crossfire. As evening approached the marines called off the operation.

That evening the American public saw the "Battle of Cam Ne" on their television screens. Morley Safer of CBS News had been lifted by helicopter into Cam Ne with General Walt early on the morning of August 3. On Walter Cronkite's "CBS Evening News" he reported that over one hundred fifty huts had been burned, an estimate later confirmed from the air by Charles Mohr of the *New York Times* but not by the marines. Safer reported that two of the wounded marines had been hit by friendly fire; this

---

A picture seen 'round the world. CBS television cameras capture the moment this marine set fire to a peasant's hut in the village of Cam Ne in August 1965, a scene forcefully reported by CBS correspondent Morley Safer (inset).

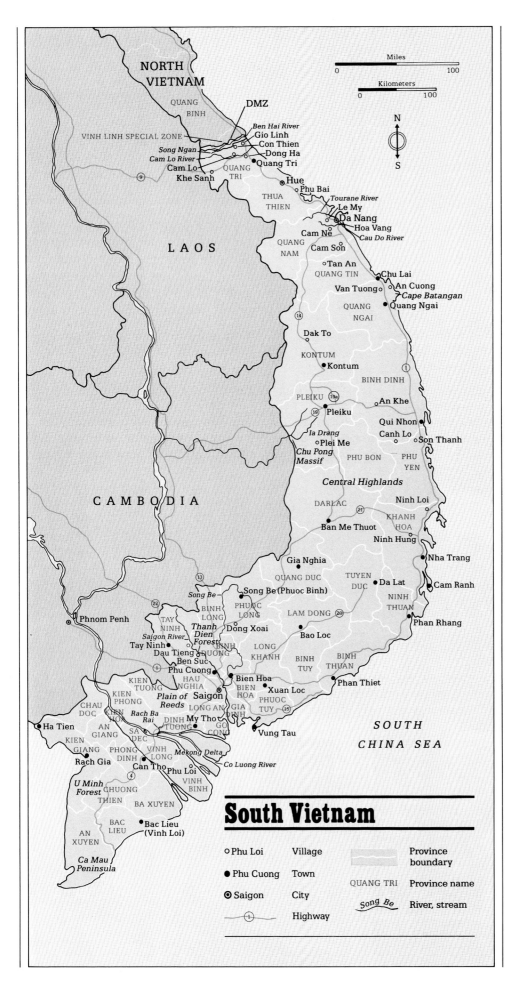

NORTH
VIETNAM

QUANG
BINH

DMZ

VINH LINH SPECIAL ZONE

Ben Hai River
Gio Linh
Con Thien
Song Ngan
Cam Lo River
Dong Ha
Cam Lo
Quang Tri
Khe Sanh
QUANG
TRI

Hue
Phu Bai

THUA
THIEN

Tourane River
Le My
Da Nang
Hoa Vang
Cam Ne
Cau Do River

QUANG
NAM

Cam Son
Tan An
QUANG TIN

Chu Lai
An Cuong
Van Tuong
Cape Batangan
Quang Ngai

QUANG
NGAI

Dak To

KONTUM
Kontum

BINH DINH

PLEIKU
An Khe

Pleiku
Qui Nhon
Canh Lo
Son Thanh
Ia Drang
Plei Me
*Chu Pong
Massif*
PHU BON
PHU
YEN

Central Highlands

DARLAC
Ninh Loi

KHANH
HOA
Ban Me Thuot
Ninh Hung

Gia Nghia
Nha Trang

QUANG DUC
TUYEN
DUC
Da Lat
Cam Ranh

NINH
THUAN

Song Be (Phuoc Binh)
Song Be
PHUOC
LONG
LAM DONG

BINH
LONG
*Thanh
Dien
Forest*
Dong Xoai
Bao Loc
Phan Rhang

TAY
NINH
Saigon River
Tay Ninh
Dau Tieng
Ben Suc
DUONG
LONG
KHANH
BINH
TUY
BINH
THUAN

Phu Cuong
KIEN
TUONG
HAU
NGHIA
Bien Hoa
BIEN
HOA
Xuan Loc
Phan Thiet
KIEN
PHONG
*Plain of
Reeds*
Saigon
PHUOC
TUY

CHAU
DOC
*Rach Ba
Rai*
LONG AN
GIA
DINH
My Tho
GO
CONG

Ha Tien
AN
GIANG
SA
DEC
DINH
TUONG
Vung Tau

KIEN
GIANG
PHONG
DINH
VINH
LONG
Mekong Delta

Rach Gia
Can Tho
Phu Loi
Co Luong River
VINH
BINH

*U Minh
Forest*
CHUONG
THIEN

BA XUYEN

BAC
LIEU
Bac Lieu
(Vinh Loi)

AN
XUYEN

*Ca Mau
Peninsula*

LAOS

CAMBODIA

Phnom Penh

SOUTH
CHINA SEA

South Vietnam

○ Phu Loi	Village		Province boundary
● Phu Cuong	Town		
◉ Saigon	City	QUANG TRI	Province name
		Song Be	River, stream
─①─	Highway		

The Big Build-up

Between March 1965 and early 1968, the number of U.S. military personnel in South Vietnam rose from 29,100 to over half a million. The logistical effort required for this massive troop build-up in an underdeveloped country halfway around the world was enormous. By 1968 monthly shipments of military equipment, ammunition, and supplies to South Vietnam had surpassed World War II figures. Yet at no time during the war was a major tactical operation impeded by a logistical failure. Supplying American troops in South Vietnam was a significant logistical achievement and, as General William Westmoreland pointed out, "Surely ... one of the more remarkable accomplishments of American forces in Vietnam."

In the three years following the decision to escalate, Defense Department expenditures in Southeast Asia not counting economic aid rose from $103 million to $28.8 billion per year, of which over $21.5 billion was directly attributable to the war. During this time over $2.6 billion was spent on construction projects carried out by a combined work force of fifty-one thousand civilians—Vietnamese, U.S., and allied nationals—and fifty-seven construction battalions and squadrons from all the U.S. services. At its peak, MACV's military logistics personnel alone made up 45 percent of all U.S. forces in Vietnam.

was denied by the marines. Safer charged that the marines had taken only one isolated sniper shot after entering the village. "If there were Vietcong in the hamlets they were long gone," Safer stated. Finally, Safer reported that the marines had been ordered to burn down the entire village if they received any enemy fire, a fact never denied by the marines and later confirmed by General Walt. But the image that lived with the American public was that of a solitary marine shown on the TV screen setting fire to a peasant hut with his cigarette lighter.

Safer's reporting and the vivid television pictures set off a wave of indignation that ranged from "highest authority" in the White House to the marines in the field. But Safer defended his reportage: "We'd seen war on television [before]. . . . The American public wasn't new to it; what they were new to was seeing American soldiers."

If nothing else, Cam Ne made it clear to the American public that this was going to be a different sort of war, according to the *Marine Corps Gazette* shortly after the incident, a "brutalizing affair" and one filled with ambiguity. Cam Ne was clearly controlled by the enemy. What did that make the civilian population, enemy or victim? Cam Ne's village huts were certainly fortified with bunkers, but were they for civilian defense or to protect the enemy? A MACV spokesman later admitted that most villages were "fortified." To the American troops, most frustrating of all was that they did not know how to react to an enemy so adept at hit-and-run tactics: destroy his cover or wait to find him? One marine senior officer, an expert on guerrilla warfare, pointed out, "For the first time we're faced with a war that is 80 percent political and 20 percent conventional military. But when a man in the lines is getting shot at, he is prone to consider the war to be 100 percent military." A marine enlisted man was less sympa-

---

To handle the huge amount of cargo being shipped to Vietnam (more than 5.2 million tons by 1968), it was necessary to rehabilitate woefully inadequate South Vietnamese port facilities. There were only twelve deep draft berths in the entire country—ten of which were for civilian use—so American merchant marine ships were forced to wait offshore an average of more than twenty days for a berth. At one point in 1965, at Saigon Harbor, a flotilla of ninety-one anchored ships awaited turns for unloading. To reduce the delay in unloading, construction crews built four major deep water ports, Cam Ranh Bay, Newport (outside Saigon), Da Nang, and Qui Nhon, as well as numerous shallow draft ports. The amount of cargo handled by all South Vietnamese ports increased from 313,000 tons in the month of December 1965 to a peak of 1.3 million tons in December 1968.

The supply line also required extensive improvement of existing transportation and shipping facilities and development of new ones. Unlike the French who had relied primarily upon their vulnerable railroad network to ship cargo, the U.S. mainly used South Vietnam's roads and waterways. Water shipments grew from a few hundred thousand tons in 1965 to over 3 million in the year ending June 1968. Land shipments, negligible in the early stages of 1965, eventually reached a monthly average of over 1.2 million tons for the year ending April 1968—a significant feat given a substandard road system beset by monsoon rains, sabotage, and poor maintenance.

An equally impressive build-up was also achieved in air transportation facilities. By 1968 the number of airfields that could land jets had been expanded to 11 while an additional 200 tactical airfields were established at strategic points around the country. To handle the growing need for in-country passenger transportation, the Common Service Transport Service was established, eventually carrying over three hundred sixty thousand passengers per month.

The Americans' remarkable logistics system had some unforeseen negative side effects. Because of the broad dimensions of its supply system, the Logistical Command was never able to establish set guidelines to monitor and regulate the flow and distribution of goods ranging from military commodities like weapons and ammunition to "luxury items" like air conditioners, steaks, beer, and radios. Each unit tended to requisition supplies independently. Supply catalogs were used, as Major General Joseph Heiser, a former commander of the Logistical Command, noted, "as if they were Sears and Roebuck catalogs." Wishing to give their troops the highest possible level of comfort, commanders often ordered luxuries and other amenities far in excess of standard logistical guidelines.

This attitude found its strongest advocate in General Westmoreland. Westmoreland was keenly aware of the problems of morale in Vietnam—especially those related to controversy over the war. For this reason—and to discourage pressure in the U.S. to "bring our boys home"—he limited each soldier's tour of duty in South Vietnam to 365 days. He also attempted to provide the soldiers with "all the comforts" during their tour. Over 90 percent of the meals, for example, were served hot, often including steak and peaches. Three dairies and forty ice cream plants were dispersed around the country. It was not unheard of for soldiers weary from the torrid heat while on patrol in the bush to be treated to ice cream flown in by helicopter. Shower facilities, both stationary and mobile, could accommodate four hundred twenty thousand soldiers per week by mid-1967, and PXs offered an extraordinary range of specialty items—from pantyhose, lingerie, and diamonds to radios, televisions, and Napoleon brandy.

The U.S. Army fought in Vietnam equipped with all the conveniences that the world's richest nation could provide. For the Vietnamese peasant who subsisted on a dwindling lot, the stream of American goods pouring into the country brought little benefit and frequently generated resentment. One of the ironies of the struggle to win the trust and good will of the Vietnamese people was that the strength of the U.S., its wealth, was in some ways a liability.

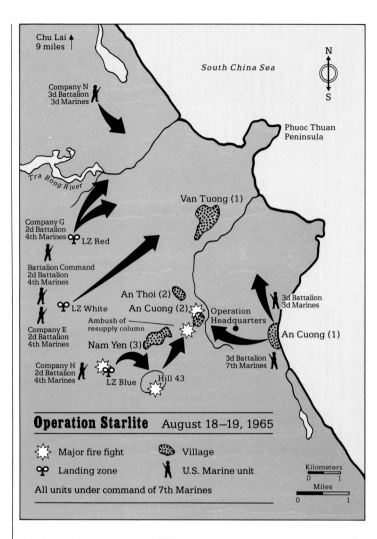

Chu Lai
9 miles

South China Sea

N

S

Company N
3d Battalion
3d Marines

Phuoc Thuan
Peninsula

Tra Bong River

Van Tuong (1)

Company G
2d Battalion
4th Marines   LZ Red

Battalion Command
2d Battalion
4th Marines

An Thoi (2)

LZ White   An Cuong (2)

Operation
Headquarters

3d Battalion
3d Marines

Ambush of
resupply column

An Cuong (1)

Company E
2d Battalion
4th Marines

Nam Yen (3)

3d Battalion
7th Marines

Company H
2d Battalion
4th Marines

LZ Blue   Hill 43

Operation Starlite August 18–19, 1965

Major fire fight   Village

Landing zone   U.S. Marine unit

Kilometers
0   1

Miles
0   1

All units under command of 7th Marines

thetic to his comrades: "There are always two ways to do something—the right way and the John Wayne way. We might as well do it the right way."

Cam Ne capped nearly five months of frustration for the marines in the Da Nang area. They were the first to be exposed to the heat and rains of Vietnam, the first to be sniped at and booby trapped by the guerrillas, and yet they were unable to find and engage the real enemy: the VC Main Force units. On August 15 they received their first break. A deserter from the Vietcong 1st Regiment informed General Thi of a major build-up of enemy Main Force units in the Van Tuong village complex, twelve miles southeast of Chu Lai along the coast. The VC goal was to achieve a great psychological victory by surprising the isolated marine base at Chu Lai in the first major engagement between American and enemy forces.

Operation Starlite

General Thi, informing none of his own subordinates, immediately relayed the information to General Walt. Marine intelligence had by this time received sufficient evidence on its own to corroborate the deserter's story. Colonel Edwin Simmons, newly arrived operations officer for III MAF, recommended a "spoiling attack" to prevent

the anticipated VC strike against Chu Lai. The timing was fortuitous. The arrival of reinforcements at the Chu Lai base on August 14 enabled Walt to reassign two experienced combat battalions, 2d Battalion of the 4th Marines *(or 2/4), and 3d Battalion, 3d Marines (3/3), to the command of Colonel Oscar F. Peatross, commander of the 7th Marines. In addition, another marine battalion, afloat offshore, served as a reserve force that could be thrown into the battle when and where necessary. Finally, two U.S. Navy ships in the area, the U.S.S. *Galveston* and U.S.S. *Cabildo*, could provide offshore fire support. The operation, code-named Starlite, would be a classic marine encounter, combining land and sea forces, including an amphibious landing and coordination with the navy. It would be a very different battle for the Vietcong, accustomed to fighting with their backs to the sea, knowing that against South Vietnamese forces the water could always be used as an avenue of escape.

Conducting an aerial reconnaissance of the operational area, which was about ten miles south of Chu Lai, Colonel Peatross found that the terrain was dominated by sandy flats, broken by numerous streams and an occasional wooded knoll. The scattered hamlets possessed paddy areas and dry crop fields. While airborne, Peatross selected the assault beach as well as three landing zones among the sand flats, about one mile inland from the coast.

Operation Starlite began inauspiciously at 10:00 A.M. on August 17, when Company M of the 3d Battalion, 3d Marines, took a short ride south of Chu Lai before marching four miles farther south and camping for the night just north of Van Tuong. They met only light resistance and, since marine patrols in the area had been frequent, aroused no suspicion. Seven hours after Company M departed, the rest of the 3/3 and the command group embarked on three amphibious ships which, after a decoy maneuver, arrived in the area of the landing beach at five in the morning of August 18. Fifteen minutes before the 6:30 A.M. H-hour, marine artillery and jets began to pound the three landing zones west of Van Tuong, LZ Red, LZ White, and LZ Blue (see map, this page). Eighteen tons of bombs and napalm were dropped, adding to the firing of 155MM guns. At H-hour the troops of the 3/3 began their beach assault and pushed inland as planned. At 6:45 A.M. Company G of the 2/4 landed at LZ Red, while Company E landed at LZ White and Company H landed at LZ Blue forty-five minutes later. The 3/3 approached Van Tuong from the south, while companies E, G, and H of 2/4 were to move in from the west. Company M blocked any retreat to the north by the VC, and the navy ships prevented an escape to the east via the South China Sea. Van Tuong

---

*The marines do not use the word "regiment" to designate their units; "4th Marines" refers to the 4th Marine Regiment; "3d Marines" the 3d Marine Regiment, and so on.

and the Vietcong were surrounded. For the most part, the marines met little resistance as they closed in, but fierce fighting broke out near LZ Blue.

In the Vietnam War, intelligence was never precise, and Company H had landed right in the middle of the Vietcong 60th Battalion and found itself surrounded. The VC let the first helicopters land without incident, then opened up on succeeding waves, a tactic they had used so successfully against ARVN. Three U.S. Army UH-1B helicopter gunships were called in to strafe the VC stronghold, a small knoll just east of LZ Blue called Hill 43. (Hills were given numerical distinctions according to their height in meters.) Meanwhile the infantry protected the LZ until the full company had landed. Company H commander, First Lieutenant Homer K. Jenkins, ordered an assault on the hill by one platoon, but it quickly stalled. Regrouping his men, and realizing that he had happened upon a heavy concentration of VC, Jenkins ordered in air strikes against Hill 43 and then assaulted it with all three of his platoons. Reinforced by close air support and tanks,

the marines overran the enemy position, claiming six KIA at one machine-gun position alone. Hill 43 was taken.

Heavy fighting also took place in the village of An Cuong (2)—approximately two miles northeast of Hill 43—when two platoons of Company I attempted to clear the village of enemy snipers. After an initial setback, the company's reserve platoon was thrown into battle and the troops cleared the village. Company I's commander, Captain Bruce D. Webb, was among those killed in the early fire, and his company executive officer, First Lieutenant Richard M. Purnell, assumed command of the successful counterassault. Purnell counted over fifty enemy bodies when the fighting ended. One Company I squad leader, Corporal Robert E. O'Malley, single-handedly killed eight Vietcong that day and became the first marine to win the Medal of Honor in Vietnam. (Later, a posthumous award was made to Captain Frank S. Reasoner, killed in action in July.)

The most dramatic fighting of the day was the result of another favorite VC tactic: ambushing a relief column. Be-

Marines rush a wounded Vietcong prisoner—one of more than one hundred captured in Starlite—to a Huey helicopter. The sandy terrain of Operation Starlite evoked in veteran reporters memories of the Normandy beachheads, but the rice fields were a reminder that this was a different war.

tween 11:00 A.M. and noon Major Andrew G. Comer sent a resupply column to aid beleaguered Company I. The column, which included three flame tanks, the only tactical fire support available, quickly lost its way. Suddenly, VC recoilless rifle fire and a barrage of mortar rounds rendered the tanks useless in providing fire support. Using only their small arms, the entrapped marines attempted to hold the advancing VC infantry. The marine radio operator panicked and, according to Major Comer, "kept the microphone button depressed the entire time and pleaded for help. We were unable to quiet him sufficiently to gain essential information as to their location." Finally Comer organized a rescue mission, led by the already exhausted Company I and including the only available M48 tank. By luck, one of the trapped flame tanks managed to break through the VC infantry and return to Comer's command post. The crew chief was able to lead the rescue mission to the location of the column. Approaching the besieged supply column, the relief force quickly drew heavy fire. Recoilless rifle fire knocked out the M48. Within minutes five marines lay dead and seventeen wounded. Comer called for artillery fire and air support, and enemy fire soon subsided. As Comer put it, "It was obvious that the VC were deeply dug in, and emerged above ground when we presented them with an opportunity and withdrew whenever we retaliated or threatened them."

The heavy fighting of the first day proved to be the only major contact of the seven-day operation. For Companies H and I it had been an exhausting time. Together the two companies had sustained casualties amounting to over 100 of their original 350 men, including 29 dead, but in return they claimed 281 VC dead.

Aftermath of victory

On August 19, Starlite's second day, sporadic and isolated fire came from enemy soldiers covering their main force's retreat, but organized resistance had ended. The operation extended for five more days with the marines, now joined by ARVN troops, conducting village-by-village searches. At its conclusion the marines could claim 573 confirmed enemy dead and 115 estimated, while suffering 46 deaths themselves and 204 wounded. The battle had been won by overwhelming American firepower. Artillery support from Chu Lai had fired over three thousand rounds while the navy ships had supported the infantry with 1,562 rounds, sunk seven sampans apparently carrying fleeing VC, and pinned down one hundred enemy soldiers attempting to escape from the beach. Moreover, the marines had benefited from the close coordination of tactical air power, a coordination that ARVN never seemed to achieve. General Walt later commented that air support was used "within 200 feet of our pinned down troops and was a very important factor in our winning the battle. I have never seen a finer example of *close* air support." The

marines had won by doing what American troops do best—coordinating their firepower on land, sea, and air. But most important, the marines had learned at least one valuable lesson from Starlite.

At General Thi's insistence no ARVN commander was even aware of the planned operation. At the last moment, General Hoang Xuan Lam, whose men augmented the marines during the second day of operations, was informed of his role. Even American reporters did not arrive on the scene until the second day. As a result the VC were caught by total surprise. Future operations, similar in nature to Starlite, were much less successful. For political reasons the marines had to inform ARVN of future operational plans and thereby risk the likelihood of this knowledge somehow reaching the enemy.

The experience taught many minor lessons as well. The planned ration of two gallons of water per man each day was insufficient in the heat of Vietnam. The M14 automatic rifle proved too heavy and bulky, especially for support troops who often crammed into small personnel carriers, and the search began for a lighter, more maneuverable basic weapon.

Finally, for the marines the operation dramatized the complexity of fighting a war among civilians. Publicly the marines declared that only fortified enemy villages were destroyed, but the official "after-action" report stated: "Instances were noted where villages were severely damaged or destroyed by napalm or naval gunfire, wherein the military necessity of doing so was dubious."

Perhaps the most important outcome of Operation Starlite was its psychological lift. In the first major engagement between American troops and Main Force Vietcong soldiers the Americans had been victorious. Had the American forces lost—a real possibility given their inexperience—the effects might have been severe indeed. The old tactics of the VC, which had worked so well against ARVN, failed to rout the marines. So the enemy learned a lesson as well; it would be many months before they would again stand to fight against the marines.

For the marines, Starlite, or the Battle of Chu Lai as it became known in their lore, took on an almost mythical importance. For those marines who came later and for whom the landings at Iwo Jima and Inchon Beach were the glory of another generation, the Battle of Chu Lai remained for many months the only evidence of what the marines could do if the enemy stood and engaged. Now, in late August 1965 the number of marines—and soldiers, airmen, and sailors—arriving in Vietnam was no longer a trickle, but a torrent. Fateful decisions had been made in Washington, by one man, sitting alone in his office: the president of the United States.

Cam Ranh Bay

The French ship Le Marne weighs anchor opposite a fishing village on Cam Ranh Beach in 1940. Although its beautiful natural harbor had been known to European and Asian mariners since the days of Marco Polo, Cam Ranh Bay was untouched by development until the early 1960s.

Preceding page. A road cut by the 35th Engineer Group bends between two large sand dunes on the U.S. base at Cam Ranh Bay. The most intractable enemy at the immense American military installation was the wind-swept sand that clogged vehicles, buried roads, and shifted under heavy machinery.

Cam Ranh Bay

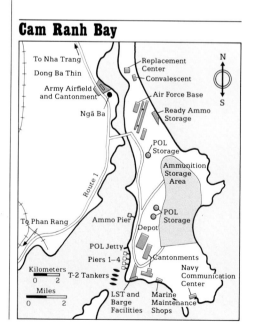

Much has been written about the imprint that America made on Vietnam and its people. Nowhere was this more evident than in the colossal base the U.S. left behind at Cam Ranh Bay. Sprawling across the golden sands of the South China Sea coast, the American complex at Cam Ranh—which in Vietnamese means "sweet stream"—in many ways came to symbolize the vast amount of military resources that the U.S. channeled into its war effort in South Vietnam.

As if drawn from the pages of *South Pacific* in its pristine beauty, Cam Ranh Bay presented newly arriving American soldiers with a sight few expected to see in Vietnam. It was not for its picturesque qualities, however, that the U.S. chose it as the sight of a major base, but for its tremendous, sheltered deep-water bay, one of the finest natural harbors in the world.

The French first called at Cam Ranh Bay in 1847 but chose to use Saigon and Da Nang as their primary ports. Over the next hundred years Cam Ranh Bay was visited by fleets from Russia, Japan, and the U.S., but it was not until 1963 that its potential as a port and military base was

exploited. On May 2 of that year, the first American construction crew—employees of Raymond International and Morrison & Knudson (RMK), two contracting firms working together—began work at the bay, then marked by only a few small fishing villages and miles of untouched beach. (Several years later on a U.S.O. tour, Bob Hope, seeing its long stretch of beaches, called Cam Ranh Bay "the world's largest sand trap.") Within fourteen months, RMK had completed work on its first pier project, making Cam Ranh Bay, along with Saigon, one of the country's deep-water ports.

The early proponent of the development of Cam Ranh Bay was Admiral Harry D. Felt, commander in chief of U.S. Pacific forces. He staunchly advocated

Above. One key to the rapid development of Cam Ranh Bay's port facilities was the Delong Floating Pier (the middle three in the photograph). Shipped piecemeal from factories in the United States and reassembled at Cam Ranh Bay, the piers enabled ships to unload their cargo quickly and efficiently.

Right. Under a searing sun, engineers from the 497th Construction Company drive piles for the construction of a new wharf in April 1965. Afternoon temperatures reaching 125 degrees forced workers to take four-hour breaks in the middle of each day.

the construction of the first deep-water pier at Cam Ranh Bay. Although the pier project was at first ridiculed by some of its critics in the military as "Felt's Folly" because of its isolated location, it played a primary role in America's escalating military commitment in the mid 1960s.

The major build-up of facilities at Cam Ranh began in June of 1965. Elements of the 35th Army Engineer Construction Group were dispatched to work with the RMK team, the first time that the army had worked in conjunction with a private construction group in Vietnam. Cam Ranh presented the engineers with a myriad of problems: lack of fresh water for making concrete, shifting sands, blistering heat, and a labor shortage. The labor problem was eventually solved by a large contingent of South Vietnamese war widows who came to be known as "little tiger ladies." Despite their diminutive stature—they usually stood less than five feet tall and often weighed less than 100 pounds—they proved equal to almost every construction task they undertook.

In the face of many difficulties, the engineers succeeded. To the single pier that had been constructed in 1963, the army and RMK engineers added five more, capable of off-loading four thousand tons of cargo per day, second only to Saigon. The army depot was also expanded to in-

clude over 1.4 million square feet of covered and 1.2 million square feet of open ammunition storage space as well as a POL storage area capable of holding 775,000 barrels of petroleum products. Also built was over 800,000 square feet of maintenance and administrative space along with barracks and recreational facilities.

Facilities were also constructed at Cam Ranh Bay for the navy and air force. The navy developed a base there to support its coast-watching operations—code named Market Time—as well as a major communications center and naval air facility. The air force base at Cam Ranh Bay, the third busiest after Saigon and Da Nang, included a permanent 10,000-foot cement runway and an equally long aluminum mat runway, both capable of handling aircraft ranging from an F-4 to a C-130. The air force also had its own barracks, recreational facilities, and ammunition depot.

Besides these facilities, Cam Ranh was equipped with a permanent laundry, a milk recombining plant built by Meadowgold Dairies, a cold storage area, an oxygen and acetylene plant, a 2,000-bed hospital (the largest of any base in Vietnam), and a power system built by Vinnell Corporation that included five navy T-2 power barges each supplying 25,000 kilo-

watts, and eight land-based generators providing 1,100 kilowatts apiece.

When Cam Ranh Bay was completed, a city had arisen almost from nothing. The base housed and employed almost twenty thousand enlisted men and officers and stretched out over an area fifteen miles long and almost five miles wide. It was, as one ARVN soldier explained, "like a small piece of the U.S. in Vietnam." Ironically, this immense complex, built at a cost of over $2.2 billion, is today a port of call for the Soviet navy.

Above. POL tanks at Cam Ranh stored much of the fuel used by the American military in South Vietnam. By 1969 steel tanks had replaced rubber bladders previously used to store oil.

Above right. An American C-5A transport takes off from Cam Ranh Bay. Cam Ranh developed into a major air terminal serving all four corps areas.

Right. In August 1972 a Vietnamese walks the deserted streets of the once-busy base. When the U.S. left, much of Cam Ranh was reclaimed by the ever-shifting sand.

LBJ: Commander in Chief

If he was generous, sometimes to a fault, he demanded loyalty and gratitude in return. If he promised more than he could deliver, he delivered more than most men dared promise. If he often played loose with the truth to gain power, he used power to help people. If he talked liberal with the liberals and conservative with the conservatives, it was because he honestly could not admit to being either. If he struggled to do what was right, he was nearly incapable of admitting when he was wrong. If he believed in himself and what he could become, he would try almost anything that would make others believe in him as well.

At six-foot three and 212 pounds he was big, like the state he came from. He was brash and vulgar ("I never trust a man unless I've got his pecker in my pocket"), brilliant and sensitive. He could be vindictive and petty and compassionate and selfless, narrow-minded and bigoted and tolerant and idealistic, and all at the same time.

He was, in short, so much like the nation he led that America would rise with his unbounded idealism and anguish with his long frustration. This was Lyndon Baines Johnson, thirty-sixth president of the United States.

He even had his own "Uncle Sam," Sam Rayburn, Speaker of the House of Representatives. Lyndon Johnson owed his success to his native qualities: his relentless determination, the brilliance of his political intuition. But he made his political career thanks to Mister Sam, who took the young Lyndon Baines Johnson, a little-known secretary to an archconservative Texas congressman, Richard Kleberg, and championed him, improbably, as the New Dealer's New Dealer. Mister Sam delivered a behind-the-scenes arm twist in June 1935 and secured for his twenty-six-year-old protégé an extraordinary political plum: the Texas state directorship of the $50 million per year National Youth Administration. Lyndon Johnson crisscrossed the vast territory of Texas carving out for his state greater and greater shares of the New Deal pie. He earned acclaim from Eleanor Roosevelt among others as perhaps the best NYA director in the country.

In 1937, at the young age of twenty-eight, Lyndon Johnson was already master of a form of patronage. With NYA jobs as both carrot and stick, he constructed a political network spanning the whole of Texas. That spring he joined the fight to fill a Congressional seat vacated by death. Never one to miss a trend or ground swell, Johnson harnessed himself securely to the FDR bandwagon. Preaching the new faith of rural electrification and river development, Johnson distinguished himself from a crowded field of contenders. It was a successful move and bold, too, for deep conservatism was still endemic in the Texas hill country when Lyndon Johnson became Congressman Johnson in 1937.

On the banks of the Pedernales

The farm lands in the hills of central Texas were flat, dry, and exposed. When the wind would blow, the soil would blow with it. Lyndon Johnson's grandfather, Sam Ealy Johnson, had settled that land in the 1850s and served in the Confederate army. He became a rancher and cattleman, often on the brink of financial disaster. The poor Johnson homestead on the north bank of the Pedernales River in Blanco County, Texas, eventually passed to Sam Ealy's son, Sam Ealy, Jr.

Despite his near poverty and reputation as a hard drinker, Sam Ealy, Jr., made a good marriage. Rebekah Baines Johnson's father, Joseph Baines, was a lawyer, educator, and lay preacher in the Baptist church. Mr.

Baines had served as Texas secretary of state and in the Texas legislature. He even made the highly unusual gesture, for 1904, of sending his daughter to Baylor University. While Rebekah was studying literature at Baylor, disaster struck. Joseph Baines lost all his money in one errant speculation. Shortly thereafter he died, and in 1907 Rebekah married Sam Ealy Johnson; Lyndon was born little more than a year later.

As a father, Sam Ealy was a taskmaster, submitting his son to humiliating tests of manhood. Johnson frequently alluded to these trials throughout his life. He recalled, "I carried a gun and every now and then I pointed it at the animals, but I never wanted to kill any of them." Finally his daddy asked him why he was the only boy who never shot an animal. Lyndon went out and killed a rabbit. "Then I went to the bathroom and threw up," he recalled. Later in life, Johnson seemed compelled to inflict these trials on others. As vice president, he all but forced one unwilling guest to shoot at and kill a deer, and the guest had felt a queasiness identical to young Lyndon's. That guest was President John Kennedy.

Johnson endured the demands of his father, never condemning him, but he was equally influenced by the more compassionate values of his mother, the student of literature. When Lyndon finished high school the conflict between the two sets of values became acute. Rebekah encouraged him to attend college, but Lyndon Johnson later recalled that he feared "it would make me a sissy again and I would lose my daddy's respect." After spending a year in California working for a law firm, Johnson found his calling and returned to Texas for a college education, choosing a career that would appease both parents:

I would become a political figure. Daddy would like that. He would consider it a manly thing to be. But that would be just the beginning. I was going to reach beyond my father. I would finish college; I would build great power and gain high office. Mother would like that. I would succeed where her own father failed. I would go to the Capitol and talk about big ideas. She would never be disappointed in me again.

The Treatment

The Congress that Lyndon Johnson joined in 1937 was filled with talk of big ideas. More important, however, was the action, making the big ideas of the New Deal the law of the land. Lyndon Johnson was in the thick of it, especially when the pork barrel was opened. Half a dozen dams for vital irrigation and flood control, a $70 million rural electrification cooperative, the biggest in the whole country, and federal loans and mortgages made the Johnson Congressional district a showcase for the plenitude of the New Deal. Most of the credit belonged to Congressman Johnson and his style of politics that gained such achievement, a style so personal that it earned its own title: "The Johnson Treatment."

Preceding page. Deep thought in the Oval Office, May 1966. President Johnson (right) confers with two of his closest aides, Special Assistant Walt Rostow (left) and Secretary of State Dean Rusk (center).

Johnson got so many things done not because he did them himself, but because he could get others to do the things he could not attend to personally. If Johnson needed a favor, especially a series of favors, he would first try flattery. One of the men near Johnson called him "smiling and deferential," then added, "But hell, lots of people can be smiling and deferential. He had something else. No matter what a guy thought, Lyndon would agree with him—would be there ahead of him, in fact. He could follow a guy's mind around and figure out where it was going and beat it there."

If flattery failed, Johnson would try empathy, presenting himself not only as an admirer, but as an embattled colleague in arms. Secretary of State Dean Rusk put it simply: "There is no person in America that can equal Johnson in knee-to-knee conversation with another man."

The trump card in the Johnson Treatment was his incredible conviction. He would stand or sit very close to men, he would touch them, and he would convey an intensity and sincerity that was overwhelming. "What convinces is conviction," Johnson would say. "You simply *have* to believe in the argument you are advancing; if you don't you're as good as dead." Johnson liked to tell the story of a young, unemployed schoolteacher who came to the Texas hill country in the depression in search of a job. When the local school board asked him whether the world was round or flat the young candidate panicked, fearing a trap. Finally he blurted out, "I can teach it both ways." It was one of Johnson's favorite stories; LBJ could always teach it both ways—and believe himself both times.

He could do so because he was unconscious of possessing any firm ideology, unless his instinctive populism could be called an ideology. Dogmatic consistency and elegant logic were not crucial ingredients in Lyndon Johnson's art of persuasion. The Treatment could survive on conviction alone.

Disorderly conviction

Johnson once remarked, "No president ever had a problem of doing what is right, the big problem is knowing what is right." Yet Lyndon Johnson was a man who valued action far more than reflective thought, a man who was more at ease "doing what is right" than in "knowing what is right." Robert Komer, Johnson's leading adviser on the complex problem of pacification in Vietnam, commented that "LBJ had no particular grasp of foreign cultures. He felt no particular need to delve into what made Vietnamese Vietnamese, as opposed to Americans or Greeks or Chinese." The notion that all peoples are responsive to material concerns particularly animated Johnson, who had grown up knowing poverty. When during the Vietnam War he announced the idea of an Asian development bank that would sponsor TVA-like projects for the Vietnamese he could not understand why Ho Chi Minh

did not leap at the chance. As Johnson's close presidential adviser, Bill Moyers, once commented, "He'd say, 'My God, I've offered Ho Chi Minh $100 million to build a Mekong Valley. If that'd been George Meany, he'd have snapped at it!'"

A revolution based on ideological conviction was something utterly foreign to Johnson's way of thinking. Rather, Johnson's view of foreign policy was based on a few simple lessons he learned from World War II. He had served in the war for only six months (including an inspection tour of the Pacific as a navy officer) before President Roosevelt ordered all members of Congress to return to their legislative duties. From his brief war experience, Johnson concluded that war came about because of two things: "a lust for power on the part of a few evil leaders and . . . a weakness on the part of the people whose love for peace often displays a lack of courage."

In Johnson's mind dealing with international aggression differed little from handling a neighborhood bully. "The one thing a bully understands is force and the one thing he fears is courage," Johnson remarked. "If you let a bully come into your front yard, the next day he'll be on your porch. . . ." During his long struggle with the Vietnam War, Johnson often saw the contest as one between individual wills—his own and Ho Chi Minh's. If the concept of North Vietnam as a complex society ever entered Johnson's consciousness, it certainly did not penetrate his gut feelings.

Lyndon Johnson was clearly uncomfortable about foreign policy and he did not like foreign policy debates, not as a senator who enthusiastically supported bipartisanism during the Eisenhower administrations, not as a vice president who contributed little to the evolution of foreign policy during the Kennedy years, and least of all as president. He believed that the president deserved support, not criticism, in the conduct of foreign policy. Above all, Johnson believed that consensus was needed in the conduct of foreign affairs.

As a senator, Johnson honed the fine art of achieving behind-the-scenes compromises and consensus and thereby secured passage of much needed legislation. In 1957 passage of a civil rights act—the first in the nation's history—was testimony to his leadership style in the Senate. Johnson's ability to line up the votes, to gain a consensus of support for legislation, was his virtue in the Senate. But what was a virtue in the Capitol proved to be a major liability in the Oval Office.

As president, Johnson used the same style among his foreign policy advisers as he had among his fellow senators. The goal was to achieve unanimity on foreign policy, to get his team to "sign on" to a course of action. Unlike President Kennedy, he could tolerate little opposition or division among his advisers. He rarely would reconsider policies once made, reminding his advisers that each of them had already signed on and agreed to its broad out-

LBJ

Above. President Johnson campaigns in New England during the 1964 election, in which he faced Republican Barry Goldwater. Johnson crushed his opponent in an unprecedented landslide.

Left. Senate Majority Leader Johnson exercises his negotiating skill on the floor of the 1956 Democratic National Convention during one of his unsuccessful presidential bids. At center is Johnson's Texas protégé John Connally.

Right. Johnson talks in May 1941 with a farmer from Corsicana, Texas, one of the "hill people."

lines. He could thereby forever after confine discussion to the realm of action rather than principle.

The style had one great flaw: Since the goal was to achieve consensus at all costs, the Johnson style tended to cover up contradictory goals and objectives. And when such policies proved less effective than hoped, or required modification, it was difficult if not impossible to go back and unravel the reasons why it had been selected in the first place. As former Secretary of State Dean Acheson said in early 1965, "Agreement can always be reached by increasing the generality of the conclusion. When this is done, only the illusion of policy is created. The president gives his hierarchical blessing to platitude." In Vietnam the result was a lack of clearly stated national objectives and, as the war escalated, a crippling credibility gap.

The air war strategy

In early 1965 President Johnson began to receive alarming reports on the fighting in Vietnam. Admiral Ulysses S. Grant Sharp, the CINCPAC, later admitted, "It became increasingly apparent that the existing levels of United States aid could not prevent the collapse of South Vietnam." As the situation worsened, the Joint Chiefs of Staff, Ambassador Taylor in Saigon, the Pacific command, and above all Defense Secretary Robert S. McNamara all pressed the president to initiate a sustained program of bombing against targets in North Vietnam. But Johnson knew full well that his political career was on the line and, more than that, did not want to become a "war president." He was unwilling to take such a dramatic step in escalating the conflict without a consensus among all his advisers. There remained at least one important holdout: National Security Adviser McGeorge Bundy. So the president sent Bundy to Vietnam for a firsthand look.

By coincidence Bundy was present in Saigon during the bloody VC attack on the U.S. base near Pleiku on February 7. That experience quickly convinced him. He called the White House to sign on, to say that he, too, now favored a tougher bombing policy. LBJ had his consensus. But there was one problem: Those forming the consensus advanced at least three distinct reasons for supporting the program of sustained bombing, and General Westmoreland had a partially unstated fourth reason.

McGeorge Bundy believed that one of the strong reasons for bombing the North was to provide a needed lift in morale for ARVN and the South Vietnamese government. It would dramatize America's commitment to "stick it out" in Vietnam and convince the South Vietnamese that the enemy was also being hurt by the war.

The Joint Chiefs of Staff and the Pacific command both felt that a program of sustained bombing could reduce or hinder the ability of North Vietnam to infiltrate supplies and men into the South. They urged a tough program of bombing aimed largely at North Vietnamese lines of communication (LOCs). Their stance was supported by General Westmoreland, although he, himself, was dubious about the effectiveness of bombing the North. He later wrote, "I still saw no hope, in view of the restrictions imposed, that it would have any dramatic effect on the course of the war."

With the air war against North Vietnam being directed by the Pacific command and the White House, Westmoreland would have little control over this escalation in the war. His support was quite likely based on a different sort of reasoning. Westmoreland had to know, as General Ridgway had warned President Eisenhower eleven years earlier during the Dien Bien Phu crisis, that a stepped-up air war would eventually mean the commitment of combat troops—to maintain, supply, and ultimately protect the air effort. Indeed, within ten days of the bombing program's approval in Washington, and even before the program was officially announced or the first sorties flown, Westmoreland officially requested the deployment of marines to Da Nang to guard its air base on the grounds that the South Vietnamese could not guarantee its security.

Each of these advisers played his role in convincing Johnson, but the arguments of the civilian secretary of defense, Robert McNamara, seemed at the time to have the largest influence on the president himself. McNamara hoped that a program of sustained bombing of the North might end the war quickly, perhaps in a matter of months.

McNamara's hope was based on his confidence in the policy of flexible response adopted by the Kennedy administration and which he had further refined in his concept of "counterforce strategy." While both the general philosophy of flexible response and McNamara's counterforce strategy remained controversial, their success in the Berlin crisis of 1961 and especially the Cuban missile crisis of 1962 had given Kennedy's advisers, most of whom now served Johnson, confidence in its soundness.

According to these theories, the decision to quarantine Cuba in response to Moscow's efforts to implant nuclear weapons there had succeeded because the United States had used firm but moderate pressure against the Soviet Union, inducing it to reach a compromise agreement satisfactory to the United States. Two factors proved crucial in that policy: (1) the United States had begun with a moderate amount of pressure on the Soviet Union so as to permit maximum flexibility, including greater pressure if needed, and (2) America provided the enemy with something in return—a commitment not to invade Cuba—if they displayed a willingness to negotiate. It was this policy of graduated pressure that governed the decision to initiate the Operation Rolling Thunder bombing.

There was, in addition, one other element in McNamara's thinking, his counterforce strategy. McNamara had shared with President Kennedy a dislike for the policy of massive retaliation which had dominated the Eisenhower foreign policy. Under the concept of massive retaliation, President Eisenhower had threatened to unleash America's nuclear arsenal against Communist China should it repeat the sort of invasion it had carried out in Korea. McNamara was uneasy about the lack of flexibility in Eisenhower's policy and the danger that it would escalate into an exchange of nuclear weapons with the Soviet Union. Still, he recognized that with China's enormous manpower pool, the United States could not afford to get involved in another "meat grinder" war if China ever again intervened in Korea or Vietnam. He therefore formulated a policy of limited nuclear response in which China's cities would be "held as hostages." In other words, nuclear weapons could be used largely against military and industrial targets, while sparing the cities. McNamara argued that the destruction of China's cities would leave little incentive to negotiate a settlement to any conflict. China would feel that it had already lost all that it could. Instead, the cities would be spared and become "hostages" of America's nuclear power, bargaining chips with which to negotiate a settlement.

The counterforce strategy had largely been designed in the hopes of preventing a localized conflict with the Chinese from escalating into a full-scale nuclear exchange with the Soviet Union, even if the United States employed tactical nuclear weapons. But a necessary corollary to this was to negotiate a settlement to the conflict before such escalation. Although he never contemplated the use of nuclear weapons in Vietnam, McNamara thought this second part of the strategy was applicable. The cities of North Vietnam could be held hostage even to America's conventional bombing because of the ever present threat of greater damage.

The theories of flexible response and counterforce strategy led to the way in which Rolling Thunder bombing was conducted. The pressure on the North would be only gradually increased while the cities would be spared the damage of America's bombing program. The goal was to provide North Vietnam with incentives, under the threat of much heavier punishment, to negotiate a settlement to the war on terms acceptable to the American government. And if the North Vietnamese remained unmoved, then perhaps the Soviet Union, fearing increased Chinese influence in Southeast Asia or an unwelcome confrontation with the United States, would apply the necessary pressure on Hanoi.

Middle-level officials opposing the bombing program pointed out that there were few parallels between China's role in the Korean War and the guerrilla war in 1965 in South Vietnam or even North Vietnam's role in supporting it. There were even fewer points in common between the Soviet Union's role in ending the Cuban missile crisis and any possible Soviet role in the conflict in Vietnam, and yet these analogies helped convince President Johnson to approve Rolling Thunder, the sustained bombing of North Vietnam.

McNamara versus the JCS

The different rationales for the Rolling Thunder program led to almost immediate conflict between civilian defense planners and the military. The role of the civilians, including the president, was to approve lists of targets submitted by CINCPAC each week through the Joint Chiefs of Staff. It was because of this detailed civilian supervision of the list of permissible targets that President Johnson was able to brag, "Hell, they can't even bomb an outhouse without my approval." But the reality of civilian control was far less substantial. After the civilians approved targets, military commanders had the option of selecting any target within the cumulative approved list whenever conditions were propitious.

The military argued that McNamara's hope that bombing would bring Hanoi to the negotiating table was unrealistic. McNamara charged that the interdiction policy would never succeed in preventing enough troops and supplies from reaching the South. The military countered that interdiction could not succeed if the civilians insisted on the restrictions placed on the bombing program. McNamara answered that the restrictions were not only necessary for international diplomatic reasons but were also an essential part of the policy of graduated pressure (that is, holding the cities hostage).

The debate began in the secrecy of the Pentagon but soon spilled over into the public arena and culminated in Senate hearings chaired by Senator John Stennis of Mississippi during 1967. The military complained about the restrictions on its bombing program but declined to predict that their removal would result in victory. After testifying that the bombing program was well equipped, the military officers complained that their greatest need was for "targets—targets."

McNamara pointed out that almost 90 percent of the targets recommended by the JCS had been approved and hit. Of those not approved, largely in the Hanoi–Haiphong area, McNamara said they were of limited military value. For instance the petroleum depots not yet hit possessed only 6 percent of North Vietnam's petroleum storage facilities. McNamara concluded that North Vietnam's limited economic development was the reason for the lack of targets, not the restrictions.

In any case, the bombing program proved a disappointment to both military and civilian strategists. Both fixed targets and LOCs had been bombed repeatedly. Joseph Hoover, a deputy assistant secretary of defense, claimed that by March 7, 1967, less than a billion dollars worth of damage had been inflicted on North Vietnam. McNamara's own estimate was even lower: $320 million. In that same period North Vietnam received more than $2 billion in economic assistance, largely from the Soviet Union and China. By 1968 North Vietnam possessed virtually a blank check for Soviet aid and had constructed an

Soviet–built SAM missiles like this one proved costly to the U.S. air campaign over North Vietnam. Enemy air defenses downed 938 aircraft valued at over $6 billion during Rolling Thunder bombing missions.

LOC system almost immune to bombing. Though about five hundred thousand people had to be diverted to the task, North Vietnam was able to repair the bomb damage. The United States during the same period suffered $6 billion in aircraft losses alone.

The plan to drive Hanoi to the bargaining table by making war intolerably costly failed, and the interdiction campaign of the JCS was not working. But the rationales for Rolling Thunder remained in force until a partial bombing halt in April of 1968. The debate between the military and McNamara would not be settled by the 1967 hearings or by Johnson's revised bombing policy of 1968, or even by the end of the war itself. At the heart of the debate was the question of restrictions.

Two sets of restrictions proved particularly bothersome to the military. The first established "prohibited areas" ten miles around Hanoi and four miles around Haiphong. The second established a twenty–five– to thirty–mile "buffer zone" in northernmost Vietnam to guard against mistaken bombing of China. In the mind of one student of McNamara's strategy "the restrictions were certainly destructive

... *if* the objective was regarded as interdiction." The problem was that Johnson's desire for consensus on bombing policy had obscured with platitudes the disagreement over objectives between McNamara and the military, and LBJ's style permitted no philosophical reconsideration of that policy until near the end of his presidency.

The effectiveness of Rolling Thunder was, however, hampered by more than the lack of clear objectives in Washington and Honolulu. The North Vietnamese themselves did much to limit its effectiveness. Within six weeks after Rolling Thunder was initiated, American pilots spotted up–to–date Soviet–built SAM II antiaircraft missile sites near Hanoi. In addition, as they so often did to counter sophisticated American firepower, the North Vietnamese avoided exposed roads and other byways for transportation and relied on bicycles capable of hauling up to five hundred pounds of supplies.

They employed a variety of techniques, some old, some new, to foil the bombers. The North Vietnamese spotted papier mâché trucks along the Ho Chi Minh Trail and papier mâché MIG–21 aircraft at Hanoi's Gia Lam airfield, built phony roads to attract American bombers, built bridges just below the water's surface so they could not be seen from the air, set fires to disorient American infrared systems, and faked explosions near trucks to make pilots think they had scored hits. None of these subterfuges, of course, stopped American bombs, but they limited the efficiency of bombing raids and reduced the damage.

Beyond North Vietnam's countermeasures, American bombing policy was also hamstrung by concerns about possible Soviet or Chinese response to the American bombing program. Whether realistic or not in hindsight, fear that the Soviet Union or China might directly enter the war if unduly provoked was a foremost consideration in Washington at the time.

Other subtle policy considerations involving the Communists also influenced the U.S. in its decision to refrain from bombing Hanoi and Haiphong. One was the probability that bombing or mining the harbor at Haiphong would have forced the Soviet Union into closer cooperation with China, a consummation the State Department

hoped devoutly to avoid but which could come about if the sea route to North Vietnam were closed and the Soviet Union felt obliged to use the overland route through China to supply the North Vietnamese. Barring such Sino-Soviet cooperation, the Soviet Union, it was speculated, might try other strong measures to retrieve its influence in Hanoi, such as providing more sophisticated weapons, provoking crises in other parts of the world, or increasing direct participation of Soviet personnel in the war effort.

A chance for peace?

If the policy of graduated pressure had any chance of working it was during its first few months, especially during April and May 1965. On April 1 Mai Van Bo, consul general of the North Vietnamese economic mission in Paris, delivered an official message to the U.S. government by way of a high-ranking official in the French foreign ministry.

The message contained the official DRV conditions for

Fifty miles south of Hanoi peasant militia swiftly fill in a bomb crater in the middle of a main road, the result of an earlier U.S. strike. By late 1966 the CIA concluded that despite an outlay of $250 million per month, the bombing campaign was not significantly reducing the flow of supplies south.

peace in Vietnam. Hanoi's "four point" program included: (1) withdrawal of American forces, (2) respect for the military provisions of the Geneva accords of 1954, (3) settlement of South Vietnam's internal affairs "in accordance with the program of the South Vietnam National Front for Liberation," and (4) the "peaceful reunification of Vietnam . . . without any foreign interference." Only the third point contradicted basic American policy, since the other three all reiterated positions that the United States had grudgingly accepted at Geneva in 1954 and later reaffirmed. Acceptance of point three, however, required the recognition of the NLF, something the U.S. had adamantly refused to do but without which surely any settlement was impossible in 1965. In 1965 the NLF controlled one-third to one-half of the South Vietnamese population and levied taxes in forty-one of the forty-four provinces.

Although it was Hanoi's first announced bargaining position, the four points could hardly have been surprising to Washington, except for the important signal that came in an attached note of explanation. Hanoi said that its four points provided "the basis for the soundest political settlement of the Vietnam problem"—not the *only* basis. In the subtle ways of international diplomacy such wording was not presumed to be accidental but implied a possible willingness to compromise.

Hopes rose further for a negotiated settlement six days later after a speech President Johnson delivered at Johns Hopkins University. At the last moment, and to the surprise of many of his advisers, Johnson inserted a line into the speech stating, "We remain ready with this purpose [to achieve peace] for unconditional discussions." In addition, Johnson offered to Hanoi the carrot which was an essential ingredient of the counterforce strategy. He invited North Vietnam to join in his multibillion dollar plan to develop the Mekong River Valley—after peace had been achieved in Indochina.

By May Johnson's advisers reached a decision to halt the bombing and extend new peace feelers to Hanoi. The initiative was code named Mayflower. Again, this consensus rested on conflicting rationales between those who felt that an honest peace effort should be made and those who merely wanted to clear the air of peace talk before intensifying the bombing.

The divided opinion seriously affected the manner in which Operation Mayflower was conducted. On May 12 Washington simultaneously ordered a halt in the bombing of North Vietnam and instructed the U.S. ambassador in Moscow, Foy Kohler, to transmit a message to the North Vietnamese by way of the Russians. It read more like an ultimatum than a peace initiative. "The United States must emphasize that the road toward the end of armed attacks against the people and government of Vietnam is the only road which will permit the Government of Vietnam (and the Government of the United States) to bring a permanent end to their attacks on North Vietnam." It contin-

ued: "If this pause should be misunderstood . . . it would be necessary to demonstrate more clearly than ever, after the pause ended, that the United States is determined not to accept aggression without reply in Vietnam."

In only two days Radio Hanoi denounced the American bombing pause as "a worn-out trick of deceit and threat." In Hanoi's view, the peace initiative represented no more than an impudent demand for surrender. Soon thereafter Johnson decided to end the pause and on May 18 Rolling Thunder sorties began anew.

Why did the initiative fail? According to Washington officials, it seemed clear that Hanoi was not really interested in serious negotiations. On May 6, CIA Director Admiral William F. Raborn concluded, probably correctly, that "the DRV is in my view, unlikely to engage in meaningful discussions at any time in coming months." Given the balance of forces in South Vietnam, Hanoi could easily have foreseen an early military victory. Why then negotiate away what seemed within its grasp through military means? On the other hand, Hanoi might well have accepted a negotiated settlement that permitted the United States a graceful exit from a difficult situation and left the NLF to cope only with the weak South Vietnamese government. To those dissidents still in the Johnson administration, such as George Ball, this prospect seemed the best means of avoiding an increasingly frustrating and costly war.

From Washington's perspective, the Soviet Union had failed to play its "assigned" role in the policy of flexible response. The Soviet Union, which had agreed to a compromise when it was one of the directly contending parties in the Cuban missile crisis in 1962, refused to intervene and pressure North Vietnam into a compromise. McNamara's reasoning, accepted by most foreign policy advisers, had assumed that the Soviets would help to find a solution to the Vietnam conflict by putting pressure on Hanoi. The fact was that even if the Soviets wished to achieve a negotiated settlement, they were essentially powerless to do so. The North Vietnamese were extremely jealous of their independence and unwilling to bend to the desires of either Communist superpower. By balancing Soviet and Chinese interests the North Vietnamese were able to keep their distance from both. The North Vietnamese and Soviets realized that any attempt by the Russians to force negotiations would be met by cries of "sellout" from the Chinese.

Added to the unwillingness of the Soviet Union to aid the American peace initiative was the attitude of Washington itself. It was no more interested in negotiations in 1965 than were the North Vietnamese. As the opponents of the bombing pause had pointed out, the American bargaining position was exceedingly weak. There was little that America could offer except the slow defeat of South Vietnam. Rather, the chief intention of the White House was to prepare the way for more intensified bombing and

Americans take the offensive. A soldier of the 173d Airborne Brigade moves into action in the Iron Triangle in 1965.

further escalation. In the words of Admiral Raborn, "it would be easier and politically more palatable to ... intensify the bombing ... *after a pause*."

There were to be more peace initiatives after the bombing resumed in May but none before 1968 that offered any real chance for peace. Instead by the summer of 1965 the United States gave up hope that the war would be short and faced the inevitability of fighting a much longer one.

The long war begins

After the failure of the May peace initiative it became clear to Washington that bombing North Vietnam alone would neither force Hanoi to the bargaining table nor measurably improve South Vietnam's (and America's) bargaining position. As a consequence Westmoreland's view, that the enemy must be convinced that it would not only pay a costly price in the North but also could not win in the South, won more adherents in Washington, and his long-standing proposals for more troops were given more careful consideration. Already in April at Honolulu, Westmoreland had won approval for 40,000 more troops. Although this was less than he requested it brought total American strength, when all had arrived in Vietnam, to 70,000 to 75,000 men. Faced with requests from Westmoreland for 45,000 additional troops, Defense and State Department officials awaited the return of Ambassador Taylor to Washington before making any new decisions.

Taylor was due on June 8, the day after Westmoreland had sent his emergency cable to the JCS detailing tremendous losses suffered by ARVN in the first days of the Communist spring offensive. Westmoreland wanted to move men "as rapidly as is practical" to stem the tide—in all, enough to increase U.S. and Third Country strength to forty-four infantry-type battalions and adequate support troops, which would increase American strength to more than two hundred thousand. The ensuing "forty-four battalion debate" was to be the last major review of American policy and objectives in Vietnam until spring 1967.

The president's top assistants, including McNamara, Rusk, William Bundy, McGeorge Bundy, Ball, and Ambassador Taylor, first turned their attention to Westmoreland's immediate request: 45,000 more troops to be in-country by mid-August, including a full division deployed in the central highlands. By June 11 a consensus emerged that satisfied even George Ball. Deployment of a division to the highlands was rejected; it was too risky without adequately secured logistical enclaves and roads. Instead, Westmoreland would receive 25,000 of the requested 45,000 troops. The remainder of his request would be postponed for future consideration. Two factors led to the decision. First, both military and diplomatic advisers were agreed that nothing could stem the tide of the VC offensive until the monsoon rains ended in the fall. In the meantime an additional 25,000 troops would stave off any immediate collapse of South Vietnam. More important, as Ball argued, the figure of 100,000 troops formed an important psychological boundary. Beyond that, the war was bound to become America's war and there would be no holding the line before 300,000 to 500,000 troops were sent.

The new troop authorizations increased the American troop level to ninety-five thousand. They formed, however, only eighteen combat battalions totaling twenty-five thousand fighting men. The rest of the American forces were made up of either advisers or support troops. In contrast, the CIA estimated that the Vietcong possessed forces of sixty-five thousand Main Force soldiers, eighty to one hundred thousand guerrillas, militia, and part-time forces, and only thirty thousand support personnel. The ratios of actual combat troops to total troop strength proved to be of incalculable importance, greatly easing the enemy's ability to match the United States escalation for escalation. The enemy needed only to augment its total forces by a fraction of the Allied increases in order to maintain the same relative combat troop strength.

The need to act on the remainder of Westmoreland's request could not be eluded and in fact became even more urgent. ARVN was now losing one battalion and/or district headquarters each week to the VC offensive. On June 28 paratroopers from the U.S. Army 173d Airborne Brigade conducted America's first officially announced search and destroy mission in War Zone D northwest of Saigon. The VC eluded attack or capture so the scheduled three-day operation was ended one day early. One American was killed and nine wounded.

The mission further clouded what had already become a murky affair. On June 8 State Department Press Officer Robert McCloskey said, in response to a question about whether America's mission in Vietnam had changed, that "American forces would be available for combat support together with Vietnamese forces when and if necessary." The American people were at that time unaware of the decision in NSAM 328 to permit wider deployment of American troops, and the New York Times on the following day wrote, "The American people were told by a minor State Department official yesterday that, in effect, they were in a land war on the continent of Asia."

Upon hearing of McCloskey's action, Lyndon Johnson went into a rage. According to journalist David Halberstam, he turned on his press secretary, George Reedy. Who the hell was McCloskey? he asked. His ass was going to be briefing people in Africa very goddamn soon. It was goddamn well treason. Only the intervention of Dean Rusk saved the press officer's position. Rusk knew that McCloskey had only been doing his job in being honest with the press.

On June 9 the White House totally denied McCloskey's report, issuing a statement that said, "There has been no change in the mission of the United States ground combat units in Vietnam in recent days or weeks." More than any other single incident, this denial opened wide the credibility gap that bedeviled Lyndon Johnson for the remainder of his term in the White House.

On June 26, in another decision withheld from the American public, General Westmoreland was granted even wider authority to use U.S. troops "in any situation . . . when, in COMUSMACV's [Westmoreland's] judgment, their use is necessary to strengthen the relative position of GVN forces." This gave Westmoreland free rein to use American troops in any way he saw fit within the borders of South Vietnam. One of Westmoreland's objectives had been achieved. Now he wanted the other: more troops.

The 100,000-troop barrier proved to be more than psychological. After the decisions of June 10-11, McNamara began consultations to determine the availability of further troops. Admiral Sharp informed him that they could no longer be deployed from the Pacific command in dribs and drabs; no more such reserve battalions existed. The next step would have to be the deployment of a division from the United States. Sharp recommended a newly organized division based on helicopter mobility—later to be known as the 1st Cavalry Division (Airmobile) or 1st Air Cav. But Sharp warned that if the division was to arrive in Vietnam by September 1, orders for its deployment would have to go out by July 10. He further informed McNamara that it would be impossible for a full division to prepare itself in secrecy; after July 10 its planned deployment would become public knowledge.

McNamara dealt with that problem by announcing on June 16 the full deployments that had been agreed upon at Honolulu in April. Although agreement had already been reached to send an additional 25,000 troops beyond that Honolulu figure, McNamara's only further comment was that "more [troops] would be sent."

Now pressed to send even more, LBJ summoned his advisers. George Ball urged that the line be held below 100,000 troops until it could be determined how well Americans operated in their newly acknowledged full combat role. Additional troops could then be discussed in the fall if things went well; if not, a graceful exit should be sought. McNamara urged that much more force be sent to South Vietnam immediately but also suggested that more intensive efforts be made to achieve negotiations with Hanoi. The president asked both Ball and McNamara to spend a week preparing their cases and scheduled another meeting for July 2.

At this juncture, the Vietcong intruded into the deliberations. Suddenly shifting the focus of their offensive away from Saigon, they opened a concerted attack on the central highlands and quickly overran six district capitals in Kontum and Pleiku provinces and countless isolated outposts. This gave greater urgency to Westmoreland's appeal for an additional American division, to be sent directly to the highlands.

July days

On July 2 National Security Adviser McGeorge Bundy sent to the president proposed action memoranda from Ball and McNamara, as well as an additional one from William Bundy. McGeorge Bundy's role in the debate had been muted. He had served more to organize the thoughts of others and convey them to the president than to originate proposals in his own office. But the power inherent in his position was clear in the covering note he sent to Johnson along with the action memoranda. Bundy suggested to the president that "you will want to listen hard to George Ball and then reject his proposal. . . . The decision . . . should be made in about ten days, which is the point at which McNamara would like a final go-ahead on the air mobile [1st Air Cav] division."

McNamara only slightly modified his earlier proposals. He urged the president to authorize the full forty-four battalions requested by Westmoreland. In addition, he suggested more extensive air and naval actions against the North. He now approved a bombing campaign against North Vietnamese LOCs and even advocated the mining of North Vietnamese ports. But McNamara no longer believed that a short war was possible. On the contrary, he offered Johnson a starkly realistic prognosis:

During operations in the Iron Triangle in 1965, two soldiers from the 173d help a wounded comrade to safety.

The war is one of attrition and will be a long one. Since troops once committed as a practical matter cannot be removed, since U.S. casualties will rise, since we should take call-up actions to support the additional forces in Vietnam, the test of endurance may be as much in the United States as in Vietnam.

Ball's memorandum, however, represented a significant change in his analysis; he was even gloomier than before. He called for the president to hold the line over the summer to avoid a South Vietnamese collapse and then find any means of negotiating America out of the war when the rainy season ended. His memo was much shorter than his earlier analysis, which Johnson had carefully read and discussed with Ball in June. He began by pointing out to the president that "no one can assure you that we can beat the Vietcong or even force them to the conference table on our terms no matter how many hundred thousand *white foreign* [U.S.] troops we deploy." Finally, Ball argued that the costs of getting out were less than what would await the U.S. in a full-scale war in Vietnam:

If we can act before we commit substantial U.S. forces to combat in South Vietnam we can, by accepting some short-term costs, avoid what may well be a long-term catastrophe.

An unexpected memorandum from William Bundy, entitled "A Middle Course," largely repeated Ball's earlier recommendation to wait and see how American troops performed in the field before making any further decision. He could not, however, accept Ball's deep pessimism.

The president declined to make an immediate decision and instead ordered McNamara to go to Vietnam on July 15 for another firsthand look. But on July 9, in a news conference, LBJ made clear how he was leaning. He indicated that more troops would likely be sent and even suggested that a call-up of the reserves might be necessary to meet America's commitment in Vietnam.

McNamara arrived in Saigon on July 15. During the first two days of discussions he determined that American commanders were confident of the abilities of American combat forces and that South Vietnamese leaders urgently wanted more American troops. More important, he became convinced that without more troops South Vietnam might collapse by autumn. McNamara immediately cabled his findings back to Washington and within hours LBJ had made his decision. On July 17 Deputy Secretary of Defense Cyrus Vance cabled McNamara in Saigon, telling him the president wanted a plan for the deployment of the forty-four battalion force, including such possible actions as Congressional approval and a call-up of the reserves.

On July 21 Johnson's senior advisers met for a final time to approve the McNamara plan. In his revised plan, McNamara had softened his advocacy of a dramatic escalation of the bombing of North Vietnam and no longer recommended the mining of ports, presumably because of

Johnson's stated opposition. McNamara's proposals called for:

- Increasing U.S. strength in South Vietnam to 175,000 by November 1, 1965;

- Calling up 225,000 U.S. reserves;

- Increasing the strength of the Pacific command by extending the tours of duty of 20,000 men stationed there each month;

- Raising the overall strength of the U.S. Army by 400,000 during the coming twelve months; and

- Doubling U.S. draft calls.

The president asked if there was any disagreement. Ball murmured that the president knew his views. All others assented. The policy debate was over. LBJ finally had his internal consensus, and it would be two-and-a-half years before its basis—an intense air war in the North to raise the cost of the war to Hanoi and a dramatically stepped-up military campaign in the South to deny the NLF victory—would be reexamined. The only remaining question was how to present the decisions to the public.

Guns and butter

Over the weekend of July 24–25, LBJ secluded himself at Camp David, conferring almost exclusively with Robert McNamara. During this period he made one major change in McNamara's program. Johnson decided against calling up the reserves. It was a delicate political decision. Only with Congressional approval could the president call up the reserves for longer than one year. By July 1965 it was clear that the war would last much longer. Even without Congressional approval the president would have to declare "a national emergency," rising to a sort of rhetoric he had already decided to avoid. Thus, when McNamara informed the president that the required troops could be raised solely through increased draft calls, one presidential dilemma was removed. Later the military would complain that by not calling up the reserves Johnson had left the military little slack. Eventually, they argued, it would drain the American strategic reserve and limit the government's ability to respond to crises in other parts of the world.

On July 28 President Johnson made his decision known to the American public. Ironically, during that last week in July the United States was suffering its highest casualty total of the war to date, 28 dead and 100 wounded, bringing the total casualties since 1961 to 503 killed, 2,270 wounded, and 57 POWs and MIAs.

Johnson decided against a highly visible prime-time presidential address and instead chose an afternoon press conference as his forum. "We did not choose to be the guardians at the gate, but there is no one else," Johnson began. Then he announced only that 50,000 additional troops would be sent now, and more would be sent later. In fact, he had already authorized an additional 150,000 men, the full forty-four battalion plan, to raise American troop levels to more than 225,000. He announced also that draft calls would be doubled. He asked for no Congressional approval of these new actions, but said he would ask the Congress for an additional $1.7 billion military appropriation for Vietnam.

Just as important as the content of this decision in shaping the future of the Johnson presidency, if not the conduct of the war, was the subdued manner in which Lyndon Johnson told the American people that the United States was now involved in a full-scale land war in Asia. He had strong reasons for doing it that way. In his memoirs, Johnson recounted a cabinet meeting held on July 27, 1965, one day before his press conference. He wrote:

In a wondrous time of hope and optimism we had begun the building of a better society for our people. The danger that we might have to slow that building, in order to take care of our obligations abroad, brought added anguish. So on that July 27, 1965, two great streams converged—the dream of a Great Society at home and the inescapable demands of our obligations halfway around the world. They were to run in confluence until the end of my Administration.

On that July day less than half of Johnson's Great Society bills had passed through Congress. Johnson had feared that any full Congressional debate on Vietnam would doom his Great Society, his ambitious domestic policy.

He further feared that the opponents of the Great Society in Congress, largely hawks on Vietnam, would seize upon the issue to deny funding for the programs already passed. Johnson himself was forced to take such steps in 1966 and 1967, but by then, he reasoned, the Great Society was law, its promise to be fulfilled in future years. Nor did Johnson want to raise taxes to support the war. One of his proudest achievements was the tax cut of 1964, and he was reluctant to take away from the American people a boon he felt he had personally given them. Furthermore the economy was sluggish in the spring and summer of 1965, and Johnson feared that a tax increase might induce a recession. He need not have feared. The war in Vietnam was beginning to heat the economy to the boiling point.

In one of Johnson's favorite phrases, a poker term, he had "thrown his stack in." His political future would now ride on his decision to support guns and butter, to arm Americans to fight in Vietnam while nourishing them through his Great Society. The policy debate was over, and the United States was in Vietnam for keeps.

Secretary of Defense Robert McNamara broods alone following the press conference in the White House East Room on July 28, 1965. President Johnson had just announced the adoption of McNamara's proposal to send fifty thousand additional troops to Vietnam, with more to come.

At one of Robert S. McNamara's many Senate grillings in the Vietnam era, Senator Wayne Morse, an early dove, called the growing conflict "McNamara's war." The secretary of defense, hunched as always at the witness table, his feet hooked behind the chair legs, came erect.

"I must say I don't object to its being called McNamara's war," he replied sternly, glaring through steel-rimmed glasses. "I think it is a very important war and I am pleased to be identified with it and do whatever I can to win it."

That was 1964, when McNamara was still optimistic about Vietnam. He regarded it as foremost a development problem. The United States, he thought, would dominate Vietnam as he dominated the military establishment and Congress, applying modern management techniques, reshaping strategies and forces. That had always been his style as he moved from one plateau to a higher one, each preparation for the next.

Old friends thought his early drive came from his mother. One of his teachers at Piedmont High School, near Oakland, California, remembered that "it was a good idea to have answers" when Claranel McNamara appeared. He excelled at Piedmont, at the University of California, where he made Phi Beta Kappa with honors in economics, and at Harvard Business School.

In 1941 he left Harvard, where he had returned to teach, to help impose statistical control over the expanding Army Air Corps. When Lieutenant Colonel McNamara was discharged in 1946, still only thirty, his Pentagon file contained no rating less than superior.

To exploit the experience, he and nine other young officers sold themselves as a team to young Henry Ford, who had just taken over from his aging grandfather. McNamara soon edged ahead of the others. One of the members of the group, who helped plan the disastrous Edsel—and was fired by McNamara—later killed himself. McNamara fathered the Falcon, the Fairlane, and the four-seater Thunderbird, all successes.

Inevitably he made enemies. A subordinate found him to be "completely deficient in human qualities." Yet he puzzled other executives by shunning fash-

McNamara

by Henry Trewhitt

Robert S. McNamara, the eighth U.S. secretary of defense.

ionable Bloomfield Hills and Grosse Pointe for Ann Arbor, the university center, where Bob and Margaret McNamara—they had married in 1940—were dedicated to civic and university affairs. It was as if there were two Bob McNamaras, one the icy manager and another the gregarious citizen and consumer of culture. At every opportunity he climbed or skied, keeping lean, always testing himself.

He was elected president of Ford on November 9, 1960, the day after John F. Kennedy was elected president of the United States. When Robert Lovett brought McNamara and the president-elect together a month later, there was not much doubt about the outcome. Given a promise of vast power, McNamara signed on, after one of the brief

reigns of corporate history, as the eighth U.S. secretary of defense.

He entered the Pentagon striding, swinging a favorite outsized briefcase. Those who arrived late, at 8:00 A.M., found the secretary's limousine parked, its engine already cold. Crises over Berlin, Laos, and Cuba dominated the early months. But more important for the long run, he set out to end historic interservice feuding by implanting civilian control and a planning-programming-budgeting system that treated defense needs as a whole. He mostly succeeded, over bitter resistance.

"They say I am a power grabber," he complained of his critics. "But knowledge is power, and I am giving them knowledge so they will have more power. Can't they see that?" Many of them couldn't.

One of his most complex achievements was the refinement of nuclear strategy. He abandoned what remained of the concept of massive retaliation against Soviet attack, which required the United States to stay ahead at enormous cost, and accepted the idea of equality for mutual deterrence. McNamara was certain that the Soviet Union eventually would match whatever nuclear power America created. In fact he thought it was a good idea: He believed the United States, out of ignorance, had built too much. But that was a heresy that had to be introduced carefully to nervous politicians and their public.

With time he also persuaded European allies to reduce dependence on nuclear weapons in favor of defense with, first, nonnuclear forces and then nuclear weapons only if necessary. His goal was not to make it easier to go to war, but to defer nuclear war as long as possible.

On some projects he lost. The services and Congress frustrated for seven years his attempt to create with the TFX a common airplane for the navy and the air force. They were helped by the suspicion that he had chosen the contractor, General Dynamics, as a favor to Lyndon Johnson.

When John F. Kennedy was killed, Johnson wanted McNamara above all others to remain in the cabinet. As early as Kennedy's first cabinet meeting, Johnson had told a reporter, "That man with the Stacomb in his hair is the best of the lot."

For more than two years after Kennedy's death that judgment held, and McNamara responded with total loyalty. He became a man-of-all-work, announcing plans to open up the copper stockpile, control imports, even making what amounted to political speeches. Bob McNamara, the president said, "is the smartest man I ever saw." He could resolve anything.

What ruined it was Vietnam. McNamara thought at first that Vietnam could be stabilized rationally, not just by killing Vietcong, though that was necessary, but by internal reform and development. "Every quantitative measurement we have shows we are winning this war," he said early, and later, more fretfully, "If we can learn how to analyze this thing, we'll solve it."

But no one ever learned, and McNamara, for too long, did not know that. He would demand statistics on pacification, logistics, and guerrilla activity from subordinates and South Vietnam's government. Lacking real figures, they supplied garbage. For years McNamara accepted it and created much of his own.

He recommended and planned carefully the escalation of 1965. But he worried over the consequences when Johnson refused to mobilize reserves and increase taxes to pay for the war. When the limited bombing of North Vietnam failed to produce negotiations, he began to turn. A colonel in the Pentagon described his reaction in human terms, "He has learned that wars kill people, innocent people."

The ambivalence began to appear in a series of speeches during the spring and summer of 1966. In the first, in Montreal on May 18, he discounted military power, though conceding it was necessary, as the essence of security. Security came from development of poor countries, with popular support, and from better understanding with adversaries. Through his remarks ran the implication that South Vietnam, lacking a sound political base, was a poor commitment. Yes, he said, "I caught hell for that one" from Johnson.

By the spring of 1967 he was in torment, apparent to all who knew him well. The president was taking military advice,

not his, about bombing targets in the North. He had dropped ten pounds from his normal 165. His wife entered a hospital with ulcers, an affliction that he felt more equitably should have been his own. In August he began to go public, arguing before a Senate committee against any increase in strategic bombing and, by implication, its continuation. In private he campaigned against further commitment of U.S. troops and for a slow turn toward what later became Vietnamization.

By then it was just a matter of time. The president was said to be worried that McNamara might become "another Forrestal." James Forrestal, the first secretary of defense, had fallen to his death from a hospital window. In November arrangements were complete: McNamara would leave to become president of the World Bank. In the public judgment he had been fired, though he and Johnson denied it then and later.

The bank offered a fresh start, a chance to satisfy the fascination with Third World development that had grown as Vietnam turned sour. Tanned and fit after a skiing holiday, McNamara pursued it with the intensity he had applied from Piedmont to the Pentagon. He remained for thirteen years in welcome public obscurity but serving as a voice of conscience to the world financial community and to Third World governments.

When he retired again on July 1, 1981, at sixty-five, he looked back at the bank's performance with satisfaction and toward its future with dismay. Under his direction it had increased lending to poor countries from $1 billion to $13 billion a year with, he reported happily, a return of 19 percent on invested capital. But support was fading, especially in the United States, and that, he warned, showed a misreading of the national interest.

Was the bank expiation for Vietnam? Nonsense, he said, though he insisted he would not talk publicly about Vietnam. McNamara, in fact, remained silent on Vietnam until May 1984 when he was subpoenaed to give a deposition in the libel suit brought by General William C. Westmoreland against CBS, Inc. The suit stemmed from allegations, in a CBS documentary broadcast on January 23, 1982, that the American military, and

General Westmoreland in particular, altered the estimates of the strength of enemy forces in South Vietnam to make it appear the U.S. was winning the war.

McNamara emphasized to attorneys in the suit that he was still unwilling to discuss his role in directing America's Vietnam policy. "I want it clear on the record," he told them, "that you are extracting these answers from me against my wishes. I have never spoken publicly on Vietnam." In two days of questioning and 440 pages of testimony, McNamara made no startling revelations, though what came through strongly was his skepticism, which he revealed to his Pentagon colleagues early in 1966, that the war "could be won militarily." The former secretary of defense under President Lyndon Johnson explained his gradual disenchantment, well documented in the *Pentagon Papers*, with the U.S. bombing program in North Vietnam. McNamara also defended his statistical approach to gauging results on the battlefield, which placed heavy emphasis on such indicators as the enemy body count and level of infiltration. "Statistics are nothing more than the means of conveying information," he said. Addressing CBS's allegation that General Westmoreland deliberately deceived the White House by suppressing high estimates of enemy strength, McNamara asserted that such a thing was "inconceivable."

At numerous points in his deposition, McNamara protested that he could "not recall his opinions or those of others during the war or basic facts about the conflict." Despite his faulty memory, McNamara's testimony occasioned his only account, since leaving the Johnson administration in 1968, of his Vietnam-related activities as head of the Department of Defense. Scholars and students of the war hoped that Robert McNamara's statements in court would not be his last word on his record as a major decision-maker during America's escalating involvement in South Vietnam.

Henry Trewhitt is diplomatic correspondent for The Baltimore Sun *and author of* McNamara: His Ordeal in the Pentagon.

American Firepower

Coming from the air, from land, and from the sea, American firepower was the great equalizer in Vietnam. It could punish enemy troops when they dared to mass into large units and extricate isolated American units from the most dangerous situations. American firepower could convert nighttime into day, turn jungle-covered terrain into charred fields, and give American combat troops a firepower edge even when badly outnumbered.

When it quickly became apparent that the enemy's strategy was designed to avoid most large-scale battles, American firepower superiority took on an even greater importance. American commanders were forced to break down their large units in order to conduct small-unit patrols in an effort to seek out the enemy. The enemy responded by choosing to attack these small units when they could count on numerical superiority. Even the major operations of divison size or larger generally proved to be a series of isolated small-unit fire fights. When Americans were outnumbered or surrounded, well-timed strikes from 105MM howitzers at a nearby artillery base, a tactical bombing run by an F-4 Phantom jet streaking across the sky, or the pinpoint strafing of enemy positions by a UH-1B helicopter gunship whirling overhead were what ground troops counted on to relieve the pressure.

The ability of American troops to

An artillery team fires an M101 105MM howitzer. The howitzer is fired by a team of four or five men, each with his own special task. From left to right: One man moves the prepared rounds of ammunition into position and removes the spent shell case; a second inserts the rounds of ammunition in the breech; the gunner uses the sight to verify the angle and direction of the gun; and a fourth soldier handles the elevation control at the gunner's direction and pulls the lanyard to fire the weapon. A fifth member (not shown here) may assist in preparing rounds.

coordinate the tactical arsenal available to them with actual ground conditions was an important factor setting them apart from ARVN. And much of the credit in the Vietnam War belonged to the commanders of small units, the NCOs, the lieutenants, and captains who led the companies and platoons in Vietnam. Perhaps more than in any other war they had the responsibility for insuring that supporting fire was brought to bear accurately. The ability and confidence of a young junior officer to call in a tactical strike almost on the heads of his own men could save not only his life, but also those of his unit.

The arsenal of tactical weapons these commanders could call upon was vast. The infantry carried their own mortars. Artillery batteries included howitzers, guns, and aerial rocket artillery. From the air, helicopters, primarily from the UH, or "Huey," series, fighter-bombers such as the F-100 or F-4, strategic bombers like B-52s, and propeller-driven gunships all provided tactical support. In addition, less common forms of support, such as naval gunfire, were often available. The following pages illustrate some of the most commonly used of these tactical weapons.

105MM howitzer

As in previous wars, in Vietnam artillery remained the "king of battle." And the king of ground artillery in Vietnam was the 105MM howitzer. The original 105s employed in Vietnam were of World War II vintage and had a "limited traverse,"

that is, they could fire only through a limited arc before the gun crew had to physically reposition the weapon. A more modern version was later deployed that had a 360-degree traverse and could be quickly repositioned to fire in any direction.

The 105 could fire a wide variety of shells, including the new "beehive" round which loosed thousands of steel darts in a shotgun pattern. The ammunition, fuse, shell, propellant powder, and casing was assembled beforehand and looked like a large rifle shell. The gunner opened the breech, shoved in the shell, closed the breech, and pulled the lanyard, the howitzer's "trigger." It could fire a round about every five seconds.

With a range of nearly ten miles, the howitzer could be brought to bear in a battle without actually being in the battle. This required sophisticated coordination between the battlefield leader and the artillery battery. The leader had to determine his exact location and the relative location of the enemy to his own position. He would then communicate the geographical coordinates to the battery. Since this knowledge was seldom accurate within 200 yards or so, artillery would first be called in to a point one felt certain was *not* the field officer's position. After seeing or hearing the shells strike, the target area could gradually be adjusted until it "found" the enemy position, a process that could take as little as five minutes or as much as thirty or more.

A related problem was inaccuracy. Generally a series of shells fired at a

single point from one gun would fall within about 50 yards of each other, but the pattern was elliptical rather than circular, offering advantages and disadvantages. Howitzers were more accurate with respect to direction than to range, so few shells fell to the left or right of the target, but many more would fall long or short. Thus the relative position of friendly and enemy forces played an important role in when and how the howitzer could be used. As with most weapon systems, the human factor—the judgment and talent of the field leader—was crucial in determining the usefulness of this weapon.

Despite these problems, the 105 was an important weapon. Unlike aerial weapons, bad weather could not limit its usefulness. Moreover, the light weight of the howitzer, especially the newer model, meant the weapon could easily be moved by helicopter. In Vietnam, not only did infantry troops possess a new dimension of mobility; so did artillery.

81MM mortar

"Eighty-ones" were the standard infantry mortar of the Vietnam War. Unlike other forms of tactical fire support, the 81MM was operated by the infantry company itself. A special mortar platoon or section could backpack the weapon, which broke down into four parts weighing a total of 122 pounds, into the battle area itself. (A newer version, introduced after 1967, weighed less than 100 pounds.) The shells were fired simply by dropping them down the tube. For short periods it could be fired as fast as the gunner could drop rounds of ammunition. This "rapid" fire could be as much as twenty-seven rounds per minute.

The weapon could employ many different shells, including high explosives, phosphorous, and illumination flares, all with adjustable fuses. The fuse could be timed to detonate in midair, upon impact, or, in order to penetrate thick jungle canopies, a few milliseconds after impact. This permitted the shell to penetrate the jungle more fully after hitting a high branch.

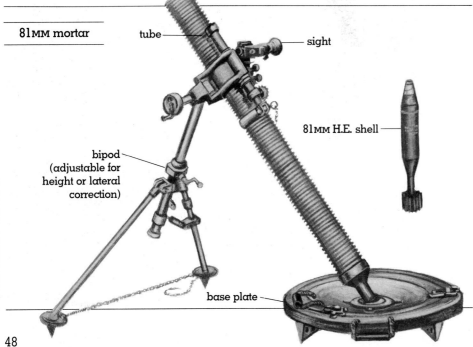

81MM mortar — tube — sight

81MM H.E. shell

bipod (adjustable for height or lateral correction)

base plate

A soldier provides nighttime support by firing an 81MM mortar. Because of its relative light weight the 81MM mortar was the most readily available form of fire support for infantry troops.

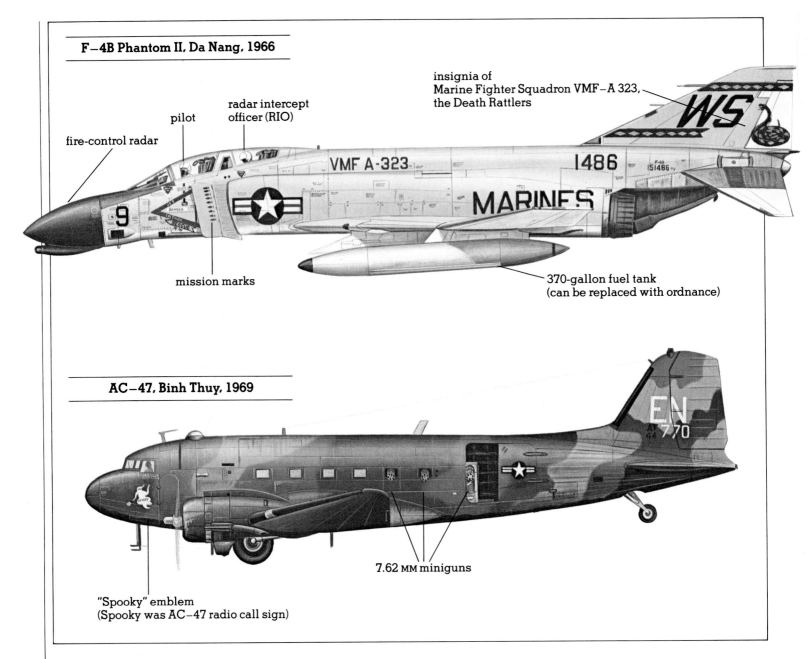

F—4B Phantom II, Da Nang, 1966

fire-control radar

pilot

radar intercept
officer (RIO)

insignia of
Marine Fighter Squadron VMF—A 323,
the Death Rattlers

VMF A-323

1486

MARINES

mission marks

370-gallon fuel tank
(can be replaced with ordnance)

AC—47, Binh Thuy, 1969

7.62 MM miniguns

"Spooky" emblem
(Spooky was AC—47 radio call sign)

The 81MM mortar had a range of two to three miles and was quite dependable within its limitations. It was known as an "area weapon," since its accuracy was confined to a fifty- to sixty-five-foot radius around its target. It thus could not be used for pinpoint shelling of a bunker or small hut. Its greatest advantage in Vietnam was its angle of fire and trajectory. Usually fired at any angle greater than forty-five degrees, the shell descends at a nearly vertical angle and could thus break through the jungle canopy more easily than shells descending at a more horizontal angle. This advantage, plus its ability to be carried along with the infantry, often made it one of the most valuable support weapons available to American troops in Vietnam.

AC-47 gunship

Among the best friends of American forces in Vietnam was "Puff the Magic Dragon," the AC-47 gunship. And no wonder, with its pinpoint accuracy and its adaptability to nighttime warfare, it was responsible for alleviating the pressure on many a trapped American platoon or company.

Adapted from the C-47 transport plane used to carry supplies and paratroopers from World War II through Korea and flown by volunteer American pilots at Dien Bien Phu, the AC-47 was equipped with fixed, side-firing machine guns. Because it was a redesigned cargo plane it could carry enough ammo to fight almost all night, even at its top ca-

pacity of 6,000 rounds per minute. The gunship also carried its own supply of parachute flares and thus could light up a nighttime battlefield to almost daytime conditions. It received its nickname in 1964 from the then-popular song because during nighttime operations its rapid firing machine guns made it look like a fire-breathing dragon.

The basic technique employed by "Puff" was to fly a controlled turn at a carefully set bank angle. This permitted the ship to fire a steady stream of rounds at a single point, almost as if someone at that point were holding the plane with a string and twirling it around. The AC-47 could thus "hose down" a selected spot of enemy concentration. A slight modification of this technique permitted "Puff" to blanket with fire an enemy perimeter rather than a single point.

F-4 Phantom

Among the sophisticated fighter-bomber jets, the F-4 was probably the most widely used in Vietnam. Guided almost entirely by ground radar, the Phantom could drop its bombs within 100 yards of a selected target. Like the Sky-raider, it could carry high explosive bombs, napalm, phosphorous, or cluster bomb units as well as rockets and the 20mm Gatling gun firing 6,000 rounds per minute.

A Phantom flying in tactical support of an engaged combat unit might come from one of two sources. Some were kept on permanent alert on the ground, ready to go whenever called upon. More often the jets were kept in the air on preplanned missions, for the express purpose of responding to emergencies. The one great disadvantage of this practice was that the aircraft in operation could not change ordnance, and thus might have only 500-pound bombs for a situation that called for napalm.

Flying high and swiftly, the Phantoms were almost completely radar directed but also required a complicated coordination with ground commanders and forward air controllers (FACs). The FACs flew in smaller, lower-flying craft and communicated directly with the ground commanders, marking the target areas with white phosphorous rockets. The jets would then follow, after receiving instructions from the FACs, zooming in on the marked target. (Ground troops referred to the jet pilots as "zoomies.") Foul weather, which might prevent a jet pilot from sighting the ground markers, might thus abort a mission.

With a high level of preparedness and with jets frequently already in the air, field commanders could count on a jet strike within a maximum of fifteen to thirty minutes from their initial requests.

UH-1B gunship

More than any other weapon at America's disposal, the UH-series helicopter—the Huey—came to symbolize the Vietnam War. Among its many uses, the helicopter was also a valuable addition to America's tactical fire support arsenal when outfitted as a gunship. The Huey gunship was armed with a variety of weapons, including rocket pods, a pair of forward-firing machine guns or miniguns, and a chin turret with 40mm automatic grenade launchers. Later improvements increased the ability to "mix and match" these basic weapons. They thus possessed a versatility exceeded by few fire support weapons.

The Huey normally fired its rockets about a mile or less from the target, each rocket armed with either ten or seventeen pounds of high explosives or phosphorous. Although they were "free flight rockets," without radar or other guidance systems to aim them and lacked pinpoint accuracy when fired in salvoes of up to twenty or more, they could saturate a wide area with deadly shrapnel or phosphorous. The smaller weapons—machine guns and 40mm grenade launchers—could be fired with deadly accuracy. So long as the targets (or friendly troops) were not obscured by bad weather or terrain, they could fire within a few yards of American positions.

The Huey could also react quickly to support ground troops. Although much slower than jets (they generally cruised at about one hundred twenty miles per hour), they were based at innumerable fire support bases throughout Vietnam. Fuel and ammo could be stocked at many locations, permitting the Hueys to

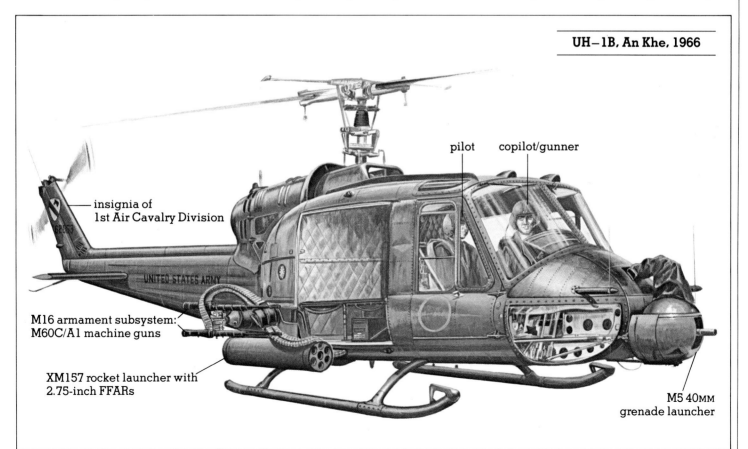

UH-1B, An Khe, 1966

insignia of 1st Air Cavalry Division

pilot

copilot/gunner

M16 armament subsystem: M60C/A1 machine guns

XM157 rocket launcher with 2.75-inch FFARs

M5 40mm grenade launcher

51

rearm and refuel quickly and return to the battlefield. This, plus an average endurance in the air of ninety minutes, meant that they could, with brief interruptions, keep aloft in the battle area all day. The Huey truly earned its reputation as the workhorse of Vietnam.

A-1 Skyraider

When choosing among fighter-bombers, the choice of battlefield commanders was often the propeller-driven A-1 Skyraider, rather than its more modern cousins, the sophisticated fighter jets. Like the jets, the Skyraider, or SPAD as it was named after the slow-flying World War I airplane, could deliver several types of high explosive bombs (up to 2,000

(Above) A camouflaged A-1E Skyraider drops a phosphorous bomb on a montagnard village. (Left) Another Skyraider drops its napalm canisters. This aircraft is probably making its first pass, as another napalm bomb and five 500-pound explosive bombs are still under each wing.

pounds), napalm, phosphorous, and cluster bomb units. The CBU broke open in midair and scattered hundreds of "butterfly bombs" over a wide area. In addition, the Skyraider could fire rockets and carried four 20MM cannons that together fired over 2,000 rounds per minute.

The A-1 had two great advantages over the jets. It could fly for long periods without refueling and thus could "loiter" near the battlefield. It could also carry more bomb tonnage than most World War II bombers. Its one great disadvantage was its relatively slow speed and low flying altitude, which made it vulnerable to enemy antiaircraft fire. But these very characteristics were what made it a battlefield favorite: It was the most accurate bomber available.

(Above) Puff the Magic Dragon. An AC-47 fires its electrically driven Gatling guns at twilight. The fire is so fast that it suggests a constant stream of fire flowing from plane to ground. (Right) An F-4C Phantom jet fires its full load of high explosive rockets: six wing pods with nineteen rockets per pod.

Search and Destroy

"You will enter the continent of Europe, and in conjunction with the other United Nations, undertake operations aimed at the heart of Germany and destruction of her armed forces." These straightforward orders of the Combined Chiefs of Staff to General Eisenhower, initiating Operation Overlord, the Normandy invasion, epitomize to most Americans the only way in which war should be carried out: Engage the enemy and destroy him. Indeed, for one hundred years this has been the American way of waging war.

The victory of the Union over the Confederacy in the Civil War ushered in a new era of American warfare. Despite experiences in such limited conflicts as the Boxer Rebellion, the Spanish-American War, and the Mexican incursion, the broad outline of American military strategy has been designed to fight wars of attrition. Like any good national strategy, this one is based on the best qualities of American society. American industry, when converted to military uses, has

been unsurpassed in producing war materiel, and American military strategy has been based on that superiority.

By the end of World War II this strategy provided America with a fighting force unequaled in the world. The United States broke the stalemate of World War I as much because of the quantity of war goods sent with American soldiers as because of the quality of those troops. Hitler's dream of European domination collapsed in the nightmare he tried to avoid, a war of attrition in which German industry was unable to match the American "arsenal of democracy," which supplied not only America's troops but those of all its allies, including the enormous Soviet army. One German soldier, when asked when he first experienced fear, replied, "When I saw my first dead American. He had new boots, a pack of cigarettes in his pocket, and two chocolate bars. Our boots were worn out and we were hungry. I knew we would lose."

American strategy, one fitting for a democracy, was based on the axiom that "bullets are cheaper than blood." Once geared up for war, American industry could provide arms and ammunition in such abundance that an economy in manpower could be compensated for with overwhelming firepower. Occasional shortages in munitions or support materiel, an accepted fact for most nations at war, are a source of twentieth century scandal for Americans. American strategy was quite simple: Find the enemy and U.S. firepower will literally blow him to hell.

But the American way of war—a war of attrition based on an aggressive engagement of enemy forces—is not the only strategy nations have employed. The Russians, who have also historically fought wars of attrition, have used not overwhelming firepower, but overwhelming manpower and territorial superiority. With a much more passive strategy, the strategic retreat, they have ground down enemy armies, avoiding direct engagement until the end. And the Germans have attempted to avoid wars of attrition altogether, knowing that they could not win them. Instead, German officers developed the *Blitzkrieg*, or war of maneuver, designed not so much to destroy enemy armies as to neutralize them through encirclement and by destroying lines of communication. Germany holds every record for the capture of whole armies still intact but unable to continue operations.

Not surprisingly, the general staff of each of these countries has been shaped by their historical strategies. American generals have learned to excel at managing resources, at insuring that war materiel is where it should be, when it should be, and in abundance. Out of World War II few American generals emerged with a reputation for tactical genius, with George S. Patton and Douglas

MacArthur the prominent exceptions. General Eisenhower, certainly a masterful leader of men and a military diplomat, really earned his reputation for the logistical innovations of the Normandy invasion and his talent for skillful blending of several nations' forces in battle, rather than for tactical judgment.

In the postwar period, these tendencies were reinforced, particularly in the army, which bore the greatest responsibility for fighting large-scale wars. Under President Eisenhower, efficiency in management became a prerequisite for the promotion-seeking career officer. Efforts at rethinking strategy and pursuing tactical innovation were in effect discouraged. Acquisition of managerial skills at such places as the Harvard Business School soon took its place beside attendance at the Army War College as a qualification for a high Pentagon position. The generation of army generals following Patton, Eisenhower, and MacArthur became America's first generation of "war managers." And no general better typified or more greatly benefited from this historical development than William C. Westmoreland.

The inevitable general

His biographer called him "the inevitable general." His West Point classmates nicknamed him "Chief" in the certain belief that William Childs Westmoreland would be the one member of their class to become army chief of staff. Even his mother recalled the qualities from his boyhood that would serve him so well in his career: "My boy always had good habits. He was always particular about his appearance and knew how to put on his clothes to make himself look good." William Westmoreland, with his square jaw, neatly trimmed hair, and lean build, certainly looked like a general.

He was born on March 26, 1914, in the small South Carolina town of Saxon. The Westmorelands, a prominent family claiming Confederate officers among its ancestors, led a comfortable existence. A servants' cabin stood in the back yard. An Eagle Boy Scout and a successful high school student, Westmoreland spent one year at the Citadel in Charleston, South Carolina, and then transferred to West Point to join the class of 1936. He finished well in the upper quarter of his class, but more important, as were Robert E. Lee, John J. Pershing, and Douglas MacArthur before him, he was named first captain, the highest honor a cadet can earn and a virtual guarantee of future success.

As for many officers commissioned in the 1930s, World War II offered Westmoreland an opportunity for rapid advancement. Early in the war, already a lieutenant colonel, he was given command of the 34th Field Artillery Battalion of the 9th Infantry Division, which he eventually led into Germany. During the summer of 1943 in Sicily Westmoreland, by then a full colonel, made a major break for himself. During a lull in the fighting he called on the commanding general of the nearby 82d Airborne, General Matthew B. Ridgway, and his chief artillery officer, General Maxwell Taylor. Learning that Ridgway was under orders to pursue the enemy swiftly, Westmoreland placed his battalion's forty trucks and jeeps at the disposal of the 82d, earning a place in the book Ridgway kept to note promising young officers. Westmoreland's career would rise in peacetime under the tutelage of Ridgway and especially Taylor.

Shortly after World War II ended, Westmoreland headed to jump school at Fort Bragg, North Carolina, becoming one of the army's elite soldiers, airborne qualified. In the Korean War he commanded the 187th Airborne Combat Team. In late 1953 he obtained his first important position in the army bureaucracy, heading the army's manpower office in the Pentagon. This post gave him the opportunity to attend Harvard Business School. While many officers fidgeted under the B. School's exacting curriculum, Westmoreland adopted many of the management concepts he learned there and became one of the school's leading advocates within the military. The stint at Harvard prepared Westmoreland for his next assignment as secretary of the general staff for Army Chief of Staff Maxwell Taylor. In 1965 Taylor awarded him his second star, and Westmoreland became at age forty-two the youngest major general in the army.

In 1960 Westmoreland received another choice assignment: superintendent of West Point. After a three-year stint there he received the command of the XVIII Airborne Corps at Fort Bragg, North Carolina. One of his assignments there was to refine contingency plans for military action in the Caribbean after the Cuban missile crisis. Westmoreland's role in preparing the corps and his careful attention to logistics and interservice coordination helped gain him the attention of Defense Secretary McNamara and other high officials.

There seemed to be only one more step to cap his career—army chief of staff. He would eventually achieve that position but first, Lyndon Johnson intervened. In 1964 the president named Westmoreland deputy and then, in June, successor to General Paul Harkins, COMUSMACV, commander, U.S. Military Assistance Command, Vietnam.

In Westmoreland, Johnson had selected the best of the new generation of generals: a superb manager, an experienced commander in war and peace, and a seasoned veteran of Pentagon battles. Westmoreland was a logical choice, a general who had succeeded with the qualities so many other prominent generals—not the least of whom was Eisenhower—had possessed. Had the war in Vietnam been more like World War II, there seems little doubt that General Westmoreland would have returned home to the same acclaim his predecessors had enjoyed.

But the United States Army had neither prepared Westmoreland—nor perhaps any other general—for what

The commanding general. General William C. West-moreland addresses American soldiers at a Special Forces camp in 1966.

proved to be America's most complex war, one in which the traditionally sharp distinctions between military and political tasks blurred. The war, as Westmoreland himself well understood, could not be fought as an American "war as usual." The greatest challenge to Westmoreland was to grow beyond the old lessons. For the next three years Westmoreland would attempt to adapt to this new face of war in Vietnam.

The development of a strategy

Within weeks after assuming command of MACV, Westmoreland developed the military strategy with which he guided South Vietnamese forces and later commanded the torrent of American troops arriving in country. Westmoreland's strategy was divided into three components. The first was "search and destroy," a process by which large units would "find, fix in place, fight, and destroy (or neutralize) enemy forces" and their base areas. Next, "clearing operations" would find those guerrillas who remained in an area after the larger-scale search and destroy operations ended. Finally, "securing operations" would be undertaken to guarantee permanent defense and provide the stable environment in which village pacification efforts could be conducted.

Westmoreland faced one immediate problem: There were insufficient American troops, even at the height of the war, to undertake all three operations simultaneously throughout the country. His solution was to divide responsibility. American troops would carry the brunt of search and destroy operations, freeing ARVN to conduct clearing operations. Finally, South Vietnamese Regional Forces (RFs) and Popular Forces (PFs), backed by ARVN, would assume the burden of securing the countryside.

Westmoreland's strategy rested above all on his confidence in the superiority of American tactical firepower. Search and destroy operations were continuously carried out in the belief, proven correct, that once caught enemy troops would be no match for the tactical fire support that American field officers could call in: artillery from nearby bases, helicopter gunships, and fixed-wing jets strafing and bombing, including giant B-52 bombers from Guam and Thailand, first introduced into the war in late 1965. The major responsibility of American ground troops was to locate enemy units, pinpoint their locations, and call in supporting fire.

These tactics dictated the war in Vietnam as it was experienced by most American combat troops. Their typical assignment, when they were not engaged in a large-scale operation, was "reconnaissance in force." A small unit, perhaps as large as a battalion, would conduct patrols along predetermined paths, eventually linking up with other friendly units. There might be hope, especially in planned operations, that a large enemy unit could be located and destroyed by a classic "pincer" or "hammer and anvil" movement. Most often, however, the enemy merely hid in the bush or, in the case of the Vietcong, disguised themselves as civilians. If the American soldiers were attacked they had in a sense achieved their immediate objective. They now knew where the enemy was and could attempt to call in supporting fire. Reconnaissance in force meant that American troops were, in reality, used as bait in the hope that the enemy would strike or ambush them and thus divulge their location.

From search and destroy to attrition

Westmoreland's battle plan became the basis of the American ground strategy of attrition: to neutralize effectively through death, severe wounds, or the destruction of supplies and rear base areas, enough enemy troops so that the enemy would be unable to continue fighting. Or as Westmoreland expressed it more graphically, "We'll just go on bleeding them until Hanoi wakes up to the fact that they have bled their country to the point of national disaster for generations." The strategy met the immediate emergency of 1965 by blunting the enemy's spring-summer offensive. However inconclusive many were, no major engagements ever resulted in battlefield defeat for American units. When American artillery and air power could be called in, they exerted a devastating effect.

But Westmoreland had difficulty translating the tactical successes he enjoyed into a winning strategy. Until late 1966, neither Westmoreland nor anyone in the Pentagon made any study to determine how many enemy troops would have to be neutralized for the strategy to succeed. When they did so, they saw how difficult the task was they had set for themselves. From 1965 to the end of 1967 the enemy lost a maximum of three hundred fifty thousand soldiers, including attrition from death, severe wounds, desertion and defection, and capture. Yet enemy strength increased rather than decreased. From a total of about one hundred eighty thousand men at the end of 1964, combined VC/NVA strength reached more than two hundred fifty thousand in December 1967. According to Westmoreland's own estimates, the enemy was able to augment its forces by one hundred thousand per year from the infiltration of NVA regulars and by about fifty thousand per year by recruitment within South Vietnam. The total of one hundred fifty thousand per year easily made good all of their losses. Westmoreland later revised even those figures, reporting from his intelligence estimates that by 1968 the enemy was able to infiltrate or recruit three hundred thousand men per year.

Westmoreland's battle plan also proved to encompass a much less comprehensive battle plan than appeared on paper. The division of responsibility just didn't work, an outcome Westmoreland must surely have contemplated. American combat troops had been called into Vietnam in the first place because ARVN units had shown that they were unable to guard American air bases. Now in mid-1965, after ARVN had suffered tremendous casualties during the Vietcong spring offensive, Westmoreland asked it to provide the needed security for Vietnam's twelve thousand hamlets. ARVN forces were no more up to this task than they had been up to the much easier task of protecting military installations.

In addition, the ARVN commanders resented being assigned the duller task of providing local security while American troops grabbed glory in large-scale operations. Having been trained by the Americans to fight more aggressively, they now refused to accept this secondary, passive task, no matter how crucial it was to a winning strategy. Westmoreland further contributed to the unwillingness of ARVN troops to accept a revised role by insisting that South Vietnamese units also be available to augment and back up American troops during large-scale search and destroy operations. One result was that ARVN failed to develop training methods and a more flexible command structure adapted to the needs of clearing and securing.

The problems of developing effective South Vietnamese forces to engage in clearing and securing operations, though admittedly complex, might have been addressed by a more vigorous MACV advisory role among those troops responsible for the tasks, especially ARVN forces at the district level and RFs and PFs in the villages. MACV

In the wake of a VC ambush in the Iron Triangle, men of Company B, 2d Battalion, 503d Infantry, 173d Airborne Brigade, await a medical evacuation helicopter to carry away their dead and wounded. The VC have slipped away.

advisers had first been assigned to some (but not all) districts in 1964. By 1965 a total of 765 army advisers (226 of them officers) were assigned to district duty.

The role of these new district-level advisers was to improve "the effectiveness of these paramilitary units [RFs and PFs] in the Vietnamese pacification plan." MACV had rejected the Pentagon's suggestion that the district advisers be used largely to train the local forces and instead believed that they could be more effectively used in the "supervision and coordination in the employment of paramilitary forces and a general reinforcement of the pacification effort at the district level."

The major problem was that the advisers did not live with these paramilitary forces but rather retired to a district capital at night, the time when local guerrillas most often struck. The role of the local forces was to deter guerrilla attacks, but since these attacks were usually of extremely short duration, amounting to a hit-and-run attack, the usefulness of the district advisers in coordinating a response was limited. Moreover, the program in 1965 had begun in a few high-priority districts, and expansion came very slowly. Two years later their number had grown to only 969. The reason, according to the *Pentagon Papers*, was that during the build-up of American forces "the advisory effort sank into relative obscurity."

Only in mid-1967, after Washington sent unmistakable signals to Saigon that a much greater effort should be made at pacification, was the commitment of advisers at the lowest levels substantially increased. In June 1967 MACV requested the assignment of 2,243 Americans to advise South Vietnamese Regional and Popular Forces at the *village* level. For the first time MACV's advisory program would be in operation at the basic unit of Vietnamese society, the village, where it could exert a continual influence on the Vietnamese forces responsible for clearing and securing. MACV's earlier reluctance to back up its verbal commitment to these operations with sufficient resources only served to convince ARVN leaders that this was not a matter of high priority.

"Breaking boulders"

As a result, the Westmoreland strategy came to mean a lot more "searching and destroying" than "clearing and securing." Westmoreland justified this imbalance by recalling an analogy which likened an insurgency to a boulder: "A sledge first has to break the boulder into large fragments; groups of workers then attack fragments with spalling tools; then individuals pound the chips with tap hammers until they are reduced to powder and the boulder ceases to exist."

But the enemy Main Force units, the primary target of search and destroy operations, were not inanimate objects like boulders. Insurgent generals often took the first step on their own, breaking down regiments and battalions

into smaller units in order to avoid the sledge hammer. Even when broken down, or broken into "large fragments" by American firepower, enemy units were able to reorganize, regroup, and re-recruit, forming another "boulder." And with so little "clearing and securing" conducted by ARVN, they enjoyed the time and safety to do so. Meeting the danger of enemy Main Force units was an essential step in any strategy, but Westmoreland's seldom went beyond this first step.

Westmoreland apparently adopted these priorities because he believed that "the enemy was moving into the third phase of revolutionary warfare," in which the insurgents, according to Giap and Mao, would adopt the tactics of conventional warfare. However, when the State Department Office of Intelligence and Research examined this assumption in June 1965, it argued against "the hypothesis that the Communists are preparing to enter the third stage. . . . We do not believe that the criteria established by Giap for the third stage—size of unit, scale of operation, and nature of attack—have been or are about to be met in South Vietnam." George Ball, arguing against the accelerated deployment of U.S. troops in July 1965, cited this State Department study but added that even if the enemy had moved into the third stage, "we have no basis for assuming that the Vietcong will fight a war on our terms. . . . There is every reason to suppose that the Vietcong will avoid providing good targets for our massive bombing and superior firepower."

In fact, the danger even from enemy Main Force units was never eliminated, because it was the enemy, and not Westmoreland, who was able to maintain the tactical initiative, a fact that contributed to the increasing frustration of American troops. In 1972 the JCS reported that of all the American patrols conducted in 1967-68 "less than 1 percent . . . resulted in contact with the enemy." When the patrols of ARVN units were included, the percentage dropped to one-tenth of 1 percent. Most patrols ended in failure, because enemy troops refused to fire and thereby divulge their location. And when Americans did make contact with the enemy, it was all too often a solitary sniper or perhaps a few guerrillas covering the retreat of the real prize, a Main Force unit, which could then slip back into the safety of its rear base areas inside and beyond the borders of South Vietnam. During the entire course of the war more than 50 percent of all fire fights were either too small or too quick to warrant a request for tactical fire support. In most cases, American might—artillery and air support—simply could not be brought to bear. Major General William E. DePuy, then commander of the U.S. 1st Infantry Division and a major architect of MACV's strategy, elaborated on the frustration: "The game in the jungle is to send in a small force as bait, let the enemy attack, and be able to react with a larger force in reserve nearby. But if the enemy doesn't want to fight, then the jungle goes off in 360 directions."

In this war without fronts, in which territorial advancement was not a goal, MACV and the Pentagon developed a series of quantifiable indices to measure progress. The most famous of these was the "body count." Originally the body count was instituted to replace "estimated killings" reported by ARVN in the early 1960s, estimates ridiculed by most of the American press. Orders were issued to count actual bodies to insure accuracy. Soon the body count became a measure of progress in itself. Had the enemy (including North Vietnam) already been stretched to the limits of mobilization in 1965—as America's enemies had been when the U.S. entered World Wars I and II—this might have made sense in a war of attrition. But the enemy was not stretched to its limits and never would be until it chose to mount its final offensive in 1975. As long as the Vietcong and North Vietnamese were able to replace and augment their forces, body counts offered no more than an illusion of progress.

Another, even more delusive, measure of progress was "battalion days in the field," days in which battalions, in part or whole, were merely in the field patrolling. This index was important in gauging the effectiveness of ARVN commanders, notorious for their unwillingness to "get out into the field," but it was a poor way of evaluating American battalions, which were not so inhibited. The fact that most patrols ended in no contact with the enemy was obscured in the statistical compilation. Similar results were obtained by measuring sorties flown by jets or helicopters. The accumulation of "sorties flown," like battalion days in the field, became an end in itself.

A final category of statistics was so subjective that its reliability was open to great question. Stress was put on the number of roads and railways open for use or the number of enemy base areas destroyed. Almost any road or railway could become the scene of an enemy ambush. A damaged enemy base area rapidly redeveloped. But officers in the field were expected to decide whether security had been guaranteed. Not surprisingly, since efficiency reports on all officers reflected their ability to present evidence of progress in their statistical summaries, a certain institutional bias toward exaggeration developed. Military careerism took its place among the problems inherent in Westmoreland's command.

What was most serious of all was that every statistical indicator could point to progress where none really existed. American officers and their troops could be meeting every objective required of them and the war would drag on. The statistics could be fed into a computer to show how much the enemy was hurting. But in the end one variable was missing: the attitudes of the people of Vietnam. As long as their loyalty and their security remained in doubt, the enemy could make good its losses and even grow no matter how much it was damaged.

Ultimately, even the army had its doubts. General DePuy, who as Westmoreland's operations officer in 1965

had pressed hard for a search and destroy oriented strategy, later admitted to another general that he "had not been perspicacious enough in those days. We should ... have thought through the military problem better."

In fact, some military experts have questioned whether a broad strategy of attrition that does not encompass more carefully defined strategic goals can really be called a strategy at all. Lieutenant Colonel Dave Richard Palmer, a leading military historian at West Point, described the strategy of attrition employed in Vietnam as "irrefutable proof of the absence of any strategy":

A commander who resorts to attrition admits his failure to conceive of an alternative. He turns from warfare as an art and accepts it on the most nonprofessional terms imaginable. He uses blood in lieu of brains.

The marine alternative

Westmoreland's strategy did not go unchallenged by his comrades in arms. The *Pentagon Papers* note, though only cryptically, that the air force chief of staff and the Marine Corps commandant were "known proponents of the enclave strategy," opposing the more aggressive search and destroy approach. But the discussions among the Joint Chiefs are still classified, and the exact content of that debate is unknown. More is known of the dispute between the marines and Westmoreland.

As the first American combat troops to enter Vietnam in force, the marines began on their own to experiment in the development of tactics. Operating on the principle that their primary responsibility lay in the enclaves that they had established, they developed tactics oriented toward providing security for the local population, or as some saw it, controlling the population.

In coming to this conclusion the marines may have been acting as much on the basis of their historical experiences as Westmoreland was in adopting traditional U.S. Army strategy. Throughout the twentieth century the marines have been called on to conduct limited military operations in support of American foreign policy, operations where political goals were often more important than strictly military ones. As recently as April 1965 the marines had found themselves in such a situation in the Dominican Republic. The marines' conclusion that the people of Vietnam were the real objective in the war, therefore, may well have been less a result of strategic or tactical innovation than of what marine General Edwin H. Simmons termed the "tribal memories" of the Marine Corps.

The differences between Westmoreland and MACV on one side, and the marines on the other, became part of a larger debate over strategy. In its broadest terms the debate was between those who were population oriented (like the marines and the VC) and those who were territory oriented. Although Westmoreland did not place a high priority on the occupation of territory, he did stress

A medical corpsman races to safety with a baby wounded by U.S. jets when they strafed the Cape Batangan operational area before the marine landing.

Operation Piranha

"Damned if we do and damned if we don't," said marine General Lewis Walt at the conclusion of Operation Piranha in November 1965 on Cape Batangan. Trying to destroy the remainder of the Vietcong 1st Regiment after Operation Starlite, the marines were met with the stony stares of villagers and the absence of guerrillas. Most of Piranha's 167 enemy KIAs came after the marines had taken fire from one well-fortified bunker. But the victims turned out to be the seriously wounded VC survivors from the earlier Operation Starlite.

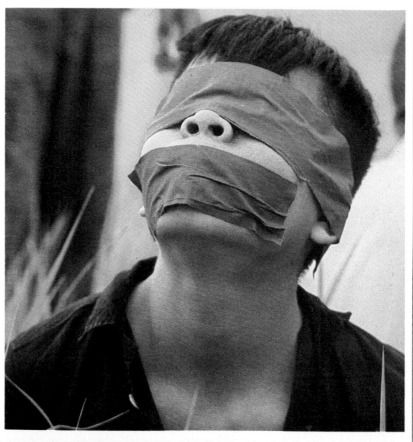

A Vietcong guerrilla captured during Operation Piranha whose eyes and mouth have been taped as a security measure.

A marine stands guard over refugees after the sweep through Cape Batangan.

Hospitalman Second Class Josiah "Doc" Lucier, attached to marines conducting pacification south of Da Nang, makes his rounds accompanied by two Vietnamese children, one of them injured by napalm. Lucier told a reporter that for the U.S. to win the trust of the Vietnamese people, "There's just got to be something more than bullets."

the importance of denying it to the enemy. In practice this meant that he placed as much emphasis, if not more, on sparsely populated areas like the highlands as he did on the heavily populated coastal regions.

Westmoreland well understood the marine tactics. "They were assiduously combing the countryside within the beachheads [enclaves]," he wrote, "trying to establish firm control in hamlets and villages, and planning to expand the beachhead gradually up and down the coast." The coast, of course, is where most of the South Vietnamese people live. But he was "concerned with the tactical methods that . . . the marines employed." Respectful of the marines' traditions and sense of independence, Westmoreland chose not "to deal so abruptly with General Walt that I might precipitate an interservice imbroglio. . . . Rather than start a controversy, I chose to issue orders for specific projects that as time passed would gradually get the marines out of their beachheads."

Westmoreland believed in the need for "spoiling attacks" to keep the enemy off balance and to use the "tactical mobility" and "shock action" of U.S. forces. The marines recognized the legitimacy of Westmoreland's concerns but objected to his priorities which too often took them away from the population in order to stalk the enemy in the mountains. The marines agreed that the enemy Main Force units posed a real threat, not the least to the population they wanted to protect. But the marines believed that this threat should be met only when superior intelligence virtually guaranteed success and where the Main Force units posed an immediate threat to populated areas (such as in Operation Starlite). They did not believe that the war against Main Force units should become the prime objective of American operations or an end in itself.

Lieutenant General Victor H. Krulak, commander of FMFPAC, the marine Pacific command, told CINCPAC Admiral Sharp:

It is our conviction that if we can destroy the guerrilla fabric among the people, we will automatically deny the larger units the food and the intelligence and the taxes and the other support they need. At the same time, if the big units want to sortie out of the mountains and come down where they can be cut up by our supporting arms, the marines are glad to take them on, but the real war is among the people and not among these mountains.

After the war, in 1978, Krulak was even more direct: "Every man we put into hunting for the NVA was wasted."

As commander of all American forces in Vietnam, Westmoreland eventually had his way. Not only could he order the marines into the mountains, but by using progress indices like battalion days in the field he could create institutional incentives to move the marines out. When the category of battalion days in the field was first announced, the marines tried unsuccessfully to gain recognition of pacification efforts as "days in the field." MACV turned them down. Brigadier General Frederick J. Karch, assis-

tant commander of the 3d Marine Division represented III MAF at the briefing where the concept of battalion days in the field was first announced. He later wrote,

I remember the day of this briefing well as it struck me as the day we changed from a high priority pacification program that could win the guerrilla war to a public relations spectacle program that would lose lives and the war.

It would be an exaggeration to suggest that the marines had developed a full-blown pacification or population-oriented strategy. Nor is there any guarantee that such a strategy would have enjoyed any greater success than Westmoreland's. In fact, the marine alternative faced many difficult problems. Defense analysts later pointed out that the marine approach "is slow and methodical, requires vast numbers of troops, runs the risk of turning into an occupation even while being called 'pacification/civic action,' and involves Americans deeply in the politics and traditions of rural Vietnam."

Marine pacification

Indeed, in the limited application of their approach the marines were often confronted by these problems. Not understanding local political traditions, the marines often met opposition by the civilian population. And as their experiences at Cam Ne so well illustrated, fighting the war primarily in heavily populated areas was fraught with danger. Yet the marines did institute some tactics which might have begun to solve these problems and form the basis of a full strategy. Among the most intriguing was the Combined Action Platoon (CAP).

CAPs consisted of a South Vietnamese Popular Forces platoon of thirty-eight men that joined with a U.S. Marine rifle squad and a medical corpsman, fifteen Americans in all, to form an enlarged platoon responsible for village security. Of greatest importance, the CAPs lived in the village, and unlike most American and ARVN troops, did not leave after clearing it of VC. With their security provided for twenty-four hours a day, the villagers were much more likely to cooperate with the CAPs, knowing that they were better protected from reprisal by the VC. Of all the problems Americans faced in gaining the cooperation of civilians, this was the most important: assuring villagers that they would not suffer if they rallied to the GVN cause.

The American marines and the Vietnamese PFs complemented each other well. The marines could supply the élan and technical know-how, especially in directing supporting fires in the event of attack, while the PFs smoothed the interaction between Americans and the Vietnamese population. In return, the marines could insure proper treatment of the population by the PFs. The villagers soon gained confidence in the CAP's fighting ability and comfort in the knowledge that their village was truly secure.

The CAPs were the only instance in which South Vietnamese troops were placed directly under the command of Americans, which might well have accelerated the training of competent South Vietnamese forces, thus hastening the long-delayed Vietnamization of the war. By this means the marines might have met the problems of heavy troop requirements and slow results cited by the Pentagon analysts.

Westmoreland recognized the virtues of the CAPs but did little to encourage their use, especially outside of I Corps, the operating ground of the marines. Westmoreland later explained, "I simply had not enough numbers to put a squad of Americans in every village and hamlet. ..." Under the marine plan, fifteen American troops were responsible for one village, on the average consisting of five hamlets. In 1967 Vietnam had approximately twenty-five hundred villages. Arithmetic shows that Westmoreland would have needed about forty thousand troops to "put a squad of Americans in every village and hamlet."

Westmoreland and General Walt, III MAF commander, both argued that their differences were more a matter of "emphasis" than of fundamental principles. However, General Edwin H. Simmons, Walt's director of operations, suggested that "that was for public consumption and there were some fairly fundamental differences in the two approaches." The differences were sufficiently great to cause General Greene to carry the debate into the Joint Chiefs of Staff. He later reported that the chiefs were "interested" in the marine approach but ultimately decided to back their field commander. In other words, the JCS decided the debate not on the substance of the dispute but according to military tradition: support for the commander in the field.

The response of the JCS pointed out another difficulty America faced in fighting this complex war. Traditional divisions of authority—ultimate civilian control of the military and military control over battle strategies—were applied in a very untraditional setting. The "interference" of civilians in military matters, which the JCS accepted as a part of the American tradition of civilian control, was never reexamined in the Vietnam context. This dimension of civilian-military conflict has been extensively reported. But less noticed was the absence of civilian input into the strategy of the ground war in which the military and political dimensions were always acknowledged as inseparable.

The marine approach was never considered by civilian foreign policy experts or debated beyond the military confines of the JCS. Brigadier General Douglas Kinnard concluded in 1974 that civilians had failed to fulfill their responsibilities in guiding the military:

The big questions about objectives or strategy were not debated until after the Tet 1968 offensive. Thus when Westmoreland writes that there were too many constraints imposed by civilians on his conduct of the war, he may be correct in one sense. From a dif-

ferent perspective, however, one can draw another conclusion: There was not *enough* civilian participation in terms of asking the big questions about what we were really doing in Vietnam.

With neither his military nor his civilian superiors willing to intervene in the debate on strategy, Westmoreland and his staff at MACV were left free to pursue the tactics of search and destroy. Given no choice, the marines followed. Ultimately the wisdom of Westmoreland's choice would be determined in two-and-a-half years of fighting. But its first real test came in the fall of 1965.

The attack at Plei Me

7:00 P.M., October 19, 1965. The scene was familiar. A unit of enemy soldiers, this time North Vietnamese regulars, attacked the isolated Civilian Irregular Defense Group/Special Forces camp at Plei Me, thirty miles southwest of Pleiku. It was the old VC tactic: Attack an isolated outpost, but don't overrun it; allow ARVN reserves to come to the rescue, and ambush them along the way. Then follow up the victory by attacking the area formerly protected by the reserve troops. The tactic had worked well all summer, providing the VC with their greatest victories in the spring offensive.

But there was a difference this time: American combat units were on the scene and available for action. When reports of the initial attack reached American headquarters in II Corps, intelligence reports immediately informed American commanders that an ambush of reserves was likely. Two full NVA regiments in the vicinity were augmented by Vietcong Main Force units and local guerrillas. It was clear that the enemy possessed more than enough strength to overrun the CIDG camp and was only waiting to spring the ambush on a relief column from Pleiku. Nor were there enough ARVN troops in Pleiku to lift the siege of the camp and also to protect the provincial capital. The orders went out to An Khe, base camp of the U.S. Army 1st Cavalry Division (Airmobile), to send a battalion to Pleiku in order to free ARVN troops, aided by American air support, to relieve the CIDG camp.

The montagnards in the CIDG camp, together with their Special Forces advisers, were encircled. When asked by radio what they needed inside the camp, an American sergeant asked for ammo and reinforcements. "Where do you want the fighters?" he was asked. "All around, 360 degrees. All you've got. Just as close as you can get," came the reply.

On October 21 the reinforcements left Pleiku as the 1st Air Cav battalion came to relieve them. Two days later the South Vietnamese rangers were ambushed, just as intelligence predicted. Major (later Lieutenant) General Harry W. O. Kinnard, commander of the 1st Air Cav, immediately asked for permission to come to their rescue. His request was approved, with the proviso that sufficient force be kept in Pleiku for security. On October 24, Lieutenant Colonel Earl Ingram's 2d Battalion, 12th Cavalry, established an artillery position in support of the ARVN Rangers and broke the ambush. The next day the relief column was moving again toward Plei Me. Over one hundred twenty enemy soldiers lay dead, victims of the 1st Air Cav's artillery guns. That same day the ARVN column arrived at the camp, only to find that the NVA had disengaged. The camp at Plei Me was saved.

Six months earlier this might have been the end of the story, a great victory for ARVN. But General Kinnard was not satisfied. Intelligence told him that the two NVA regiments, the 32d and 33d, had moved only about five miles westward and were under orders to reassemble. On October 27 Westmoreland gave Kinnard what he wanted. He ordered the 1st Air Cav "to find, fix, and defeat the enemy forces that had threatened Plei Me." It was destined to be the first major test between American combat troops and North Vietnamese regulars.

The new tactical area of operations covered 965 square miles of dense, jungle-covered mountains. The area was as large as the state of Rhode Island but with only two narrow roads. The western portion of the area, where the NVA was reassembling, stood seven hundred fifty feet above sea level. A small river traversed the terrain, providing the NVA with water in seemingly secure rear areas. It was to this area that the 1st Air Cav was drawn: the valley of the Ia Drang.*

The battle of the Ia Drang Valley

The fighting along the Ia Drang offered a test of a new concept in mobile American warfare. As early as 1946 the marines had begun to experiment with the concept of a "sky cavalry" based on helicopter mobility, but not until the idea was advanced by the army's General James Gavin in a 1954 article entitled "Cavalry, and I Don't Mean Horses" did it achieve much notice. During the Eisenhower administration, when tactical innovations were discouraged, the idea remained undeveloped, but President Kennedy's insistence on a more diversified and flexible military machine led to the creation of the 11th Air Assault Division in 1963. After two years of experimentation and testing, the division was redesignated the 1st Cavalry Division (Airmobile) and became the first full stateside division to be sent to Vietnam, closing in September. It quickly adopted its preferred name: the 1st Air Cavalry. The Ia Drang Valley was the perfect location for its initial test. The lack of major roads, and even of many jungle paths, in the area made the terrain difficult for conventional infantry to patrol. With its helicopter mobility the 1st Air Cav could spot enemy units from the air and rush assault troops to the spot to engage them.

General Kinnard designated his 1st Brigade, commanded by Lieutenant Colonel Harlow Clark, to spearhead the attack. By October 28 all was in place. For three days the 1st Squadron, 9th Cavalry, employed its new technique of aerial reconnaissance by fire. Like ground reconnaissance in force, the aerial version was designed to fix enemy units by drawing fire. General Kinnard acknowledged that "the pilots would not be likely to agree that this was a preferred way to learn of the enemy's presence." But the technique permitted Kinnard to "find and then fix [the enemy] in order to mass fires and forces against him." On November 1 Americans achieved their first real success.

At 7:20 A.M., 1/9's aerial scouts spotted an increasing number of NVA soldiers near the Tae River. Within forty-five minutes one of 1/9's rifle platoons was on the ground; it quickly killed five enemy soldiers. The men of the rifle platoon had happened upon an NVA regimental hospital. Two more rifle platoons arrived in helicopters. Meanwhile, aerial reconnaissance spotted a battalion-sized NVA force closing in on the three rifle platoons. The platoons defended themselves against heavy enemy fire while help was on the way. Six full platoons were quickly helilifted in from as far away as twenty-five miles. Within two-and-a-half hours the 1st Air Cav troops, originally outnumbered, had been augmented and regained the offensive, clearing the area and securing a solid nighttime perimeter. General Kinnard later remarked, "No other unit in the world could have marshaled reaction forces so swiftly over such terrain." The 1st Air Cav had not used forces held in reserve for the reaction but plucked units out of the field, in the midst of other tasks, to fly them to the battle scene.

The day's fighting forced the NVA 33d Regiment into retreat. First Air Cav helicopter rockets continued to harass the NVA as they withdrew. The 33d soon received a reprieve when an additional NVA regiment, recently arrived in South Vietnam, joined it in the Ia Drang area. But the 1st Air Cav had more to deliver.

On November 3, Troop C of the 1/9 Cavalry used an old VC trick. They established three nighttime ambushes on the south bank of the Ia Drang. One platoon, commanded by Charles S. Knowlen, spotted a large NVA unit at 7:30 P.M. Fighting off mosquitoes and nervousness, the platoon maintained silence as the NVA troops joked and dallied in what they were sure was secure territory. Knowlen permitted the enemy lead platoon to pass—a part of the old VC tactic—before ambushing the second platoon, one carrying the NVA's heavy weapons: machine guns, mortars, and recoilless rifles. As soon as the platoon reached Knowlen's position he fired ten Claymore mines set along the jungle trail. It was the signal for his men to unload their M16s and their M79 grenade launchers.

Fearing that the enemy would soon send reinforcements, the troops quickly withdrew. Within two hours a full

---

* Ia is one of the Vietnamese words for river.

NVA battalion came rushing toward the patrol base perimeter. The first assault was repulsed, but the base was in trouble. Headquarters sent Company A of the 1/8 Cavalry to the rescue. Shortly after midnight its third platoon, commanded by Lieutenant John B. Hanlon, was on the ground. It was "the first time," according to General Kinnard, "that a perimeter under heavy fire had been relieved at night by heliborne forces."

The relief platoon, however, quickly came under heavy fire. Hanlon was hit and his medic, Specialist 4 Raymond Ortiz, rushed to his aid, but not before a bullet tore into Ortiz's left arm. After treating the officer, Ortiz heard the cry of "Medic! Over here!" As he moved toward the sound a second bullet struck Ortiz. He recovered his breath and again moved forward. A third bullet struck him, but still he tended the wounded—six in all. For his bravery Ortiz was awarded the Distinguished Service Cross.

By morning the NVA had withdrawn and an artillery battery provided additional security for the patrol base. "The night no longer belonged to the enemy," Kinnard boasted. During November 3 the 1st Air Cav had moved the equivalent of twelve companies and two artillery batteries a total of more than two hundred miles.

The pattern of those early days of the battle continued. Continuous aerial reconnaissance fixed enemy locations. Troops and, when possible, artillery were rushed in. Reinforcements arrived quickly when needed. By the end of the operation the 1st Air Cav had established a goal of twenty minutes for reinforcements to arrive. The campaign would continue for a full month, not ending until November 26, and reached its most furious pitch in the three-day battle at LZ X-Ray.

As the first phase of the fighting ended the NVA decided to reconsider its objectives. Of the original two NVA regiments, the 32d had remained combat effective, but the 33d had lost nearly two-thirds of its manpower to death, wounds, and capture. The 33d therefore reorganized its decimated battalions into one fighting unit. By November 6 a third NVA regiment was on the scene, the newly infiltrated 66th. The three regiments were ordered to regain the offensive with a renewed attack on the CIDG camp at Plei Me. There were fresh American faces on the scene as well. On November 9, Kinnard ordered the 3d Brigade of the 1st Air Cav to relieve the exhausted 1st Brigade.

The fight for LZ X-Ray

On the morning of November 14 Lieutenant Colonel Harold G. Moore's 1st Battalion, 7th Cavalry, having found little sign of the enemy, was ordered to shift its patrols westward, near the Chu Pong hills. By noon most of his battalion had landed at the small landing zone named X-Ray. As Moore's men slowly began moving out, Company B came under attack northwest of the LZ. They had run unexpectedly into the NVA 33d and 66th regiments on their way to Plei Me. As Company A moved to reinforce Company B, enemy mortar and rocket fire began hitting the LZ. The remainder of 1/7, unable to land, was waved off. Soon Companies C and D were attacked to the east of the LZ. Close air support and artillery was directed within 100 yards of the LZ to relieve the eastern position and open the LZ for reinforcements. By nightfall an additional company from 2/7 had landed. But one platoon from Company B still remained isolated and under heavy attack throughout the night.

Next morning the NVA 66th Regiment and the remainder of the 33d launched sustained attacks on the tiny perimeter of Moore's troops before additional reinforcements could be brought in. Company C repulsed the attacks in fierce hand-to-hand combat. Soon tactical air and artillery strikes took their toll of the enemy. By nine, the enemy fire had so slackened that an additional company from 2/7 was able to reinforce 1/7. But the still-isolated platoon of Company B was taking heavy casualties. Shortly after

noon Moore ordered the newly arrived—this time by foot—rifle companies of the 2/5 Cavalry to the platoon's rescue, but it had already driven off the enemy, counting 75 KIAs. Eight men of Company B lay dead, and twelve additional wounded men had been evacuated to safety; only seven of the platoon's original twenty-seven men were unscathed. Artillery and air support protected the X-Ray perimeter through the night.

At first light on November 16, Colonel Moore ordered all his troops to open fire with small arms and machine guns, one "mad minute" of fire to flush potential snipers out of trees and bushes. He gained an unexpected bonus. A 40-man NVA unit hiding in the grass thought it had been discovered and began to run in confusion. They were gunned down by the defenders of X-Ray. During the day a series of troop rotations relieved the most exhausted units and supplied the 1st Air Cav with fresh troops. But the NVA returned to the Chu Pong Massif. In the three-day battle they had lost 834 men by count, and American estimates of additional KIAs were over 1,000, mostly victims of air and artillery fire.

Agony at LZ Albany

On November 17, as the fighting at X-Ray slackened, the 2/7 Cavalry moved out, preparing to be helilifted back to headquarters from a new landing zone they were ordered to establish at a place identified as Albany. The battalion had covered most of the six-mile march when it was discovered by a patrol from the 8th Battalion of the NVA 66th Regiment. With twenty minutes warning, the enemy commander laid an ambush. Permitting the lead elements of the cavalry column to penetrate his perimeter, he then ordered his men to open up fire from the left, right front, and right flank of the Americans.

The enemy had succeeded in engaging the 2/7 forces in very tight quarters, where supporting U.S. firepower would endanger American lives. Companies C and D of the 2/7 took the brunt of the attack. Within minutes most of the men from the two companies were hit. According to one survivor, "the sound of men screaming was almost as loud as the firing." From well-entrenched machine-gun emplacements the NVA was able to mow down the cavalry soldiers in the high jungle grass. The men of Company C, virtually without combat experience, began returning fire wildly. Later it was deduced that many of the dead were killed, or at least hit, by friendly fire.

As night fell the disorganized and leaderless survivors feared an all-out enemy assault under the cover of darkness. But illumination flares provided by air force aircraft made the NVA cautious. By morning the enemy had fled, and medical evacuation of the wounded began. General Kinnard later wrote of the battle that the 2/7 "had won the day, inflicting heavy casualties on the enemy. The enemy abandoned more than four hundred of his dead and a great many weapons."

But the victory that day was much less clear-cut than General Kinnard suggested. The enemy had demonstrated that it could neutralize the effects of American firepower by close-in fighting. Reinforcements were unable to land to augment the companies under attack. During the battle no medical evacuation helicopter even attempted a landing. Of the 500 men in the original cavalry column, 150 had been killed and only 84 were able to return to immediate duty. Company C suffered 93 percent casualties, half of them deaths. Most of the wounded had been exposed to the central highlands heat for twenty-four or more hours, and this caused greater deterioration of their condition. Many were crippled for life. Victory at LZ Albany had come at a very heavy price.

During the battle for LZ X-Ray in the Ia Drang Valley, the men of Company B, 2/7, fire at NVA soldiers just outside the American perimeter.

Isolated fighting in the Ia Drang Valley continued for ten more days. It ended only when aerial reconnaissance by fire failed to reveal any more enemy locations. It was presumed that the three NVA regiments had crossed the border into Cambodia to nurse their wounds. In all, the enemy had suffered severe losses: nearly 1,500 men by body count and an additional 2,000 estimated KIAs. The NVA had lost the equivalent of nearly one-half of a full division in manpower. In contrast, MACV reported the loss of 240 Americans killed in action.

Statistics of the 1st Air Cav's engagements substantiated the battlefield tactics and the concept: Entire infantry battalions had been moved by air. Sixty-seven times artillery batteries were deployed by helicopter, often in the midst of trackless jungle where they could provide maximum close support for combat troops. During thirty-five days of fighting, tactical support fire had been overwhelming: 33,108 rounds of 105 MM howitzer ammunition and 7,356 rounds of aerial rockets. Out of perhaps fifty thousand helicopter sorties, only fifty-nine ships had taken any enemy fire, only four were shot down, and only one was lost. Over seventy-five hundred tons of supplies had been shipped in.

The Ia Drang fight contributed to the American forces' continuing education in Vietnam. Radio sets had become inoperable during periods of heavy rain. Kinnard suggested the use of plastic bags as a stopgap measure but called for the procurement of radio "boots." Combat units pointed out many problems in the use of newly arrived M16 rifles, and new methods of caring for the weapons were recommended. First Air Cav troops also found pole litters difficult to use for the evacuation of the wounded in dense vegetation. They recommended the employment of poleless nylon litters, pointing to their own improvised use of ponchos as litters. Finally, they were impressed by the superiority of the NVA rain ponchos, which were very lightweight and "did not make noise," and asked for nylon ponchos.

The North Vietnamese also learned from the battle of the Ia Drang Valley. In addition to their discovery that they could minimize the devastating effects of American firepower superiority through close-in fighting, they also discovered that the low-flying scout helicopters were poor targets and that firing at them only revealed their own locations.

General Giap's protracted war strategy

More important to the North Vietnamese than these tactical lessons was the reexamination of their strategy provoked by their losses in the Ia Drang Valley. The reexamination was a new round in a long-standing debate between General Vo Nguyen Giap on one side and Truong Chinh and General Nguyen Chi Thanh on the other.

Giap and Chinh had been engaged in extensive debate ever since 1950. Giap was the most identifiable pro-Soviet member of North Vietnam's politburo, while Chinh was the leading exponent of the Chinese revolution. Their two careers seemed to be part of an hydraulic system: When one rose, the other declined. Chinh had suffered a severe defeat in the late 1950s when his land reform plans led to a peasants' revolt. But by 1964 he had recovered much lost ground and was able to place one of his protégés, General Nguyen Chi Thanh, as commander of COSVN (Central Office for South Vietnam). Under Thanh's direction the guerrilla movement in the South moved into an intensified stage in 1964, including eventually the commitment of North Vietnamese Army regulars.

At this point Giap called for a new debate on strategy. Probably mindful of his experiences in early 1951 when he had prematurely committed his best troops against the French army, Giap urged caution, pointing to the overwhelming superiority of the Americans in firepower and mobility. Thanh disagreed. Victory was so close, he argued, that South Vietnam could be liberated before American troops had sufficient time to acclimatize themselves to the Vietnamese weather, terrain, and battle conditions. With Le Duan, first secretary of the party, tipping the balance, Thanh was given the go-ahead to mount the spring-summer offensive of 1965. After initial successes, American air power and ground combat units stopped the Communist offensive, culminating in the battle of the Ia Drang Valley. The architect of that strategy was Thanh, not Giap.

The events in the Ia Drang Valley provided Giap with an opportunity to reopen the debate, and this time Le Duan tipped the scales in the opposite direction. He permitted the continued infiltration of NVA troops (which Giap opposed, believing that guerrillas must have firm roots of support in the population) in order to counter the weight of American troops. But he called for a renewed emphasis on guerrilla, rather than Main Force, tactics. Of greater importance, the North Vietnamese Communist party endorsed Le Duan's plan to make U.S. forces their main objective, setting a goal of fifty thousand U.S. troops to be killed or disabled. The objective was to destroy U.S. morale and set the stage for the day when American forces would leave and only ARVN troops would stand between them and "liberation of the South."

No longer was Hanoi seeking immediate victory. Instead, it was aiming for a stalemate: the return to Giap's protracted war strategy. These decisions marked the beginning of Thanh's decline, which would continue slowly until his death in July 1967, and Giap's return to his position as North Vietnam's leading strategist.

The revised enemy strategy was immediately apparent. In his Monthly Evaluation Report of December 1965, the month following the conclusion of the Ia Drang campaign, Westmoreland wrote:

A wounded soldier from the 1st Air Cav is handed a cigarette as he awaits evacuation during the battle at LZ X-Ray. His company had been ambushed by the NVA.

Military activity in December was highlighted by an increase in the number of VC/PAVN attacks on isolated outposts, hamlets, and districts, towns [sic] and the avoidance of contact with large GVN and Free World Forces. The effectiveness of this strategy was attested by the highest monthly friendly casualty total of the war, by friendly weapons losses in excess of weapons captured for the first time since July, and by 30 percent fewer casualties than in November.

The enemy, by adopting again a protracted war strategy, was employing a war of attrition of a different kind, through a tactical defensive, instead of the aggressive warfare of Westmoreland's strategy. The enemy was willing to engage American troops and suffer the inevitable consequences of U.S. firepower superiority but only when they felt the loss was justified. The objective was to weaken gradually America's will to fight by increasing its costs in manpower, money, and time. According to the JCS, "three-fourths of the battles are at the enemy's choice of time, place, type, and duration." An army study reported that 46 percent of all battles began as enemy ambushes, and in 88 percent of the fighting the enemy initiated contact.

Attrition: ours and theirs

While Westmoreland pointed to the ever-rising enemy deaths as evidence of progress, the ratio of deaths between the two sides is probably a better index of the manner in which the enemy maintained the initiative. In the first quarter year after the full deployment of U.S. combat troops (July to September 1965) the enemy suffered forty deaths for every American killed. By the end of 1965 they

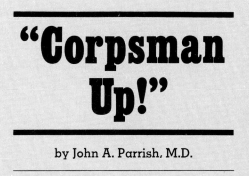

"Corpsman Up!"

by John A. Parrish, M.D.

Because I am a doctor, I was assigned to the 3d Medical Battalion, 3d Marine Division in Phu Bai. We held sick call for marines at usual office hours and received casualties directly from the field by helicopter at all hours. Our compound was protected on all sides by sandbags and marines. After six months I left the medical group and was sent into the field with the 3d Marines along the DMZ near Cam Lo.

Life was much different in the bush. I lived with my corpsmen and with the marines instead of with other doctors. Marines did not seem to get sick as much in the front lines as in the rear, and we did not take care of casualties because they were usually flown directly from the site of impact to the rear by helicopter.

One of the corpsmen in the field was Robby Wills* from Albany, Georgia. He seemed like an ordinary boy, possibly too vulnerable to be a soldier and too young to be a medical corpsman. However, one thing I learned in a combat zone was how much I could come to care about or-

* Robby Wills is a pseudonym given by Dr. Parrish.

dinary kids and how unordinary each of them could become. Wills had just arrived in Vietnam about the time I went to the infantry unit, and he became my personal assistant for several days before he was assigned to a combat company and began to go with them on patrols.

Wills's first patrol was a disaster for the company. They lost several marines and Wills lost control of his emotions and composure. The very next day, however, he went again with the marines far into enemy territory and managed to be a useful part of a routine operation with few casualties. Eventually, working and walking with a marine company got to be a regular part of his life.

He got to be a good corpsman. He began to bug the guys to take their malaria pills. He began to volunteer for missions and carry less ammo and more medical supplies. It was the coldest night of the rainy season when Wills secured a permanent place in the lives of a few marines who probably will never know him.

It was cold and the rain had increased from its storm-like base line to full-fledged monsoon. The mud in the shallowest places was ankle deep, and in the basins one could sink up to the waist and not be able to walk. The marines were to join up with a company of ARVN soldiers and walk to the highway to provide temporary protection for a bridge, a village, and the highway. The battalion that had been providing this security was pulling back toward the rear. The rains had made it impossible to hold all that had been held two weeks earlier. It was a routine operation. No contact was expected.

But the ARVN company didn't show up. The marines waited three hours in the rain before continuing without them. Because of the delay and the mud it became clear that they would not reach high ground by dark. When it grew too dark to see well, it was decided to kneel in place and wait until first light.

It was too muddy to dig in. Anyone who lay down or fell asleep without positioning his head correctly on his helmet would drown. A loose perimeter was established in hopes that the mud would discourage any enemy attack. It was hoped above all that the NVA mortar teams did not know the exact position of the marines, who were in the open.

A no light, no fire, red alert was ordered, and man-to-man communication in the darkness consisted only of an occasional touch or whisper. When a form sloshed by no one could be sure if it was friend or foe.

Suddenly automatic weapon fire began cracking repeatedly about 200 yards from the main body of marines. No one was sure if it was marine or NVA fire. Soldiers began yelling at one another. One marine opened up in the direction of the automatic weapons.

Then all hell broke loose.

Weapons were firing everywhere. Creatures sloshed back and forth in the mud in all directions. No one was sure who was moving and where they were going. Just as the marine captain started screaming orders, enemy mortar rounds began to sock into the mud with dull, deep, sickening belches.

had reduced that ratio to about fifteen to one, and it fluctuated around the ten- or twelve-to-one mark through the end of 1967. The enemy was determining the extent to which it was willing to suffer casualties, and no matter what the United States tried, it could not increase the ratio for any sustained period of time.

The war was shaping up as a battle between two strategies of attrition. The United States' objective was to attrite men, while the North Vietnamese were attriting time. But the choice of battlefield tactics was working to the advantage of the North Vietnamese and Vietcong, not the United States. The Communists were controlling the tempo of the war and thereby limiting their own casualties to an acceptable level. And they were being given the time and safety to augment their forces and make good their losses by the inability and unwillingness of the Americans to prevent the recruitment of new guerrillas from within the South or through infiltration from the North.

The enemy had one other very telling fact on its side. No matter how long the Americans chose to remain in Vietnam, the Vietnamese (and by that, the enemy meant themselves) would be there longer. Giap had already learned fifteen years earlier that in a guerrilla struggle, survival is the first step toward victory. Only a belief that the government can outlast the guerrillas will ultimately deter the insurgents, as the Philippine and Malayan governments had shown. The power to survive and outlast the guerrillas was the most crucial challenge of the war, and it was a challenge, not to the American troops or their government, but to the government of the Republic of Vietnam. In the spring of 1965 it was not doing a very good job.

A B-52 bombing raid began in the mountains several miles to the north, and the rumble occasionally lit the northern sky. Under cover of the confusion, while the mortar shelling continued, NVA began to wade right into the marines.

The marines started firing flares into the air. As they intermittently floated to earth, bright light and good visibility alternated with complete darkness. Just as one flare exploded Wills saw two NVA who had already passed by him. He stood, turned, fired his M16 from the hip, and cut them down at close range.

Most marines squeezed deeper into the mud and kept firing. A few tried to run but were unsure where to go and almost unable to move about in the mud. Everybody was firing at anything that moved.

"Corpsman up." A cry about sixty-five feet from Wills. He began crawling toward the cry. Automatic weapons fire whizzed by him. Probably both marines and NVA were shooting at him. A mortar shell socked into the mud just behind him and pushed him face forward deep into the mud, wounding him in the buttocks and propelling him closer to the wounded man.

"Corpsman up!" A black marine had a chest wound and a missing left hand. Wills pulled up beside him.

"Hey, Doc, I got it in the chest, man. I can't breathe."

Wills found a Vaseline gauze in his pack and dressed the chest wound as he lay on his side next to the lance corporal.

"I'm freezing. I'm cold as hell, Doc." The marine was shaking. Most of what Wills did was by feel and not by sight.

"This should plug the hole."

"Hurry, Doc. Can't breathe."

Wills put a tourniquet on the left wrist and gave the marine a shot of morphine.

"Doc, I gotta stay out here all night, don't I?"

"Right."

"Doc, stay here with me. I don't wanna die."

"You'll make it, man."

"I'm cold as hell, Doc."

Wills didn't answer. He crawled back to the two NVA bodies. Bullets flew everywhere. He felt one rip into the NVA body. The NVA were walking the mortar shells systematically back and forth in rows across the mud plain. Wills froze as they came closer to him on one pass. He put his whole body face down as low as he could in the mud. A mortar shell landed fifty to sixty-five feet to his left in the mud and the next one sixty-five feet to his right, and then he began to crawl again. He dragged one of the NVA bodies back to the wounded marine and curled it around his upper body for protection. The marine let his legs and hips slide down deeper into the mud and hid his upper body in the crook of the NVA's body.

"Corpsman up! Corpsman up!" from behind Wills. "Corpsman up, goddamnit, hurry!" Wills was off again.

Wills was at it all night. When first light arrived the enemy fled. Wills was found nude except for his boots. Six wounded marines were huddled in a pile in a mud hole protected on three sides by bodies (two NVA and one marine). They all had well-placed battle dressings and were covered up with the clothes and the flak gear of Wills and the three dead men.

Wills lay face up next to his human-body-and-mud bunker with his head resting on a dead marine's leg. The rain beating on his face had washed it clean. The rest of his nude body was partially submerged in the sea of mud.

Marines began to pick up the wounded and carry them to the highway and ground transportation to Dong Ha. Wills came to while the wounded were being loaded. Then he bandaged his own ass, wrapped himself in a blanket, and got in the truck to attend the wounded en route to the clearing station.

Three of six men from Wills's homemade fortress were dead when they arrived in Dong Ha—two had died during the long night and one more en route to the clearing station.

When the truck pulled up at Dong Ha, Wills looked over at the black marine with no left hand. "You got it made now, man. Doctors. Gear. Operating rooms. You've made it."

"Thanks, man," the marine said holding out his one hand palm up.

"Three for six," Wills slapped his palm. "Fifty percent." He hopped off the truck to help with the litters. "I'll do better next time."

John A. Parrish, M.D., served in Vietnam as a navy medical officer assigned to the 3d Marine Division in 1968-69. He is currently associate professor of dermatology at the Harvard Medical School, Massachusetts General Hospital.

The "Other" War

The mood in the headquarters of the III Marine Amphibious Force was tense. It was May 21, 1966, little more than a year after the marines had first landed at Da Nang, and now it had come down to this. A squadron of South Vietnamese Air Force (VNAF) jets, under orders from Saigon, was buzzing Da Nang and preparing to wipe out the last pockets of resistance in the two-month-old confrontation between the South Vietnamese government and the Buddhists. General Lewis Walt had already complained, fearing that American installations in Da Nang might be hit by an errant bomb. Almost immediately thereafter Walt's worst fears were realized as two Vietnamese pilots badly undershot their target, hitting a U.S. Marine compound and wounding eight marines, two seriously. Walt immediately dispatched two marine F-8 Crusaders to circle above the Vietnamese Skyraiders and informed the VNAF commander that he would shoot down the first plane that dropped another bomb or fired

another rocket. Several minutes later Walt received a call from Washington, questioning him about a complaint from the South Vietnamese government that he was interfering in internal matters. After explaining the situation, Walt received the full backing of the White House with orders to take any appropriate action.

The VNAF responded with a dangerous game of one-upmanship, dispatching another four aircraft to circle above the U.S. jets. Walt scrambled another two F-8 Crusaders to fly above them. For two full hours this four-tiered aerial stand-off circled and pirouetted in the skies over Da Nang, with neither side showing any signs of backing off. Suddenly the Vietnamese pilots peeled off and returned to their base.

The South Vietnamese government, already involved in one bloody civil war with the Vietcong, had for the previous two months been on the verge of a second civil war with the Buddhists, headquartered in Da Nang and Hue. Now for two hours on May 21, 1966, it came close to battle with the United States. The United States had come to Vietnam to insure a free and democratic government and secure it against internal and external aggression. On May 21, 1966, almost a full year since Nguyen Cao Ky had taken the reins of South Vietnam with little concern for either freedom or democracy, it would not have been inappropriate for Americans to ask if there were any South Vietnamese government able to be saved or worth saving.

Nguyen Cao Ky was born in 1930 in Son Tay Province, just west of Hanoi. After attending high school in Hanoi, Ky immediately joined the French air force. Trained as a fighter pilot by both the French and U.S., he rose quickly through the ranks, earning through his own personal skill and courage the loyalty and respect of his troops and the admiring title of "Warlord of the Air." By age thirty he had become one of the leading military figures in South Vietnam and at age thirty-five, his country's premier.

Clad in one from his array of canary yellow, purple, and black flight suits and his ever-present lavender scarf, and packing matching pearl-handled revolvers, Ky cut a dashing and flamboyant, though often ludicrous, figure. On one occasion in early 1966 Ky dumbfounded a group of peasants and one American observer when he visited a newly pacified village with his beautiful wife, Mai. Clothed in matching black flight suits, flight boots, lavender scarves, sunglasses, and blue flying caps, the premier and his wife looked more like fashion models than the leader of a country and his first lady. As the local populace stared on uncomprehendingly, the flabbergasted American exclaimed, "My God, they look like Captain and Mrs. Midnight."

Preceding page. Caught in the middle: Peasants from a VC-controlled village in Quang Ngai Province are confronted by members of the U.S. American Division in 1967.

Unfortunately, the premier's flair for the outrageous was not confined to his wardrobe. Hardly had he taken office when he declared that Vietnam needed someone like Hitler to solve its problems. Although he later explained that he meant only "Hitler's leadership and sense of discipline" and not his inhuman methods, the damage had been done. Equally damaging was Ky's tendency for dramatic overreaction. Before the war was over, he would gain the unusual distinction of being the only man to threaten to bomb both Hanoi and Saigon. While to his troops Ky's glamorous appearance and swaggering, romantic style were cause for endearment and emulation, to many western observers they were often cause for contempt and dislike. Despite his many attempts to erase this image, Ky was never able to establish himself fully as a credible and capable leader.

The last coup in Saigon

Ky's assumption of power was anything but dramatic. On June 12, 1965, with the backing of the Armed Forces Council, Ky was appointed premier, replacing the civilian government of Dr. Phan Huy Quat. Quat himself had come to power as a result of a coup in February 1965. The Quat government had seemed the answer to American prayers. Since the ouster of the Diem government in November 1963, Vietnam had experienced six major changes of government, none lasting more than six months, and countless minor shuffles in leadership. In late 1964 Ambassador Taylor cabled Washington, suggesting more realistic expectations of what to hope for from a Saigon government:

We must accept the fact that an effective government, much beyond the capacity of that which has existed over the past several months, is unlikely to survive. We now have a better feel for the quality of our ally and for what we can expect from him in terms of ability to govern.

Taylor called for the acceptance of a government "which will have definite limits of performance," by which he meant one that would bring civil unrest under control while allowing the United States to prosecute the war as it wanted. After stability, the U.S. was most interested in finding civilian leadership that could remove from the U.S. the onus of supporting a military dictatorship. The Quat government seemed to answer such concerns. Its leadership under Quat and Chief of State Phan Khac Suu was civilian, and the support it received from the Armed Forces Council, headed by General Nguyen Van Thieu, promised to provide stability.

Even this strong military backing was not enough. The AFC, which had been formed in December, established some cohesion among the generals, but Saigon's civilian leaders were still capable of indulging in sufficient bickering to make governing difficult. Quat immediately faced the protests of Father Hoang Quynh, a militant Catholic

Wearing one patch that depicts a dragon's fiery breath burning a Communist flag (left) and another that translates as "magic wind" (right), two-star General Nguyen Cao Ky, the "Warlord of the Air," poses with his fellow VNAF pilots.

priest, who accused Quat of being "too soft" on communism and giving in to Buddhist demands. He warned his parishioners to arm themselves in case of an accommodation between the Vietcong and the Buddhists.

Quat attempted to counter Quynh by dismissing two Catholic ministers in his cabinet. But Chief of State Suu, himself a Catholic and under intense pressure from Catholic groups, declared that the dismissals were unconstitutional. Quat pleaded that if a premier did not have the right to name his own cabinet, the position was of little use. Quat, believing that the AFC was interested in a strong civilian government, asked the generals to mediate, apparently confident that they would side with him. He guessed wrong. Having had enough of civilian bickering, the AFC disbanded the government and assumed control. At the same time the military all but extinguished any remaining hopes of establishing civilian rule. There were few people who would have bet on it, but the bloodless coup of June 12, 1965, was the last Saigon was to see.

The new regime consisted of a triumvirate backed by the Directorate of Generals, a newly renovated AFC. Ky held the positions of premier and chairman of the Executive Council. Thieu became chairman of the Directorate and chief of state, and General Nguyen Huu Co was made commissioner-general of the armed forces. Also included in the government were seven other generals, including all four corps commanders. This was done both to broaden the power base of the government as well as to

keep General Nguyen Chanh Thi, commander of I Corps, within the government. Ambitious and certainly the single most powerful man in the military, Thi would have been much more dangerous outside the government than in. Only Ky's appointment to the premiership aroused any opposition. Both Catholics and Buddhists spoke out against Ky's appointment, while members of the Directorate of Generals questioned his rash temperament. But with Thieu's backing and the military rejection of civilian leadership, Ky's appointment stood.

While Ky held the limelight of South Vietnamese politics and handled the day-to-day running of the government, control of overall decision and policy making lay principally in the hands of Nguyen Van Thieu. A quiet, urbane man, the forty-two-year-old Thieu provided a moderating counterbalance to the rashness of the younger Ky.

A southerner by birth and a Catholic by conversion, Thieu was the first choice of the U.S. to lead the new government. Like Ky he had been trained at military bases in America (Fort Leavenworth, Kansas, and Fort Bliss, Texas). But unlike his junior colleague he was also skilled in the political intrigues of South Vietnam. Thieu was considered by the U.S. State Department to be "the most sophisticated politician on the Directorate." He was careful to maintain a balance of power among the members of the Directorate, insuring that none could rise above the others and topple the government. He also assiduously sought the opinions of both Catholic and Buddhist leaders, especially in the early stages of his regime, trying to show as little favoritism as possible without compromising his own independence.

Although as chief of state his power was theoretically less than Ky's, his real power stemmed from his position as chairman of the Directorate, the true ruling body in South Vietnam. Confident of his own power and position, he was content to allow Ky to hold the spotlight and battle with the press while he remained in the background quietly puffing on his pipe, smoothing out differences within the Directorate and charting the government's course. Thieu realized only too well the role that internal strife had played in the fall of previous governments, and at least for the first nine months of his new regime he was able to avoid it.

Trouble in the North

From the beginning of the Ky-Thieu regime, it was apparent that eventually either General Thi or the Buddhists, or both, would begin some form of protest. The Buddhists had been relatively quiet since the anti-Diem demonstrations in 1963; Thi, however, was another story.

Nguyen Chanh Thi was a capable and ambitious man, and not one to take a back seat for very long. He resented taking orders, especially from Ky, whom he considered an inferior and openly patronized by calling him, "My little brother." Thi was one of the most powerful men in the country and a formidable challenger to Ky's position. In I Corps he was known as the "Warlord of the North," and his power was equaled only by that of the Buddhist Thich Tri Quang. Thi's U.S. military counterparts, the marines of I Corps, considered him a man of great personal courage (he had been a paratrooper and survived capture by both the Japanese and the VC) as well as a very capable tactician. A "real fighting general," marine General Edwin Simmons called him.

Early in March Thi gave Ky the opportunity he had been waiting for. Ky traveled to Hue to meet with Thi but was publicly insulted when Thi loudly inquired of an aide, "Should we pay attention to this funny little man from Saigon or should we ignore him?"

Ky immediately summoned the Directorate, and on March 10 the generals voted unanimously to dismiss Thi. But Thi refused to leave the country peaceably, and Ky was forced to arrest him in Saigon. Even more disturbing were the resultant demonstrations that broke out in Da Nang on March 12.

In dismissing Thi, Ky had played right into the hands of Thich Tri Quang, and the politically astute Buddhist was quick to exploit the young general's mistakes. Thi's dismissal was an excellent catalyst for a political uprising, just as the May 8 riot in Hue in 1963 had been, but it was not an issue around which a national movement could be fashioned. Instead Tri Quang called for constitutional re-

form and a civilian government. It was an even better issue than the charges of religious persecution had been three years earlier. Whereas that issue had isolated the Buddhists, the cause of civilian government allowed them to form a united front of opposition which included not only Buddhists and students from all over the country, but also Cao Daists, intellectuals, and even some Catholics.

Attempting to quiet the protesters, Ky announced on March 25 the formation of the Constitutional Preparatory Commission, which was slated to produce a new constitution at the end of two months, with elections to follow by the end of the year.

This conciliatory move failed to mollify the Buddhists and their supporters, who demanded the immediate resignation of the military government. On March 26 the radio stations in Hue and Da Nang were taken over by the demonstrators. As March drew to a close the mounting civil strife in central Vietnam had wrenched the war effort there to a grinding halt. In dealing with the growing unrest Ky was still determined to avoid physical confrontation and the fate of the Diem government.

It was quickly becoming apparent, however, that force would have to be used. In Hue, police and I Corps troops had either actively joined the movement or were maintaining a guarded neutrality; in Da Nang, the mayor of the city openly joined the antigovernment forces on April 1, and rebel troops began establishing independent control of the city. After discussing the situation with U.S. Ambassador Henry Cabot Lodge, Ky became convinced that the use of force was necessary.

Ky announced the change in policy in his own unique way. On April 3, he stunned a group of reporters when he informed them that Da Nang was "held by Communists and the government will undertake operations to clear them out." He declared, "we will liberate Da Nang," and went on to accuse the mayor of Da Nang of "using public funds to organize antigovernment demonstrations. Either this government will have to fall—or the mayor be shot."

Personally leading two Vietnamese marine battalions, Ky headed to Da Nang on April 5 for a planned dawn raid. Upon his arrival at the U.S. air base outside of Da Nang, however, he found the roads to the city blocked by a mixed force of about three hundred rebel I Corps troops and Buddhists. Ky felt it prudent to put off the confrontation and retract his earlier statement about Da Nang and its mayor in order to seek again a peaceful solution. But he left the marines bivouacked at the air base.

As the crisis worsened the U.S. began to withdraw its personnel from Hue, Da Nang, and several other trouble spots, seeking to avoid any involvement in the civil strife and to maintain its neutrality in the fighting as much as possible. But as the situation deteriorated the neutrality became more and more difficult to maintain, especially in the Da Nang area where some sort of armed confrontation seemed imminent.

On April 9, the U.S. was finally forced to step momentarily into the conflict. Under the command of Colonel Dam Quang Yeu, a force of dissident I Corps soldiers, with their artillery, assumed positions opposite the Da Nang air base. Although their announced target was the marine battalions left behind by Ky, they also posed a threat to the nearly twenty thousand U.S. Marines stationed there. Marine General Lewis Walt dispatched Colonel John Chaisson to talk with Yeu. After several tense moments the rebel commander withdrew his troops and a bloody incident was avoided.

Although Walt and the U.S. had at least temporarily avoided trouble, the Ky-Thieu government was now staring down the barrel of a loaded gun. Rather than pull back completely, Ky and Thieu chose instead to bend a little. They met privately with Buddhist leaders and at last promised them a civilian government within three to five months. They would call for the election of a constitutional assembly, which would form a provisional government, pending elections by the end of 1967. Almost immediately the storm subsided.

A dark cloud hovered, however. Ky refused to announce publicly what he had guaranteed the Buddhists in private. Instead, on May 6 Ky told a group of American reporters that the promised constituent assembly would not form an interim government, as the Buddhists believed. Ky further remarked that he expected to stay in office for at least another year. While the Buddhists expressed anger at this sudden reversal of the government's position and began to revive the protest movement, Ky and the generals prepared to crush the dissidents with force.

The siege of Da Nang

On May 14 Ky moved on Da Nang for the second time in a month, catching both the Americans and the rebel forces by surprise. Deploying quickly around the perimeter of the city, 3,000 Vietnamese marines steadily pushed back the 1,200 dissident I Corps troops and Buddhists, seizing Da Nang City Hall and the radio stations as well as other key points. Eventually they forced the dissidents into a section of the city on the east bank of the Tourane River, and again the U.S. Marines found themselves in an uncomfortable position.

A confrontation soon arose over a bridge spanning the Tourane River. The bridge had been seized and mined by I Corps troops to prevent loyal ARVN forces from reaching the munitions depot on the other side. This bridge, however, was also heavily used by the U.S., so Walt moved to prevent its destruction.

After an initial discussion between Colonel Chaisson and an I Corps officer who mined the bridge yielded no results, Walt and his officers decided that the charges would somehow have to be defused. As Walt recalled it, he occupied the Vietnamese officer at the middle of the bridge while a U.S. adviser and two marine engineers clambered unseen beneath the bridge and slowly began the dangerous job of defusing the charges. After several tense minutes Walt was finally given the thumbs-up sign from the sweat-soaked adviser. Breaking off their conversation, the marine general informed the Vietnamese officer that he had five minutes to remove his men and disarm the detonator. Slowly the minutes ticked by until, finally, praying that the adviser had done his job well, Walt signaled his marines to cross and hold the bridge. Suddenly the Vietnamese officer raised his arm and looking at Walt said in good English, "General, we will die on this bridge together." As he snapped his arm down sharply to his side, a Vietnamese soldier slammed the plunger down on the detonator. The explosion never came; the U.S. Marines swarmed across the bridge and took control of it without firing a round.

As the attack on Da Nang progressed, the fighting turned from sporadic and tentative to bitter and intense. The battle now degenerated into an ongoing series of short vicious sniper attacks as the rebel forces abandoned all but a few strongholds and fanned out over the city. And so came the May 21 confrontation, the third and most dangerous between the South Vietnamese and their United States ally: the Vietnamese decision to wipe out the resistance by bombing the remaining rebel strongholds; General Walt's decision in turn to threaten the destruction of the VNAF aircraft with marine jets; the incongruous four-tiered standoff in the air over Da Nang; and the sudden backdown of the Vietnamese.

Though foiled in its attempt to wipe out the rebels by air, on May 22 the South Vietnamese government broke the remaining rebel strongholds with ground assaults. At Tan Ninh Pagoda the rebel forces withstood four hours of bombardment before the onslaught ended. Breaking through makeshift barricades the ARVN troops found eight dead rebels and two dead monks. Ripping down a Buddhist banner, one soldier muttered, "*Fini.*"

With the fall of the protesters in Da Nang, the drive and strength were knocked out of the Buddhist organization. In Hue, the last major Buddhist stronghold, the rebels, lacking direction and guidance, struck out randomly at anything connected with the U.S. or the government. On May 26 rioters burned the United States Information Service library. Four days later the violence in Hue reached its peak as Buddhist youths burned the U.S. Consulate. The government, however, simply sat back and waited, having stopped all movement in and out of the city. Finally, on June 8, with almost all the rebel troops and officials back in the government, Ky reoccupied the city using only four hundred policemen in an almost bloodless action.

The breaking of the Buddhist uprising marked the end of the Buddhists as a dominant political movement, the passing of the last major political rival of the Directorate and, with that, the last hope for a civilian-based govern-

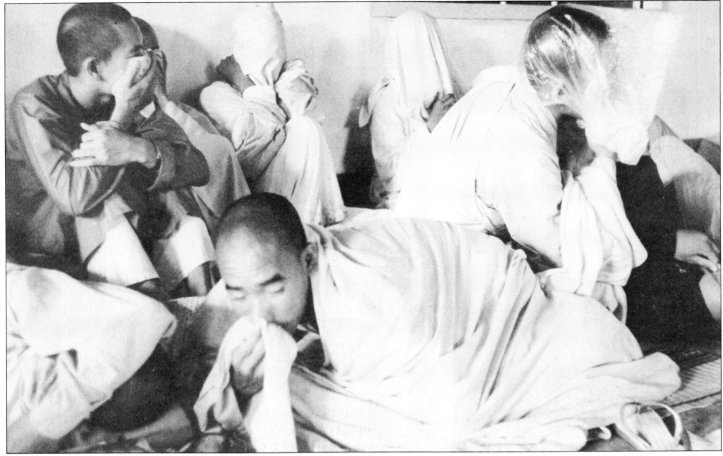

Assailed by tear gas, rebellious Buddhist monks huddle within Saigon's Vien Hoa Dao Pagoda on May 22, 1966. For many during the Buddhist uprising, protest ended in imprisonment and/or death.

ARVN airborne soldiers hunt down dissident ARVN and Buddhist forces in Da Nang, May 1966.

A rebel soldier lies dead in Da Nang moments after being summarily executed by loyal ARVN troops. After taking control of Da Nang on May 22, Ky had effectively crushed the Buddhist uprising.

ment. After three years of almost constant internal political strife, after three years in which no government was able to fulfill even the most minimal duties of a political leadership, South Vietnam at last found a measure of stability. In the interim more than two hundred fifty thousand American troops had arrived. They had carried the brunt of fighting against Main Force VC and NVA troops and provided most villages with the only security they would find. Other Americans—civilians—had manned South Vietnamese ministries in their roles as advisers and had supervised the distribution of goods and services on the province and district level.

But Americans were no substitute for Vietnamese, especially in gaining the loyalty of the population for the government cause. Enormous tasks were left undone, tasks which only the South Vietnamese government could complete. Beyond the large-unit war, in every village and hamlet, another war was being waged by the enemy, and without effective opposition. With their political enemies defeated and with unprecedented cohesion among the military leaders, the long-term stability of the Ky-Thieu government would now depend on how well they fought this "other" war.

Hearts and minds

No one really knew what to call it. The French had called it "pacification," and so the Americans and South Vietnamese tried to avoid the use of that term. President Johnson liked to call it "the other war," but Ambassador Ellsworth Bunker, arriving in Saigon in May 1967, forbade the use of the term. He believed that one could not artificially divide the war effort. "The other war" was part of *the* war. Some called it a war for the "hearts and minds" of the people, but American enlisted men turned the phrase on its head, saying, "Grab them by the balls and their hearts and minds will follow." The South Vietnamese government chose to call it "rural construction," but when he was ambassador, Henry Cabot Lodge thought that smacked too much of bricks and concrete. He liked the phrase "revolutionary development." But the South Vietnamese never used that term. No one really knew what to call it, but everyone understood the problem: what was to be done *after* American and ARVN units had swept through a village clearing it of VC? How could the guerrillas be prevented from returning, leaving the government and the American military effort no better off than before?

In traditional Confucian thought a confusion over names signals a more fundamental problem, a clouded view of reality. The "pacification" program American troops found when they entered the country bore out the Confucian belief. The ultimate goal of pacification often obscured the necessary means of achieving that goal, hence the problem in finding a name.

Ultimately the purpose of pacification was to gain the positive loyalty and active support of the population for the government. This was important not merely to fulfill western notions of what a democracy ought to be, but because the loyalty of the population could become the most effective tool of the government against the VC.

In the first place, a population supporting the government would prove to be barren ground for the VC to recruit replacements for their forces as they were lost to American firepower, a crucial consideration in a war of attrition. More important, civilian villagers possessed the best knowledge of the movement and plans of guerrillas as they passed through villages collecting supplies and caching weapons. The active support of the population would enable the government to deny the enemy what was one of his most important weapons: hiding places. VC guerrillas would be unable either to blend in with civilians or conceal themselves in villages.

To gain this loyalty the government of South Vietnam had to provide the population with the first requirement of all governments: order and security. Without the certainty of security, villagers who did cooperate with the government faced the retaliation of those who could provide their own form of order: the NLF. Without providing dependable protection for those who helped them, the government of South Vietnam would have as difficult a time finding "witnesses" of VC activities as the American government has in, say, finding witnesses to testify against organized crime. The confusion over names in the pacification program was, in large measure, a result of a failure to recognize this fundamental fact. The battle for the hearts and minds of the villagers could not achieve much until their very lives had been made secure. In pacification the name of the game was security, security, and more security. In 1965 the South Vietnamese government was providing little of this precious necessity.

The statistical reports revealed just how dismal the situation was as American combat troops first arrived in Vietnam in 1965. Quang Nam Province, which includes Da Nang, had a total of 537 hamlets. In November 1963, at the time of the coup against Diem, 450 of them were officially labeled "secure." In March 1965 only 12 of them could be called secure. Whereas in 1963 most of the young men of the province still lived at home, by mid-1965 many had been recruited or coerced into joining the VC. Most families now possessed some blood tie to the insurgents which would make them all the less likely to support the government. And with the young men off to war—fighting for one side or the other—there were few good candidates for the formation of a local security force.

So desperate was the situation that the bulk of all emphasis on pacification in Vietnam had been concentrated in 1964 in one seven-province area around Saigon, in a program called "Hop Tac," or "Cooperation." (See page 122, *Raising the Stakes*, another volume in *The Vietnam*

Experience.) By September 1965 even that program was in shambles. The Vietnamese felt that the Hop Tac program was an American idea, and one in which they had little stake. Moreover, the South Vietnamese government was unwilling to create a unified command structure in the area to coordinate the program, fearing that placing so much power in the hands of one individual operating so close to Saigon would only be an invitation to a coup. In one year, twenty-four of the thirty-one district chiefs in the area and five of seven province chiefs had been changed.

As coup had followed coup in Saigon, the tremors stretched the length of the country. Each new government attempted to install officials loyal to it, especially at the province level, no matter how competent the former officials were or how incompetent the new replacements might be. In addition, the officials loyal to the central government, more often than not Catholic because of their educational advantages, were often anathema to the overwhelming Buddhist population of the countryside.

There seemed to be no one more committed to improving the dismal state of the pacification program than Henry Cabot Lodge, who had arrived for his second tour of duty in Saigon in July 1965, replacing Maxwell Taylor who departed, as he had specified he would in accepting the post, after a one-year term.

Lodge, through long experience in negotiating with the Communists, had a distinct idea of how the war would end. The enemy would never negotiate a settlement but rather would simply "fade away" as the environment became increasingly hostile to them. "This means that we would not be insisting on the complete elimination of the VC although no safe haven would be allocated them," he wrote. "The GVN would control 80 to 85 percent of the population and . . . the VC would be limited to the jungle and mountainous areas where they would go on as bandits . . . and where the GVN would have the right to pursue them and try to destroy them."

Lodge's approach shared some similarities with that of the U.S. Marines. His goal was the control of the population, permitting the VC to roam (although not at will) in the unpopulated territory of South Vietnam. The politics of pacification would often make strange bedfellows, and Lodge and the marines would soon be joined by another, very powerful voice in Washington, that of Lyndon Johnson.

LBJ and pacification

Lyndon Johnson's motives for supporting pacification differed from those of Lodge. He had no quarrel with the kind of war being waged by Westmoreland but was stung by the charges that he was employing only military means to solve what was essentially a political problem. In Johnson's mind a new emphasis on pacification would counter-

balance the emphasis on military activity and perhaps silence his liberal critics. Robert Komer, LBJ's specialist on pacification, recalled that Johnson "had a splendid sense of public relations and of the public appetite. . . . But beyond that LBJ was a genuine populist. He said, 'we've got to electrify rural Vietnam. People are all the same under the sun.' "

In February 1966 LBJ artfully combined his sense of public relations with his populist belief in caring for human needs. At a command conference in Honolulu in which LBJ met for the first time with Generals Ky and Thieu, he brought with him Secretary of Agriculture Orville Freeman and Secretary of Health, Education and Welfare John Gardner. They were present to advise General Nguyen Duc Thang, newly appointed minister of rural construction in South Vietnam, and then to continue on to Saigon for a first-hand look at how American experience in rural development programs could be applied to Vietnam. The star-studded cast at Honolulu, as well as a promise by Thieu and Ky to hold elections, grabbed most of the headlines, but the conference also committed the South Vietnamese government to its most strenuous pacification effort ever.

The South Vietnamese agreed to place special effort on four high-priority areas of pacification, one in each of the four military zones, including the area formerly under the Hop Tac program. In addition, plans were announced for the training of new fifty-nine-member Rural Construction Cadre Teams. Since the Americans chose to use the name Revolutionary Development, rather than translating the Vietnamese literally as "rural construction," the teams became known as RD cadres. The new RD workers were trained in thirteen-week cycles in which they were taught to wear "black pajamas" and practice the "three withs" of the VC: eat, sleep, and work with the peasants. It was back to step one. Diem had trained his first Civic Action cadres with the same lessons eleven years earlier.

The RD cadres were to carry the brunt of the pacification effort, but the Americans were much less satisfied with what the Vietnamese promised in the way of supporting the teams. The Americans wanted to give province chiefs greater authority to call in ARVN troops to help in securing villages, but South Vietnam's military leaders refused to take such power away from division commanders. They feared that doing so would tempt the commanders to lead another coup. Since only division commanders could order troops to engage in securing operations, province chiefs would have to make their requests through the time-consuming chain of command. General Thang also remarked that troops assigned to pacification are "liable still to be withdrawn on a temporary basis to meet situations which ARVN senior commanders judge to be critical." Westmoreland agreed, wanting the flexibility to use ARVN troops in the big-unit war. In other words, South Vietnam's leaders, backed by Westmoreland, refused to

insure that ARVN troops would be permanently committed to pacification or to modify the chain of command to permit a speedy response to guerrilla activities within the villages. Since constancy of security was the prerequisite for all pacification efforts, South Vietnam's leaders had severely qualified their new commitment to pacification.

The conflicting signals from Honolulu concerning ARVN's role in pacification were only the latest example of the confusion surrounding South Vietnamese forces since the introduction of American combat troops. The major question, never seriously addressed by MACV, whose original mission had been to advise the South Vietnamese armed forces, was what was ARVN to do as the Americans took over more and more of the fighting. In its simplest terms, the answer was everything and nothing.

Under Westmoreland's basic strategy ARVN was to carry out the bulk of clearing and securing operations. In addition, they were encouraged to initiate and carry out their own large-scale operations. In fact, ARVN carried out three times as many land operations of battalion size or larger as did the Americans. And in IV Corps, the Mekong Delta region, ARVN was given full responsibility until 1967 for the conduct of the war. Finally, ARVN forces were often held in reserve, to back up American forces in combined large-scale operations.

How effective were the South Vietnamese forces in carrying out these several tasks? The available evidence suggests that the prevailing opinion, expressed by Lieutenant General John L. Throckmorton when he said that "ARVN can't hack it," had much merit. The lack of progress in pacification was largely the result of South Vietnamese ineffectiveness. In 1967 the South Vietnamese government felt compelled to request that American soldiers reinforce ARVN forces in IV Corps because the situation there had so deteriorated. Moreover, casualty figures suggest a continuing lack of aggressiveness on the part of South Vietnamese forces. While South Vietnamese combat deaths exceeded American deaths each year, the gap narrowed considerably by 1967 when American force strength passed four hundred thousand. In that year nearly ten thousand Americans died in action compared to twelve thousand South Vietnamese, but Americans suffered twice as many casualties as did the South Vietnamese despite having forces only half as large as their ally's. In addition, many South Vietnamese casualties were suffered by the notoriously ill-prepared Regional and Popular Forces rather than by the regular South Vietnamese army.

Many of ARVN's failures during this period were a result of problems immune to an American "quick fix," such as inadequate leadership, defense-minded tactics, and poor relations with their own population. But part of the blame also lay with MACV, which despite claims to the contrary, seemed to act as if the war could be won without ARVN and thus failed to develop a well-defined mission for South Vietnamese forces in light of the American build-up. Not until General Creighton W. Abrams was sent to Saigon as Westmoreland's deputy in April 1967 did MACV address this problem. Abrams's orders, direct from Washington, were to shape up the South Vietnamese army, first to make it more effective in the pacification effort and later to improve its performance sufficiently so that American soldiers could gradually be withdrawn.

Reorganization blues

When the dust cleared from Honolulu the American civilians back in Saigon were left with the responsibility of making sure that the renewed commitment to pacification would yield results in the field. As fortune would have it, the South Vietnamese were about to be consumed by the Buddhist crisis, and for at least three to four months any movement in pacification would have to be achieved by Americans working virtually alone. The first need was to look at the American Embassy itself, to see how it could better perform its functions.

The organization of the American Embassy in Saigon had been a recurrent problem for five years. It was being run as if Saigon were no different from Paris or Manila or any other foreign capital. The operating concept was that of the "country team" headed by the ambassador, his deputy, the heads of the political and economic sections, chiefs of agencies such as CIA, AID, and USIS, and military assistance commands. With the growth of the American involvement, Ambassador Taylor had organized a "Mission Council" which met weekly to coordinate activities among the various agencies.

But the Mission Council proved to be no solution. As American troop strength passed 250,000 and as economic aid to South Vietnam passed one-half billion dollars a year (one-quarter of all the U.S. aid to the world), the embassy was still being run as if Vietnam were a run-of-the-mill country. In 1964 the embassy had employed 2,500 people (1,500 in AID). By 1967, AID alone had 6,500 employees. One presidential adviser said, "To cope with something like that you really need the president of General Motors."

The greatest problem was bureaucratic inertia. Each agency operating in Vietnam had two sets of standards: those by which progress might be measured in Vietnam and those universal standards by which agency work was measured all over the world. Since a bureaucrat's tour of duty in Vietnam was limited and his chances for advancement were dependent upon following the universal standards, "the bureaucracy," in the words of Robert Komer, "did its own thing." Rather than coordinate his activities with other agencies, each bureaucrat simply went about doing his own work, generally with the best of intentions, but designed more to make an impression in Washington than in the Vietnamese countryside.

Villagers often possessed the best information on the movements of the guerrillas but faced retaliation from the Vietcong unless the government could provide security. Here a woman weeps over the body of her husband, who had informed on the VC and was killed in revenge in mid-1967.

Pushed from Washington by Komer, more drastic reorganization measures were considered, among them placing all pacification chores under Westmoreland's command and giving him authority over civilian agencies. Lodge and the civilian agencies in Washington vehemently opposed this drastic solution. President Johnson instead decided upon an interim solution, the creation of the Office of Civil Operations (OCO), which would have command responsibility over all civilian agencies, forming, in effect, a pacification high command.

Deputy Ambassador William Porter was given the task of making the new plan work. Johnson was clearly losing his patience and told Porter that OCO had only 90 to 120

days to produce results or the whole program would be given to the military. Johnson knew that four months was insufficient time to produce any progress and was already preparing to give Westmoreland command over the pacification program.

Lodge played right into Johnson's hands, choosing that moment to go on vacation, leaving Porter with all the ambassador's duties, plus OCO. Porter had refused to have a second deputy ambassador come to Saigon and now he would pay the price. Moreover, Porter appeared not to take his authority seriously. Although given total command over civilian agencies, Porter made it clear that he "planned to suggest action" rather than to command.

With the American effort in disarray, it was not surprising that the South Vietnamese RD cadres in the field were unable to make much progress. Above all there was precious little coordination between the military side of pacification—providing ongoing and constant village security—and the social side of nation building. Thus the best laid plans of the civilian agencies and the most competent execution of those plans—and there were few examples in either of those categories—were often destroyed in one blow by local Vietcong guerrillas who attacked the instant security slackened, thus reminding local villagers who was really in control.

Under such conditions, pacification work was often incomplete. Rural Construction workers, and their successors, the RD cadres, feared staying in a village too long and involving themselves too deeply in village affairs. The results were pacification reports of villages brought under government control where VC influence had scarcely been threatened.

In December 1966 Daniel Ellsberg, at the time special assistant to Porter in OCO and once an enthusiastic supporter of the U.S. effort in Vietnam, visited the village of Loc Tien on the day it was officially declared "secure." What he found depressed him. Of six criteria used to classify a village as secure, only one—the taking of a census—had been satisfied. Not even the most elementary security had been provided. During the previous week five RD cadres had been murdered by guerrillas. The hamlet chief, elected to fulfill one of the criteria, had been assassinated and a new chief hurriedly elected to fill the gap. Of greatest importance in Ellsberg's mind was the fact that the village officials refused to sleep in the hamlet, instead retiring to the district capital at sunset to avoid the VC. And yet, Loc Tien was declared a secure village.

MACV takes over

By now Johnson had had enough. Meeting with senior officials from Washington and Saigon in Guam on March 20 and 21, 1967, the president announced that he was going to turn pacification over to MACV, to put it under Westmoreland's control. But he admonished those in the room not to mention his decision until it was ready to be announced to the press. Two months later Johnson chose a new team to head the mission in Saigon. Lodge retired at his own request and was replaced by Ellsworth Bunker as ambassador to South Vietnam. Bunker immediately announced that MACV would be placed in charge of an integrated civilian-military chain of command for pacification. OCO was transformed into Civil Operations and Revolutionary Development Support (CORDS), under the direction of a civilian deputy commander of MACV. As the first deputy commander Johnson chose his presidential assistant, Robert Komer. Komer was given the rank of ambassador and the military equivalent of three stars.

Under the New Model pacification program, as CORDS came to be called, all civilian agencies would operate within the military chain of command in order to provide the minimal level of security necessary for pacification programs to work. Changes in ARVN were coming as well. A "substantial portion" of ARVN forces—one-half was mentioned—would be assigned the permanent duty of supporting pacification by providing constant village security. Province chiefs, mostly chosen from among senior military officers, were finally given some command authority over ARVN. They were permitted to by-pass divisional commanders in requesting ARVN troops to counter guerrilla attacks in the villages. By going directly to the regimental or even battalion level and *ordering* troops into villages under attack, they could insure a speedier response to the VC.

Of equal significance, it was at this point that MACV made its first commitment to pacification and the provision of village security in the form of military assistance. It was following the creation of CORDS that Westmoreland finally requested in June 1967 that 2,243 U.S. Army advisers be assigned to permanent village duty in order to fashion the Regional and Popular Forces into a credible village defense system.

Komer spent the remainder of 1967 putting the new program into operation. He later admitted that it was unable to achieve measurable progress during those first six months. However, the creation of CORDS and the corresponding changes in the South Vietnamese pacification program showed that important lessons had been drawn in Washington from two-and-a-half years of failure:

- No pacification program could succeed without first providing permanent security within the villages.

- ARVN forces, in particular, had to be brought much closer to the village and hamlet level and had to be available to respond speedily to guerrilla attacks on villages.

- American economic and social programs had to be better coordinated with the security effort to make sure that those resources were available when they could do the most good and not be wasted or fall into the hands of the enemy.

- No amount of success in the big-unit war would bring the United States and South Vietnam closer to victory unless VC influence in the villages could simultaneously be reduced.

On paper, at least, the New Model program looked as if it might solve all of these problems by providing the pacification effort with a constant shield of security for the villages and coordination among the various social programs. The test of CORDS would come not in 1967 but after the new year began, for South Vietnam was nearing

a climactic challenge. The challenge would be directed at the heart of the pacification program, at the country's twelve thousand hamlets and twenty-five hundred villages.

The situation did not look all that promising. In November 1967 two officers from an American division, flushed with their successes in the big-unit war, visited the senior American pacification adviser in a neighboring village. The adviser complained bitterly of VC control of the area, which threatened even the district capital. The visiting officers were struck by the adviser's "negativism" and pointed out that their division had the NVA units "on the run" and had claimed more than five hundred KIAs in the previous month alone. The adviser replied, "Colonel, that's your war, not mine." That very night a team of enemy sappers, not from a Main Force NVA unit but from the VC local forces ignored by the division, destroyed the district MACV headquarters and killed the adviser.

The comment the dead senior adviser had made echoed a question that was beginning, though only dimly, to enter the minds of many Americans: Whose war was it? While he had insisted that the United States would not renounce its commitment to help save South Vietnam from Communist takeover, President Kennedy, in his last public words on Vietnam, carried over nationwide television, had issued a warning:

In the final analysis, it is their war. They are the ones who have to win it or lose it. We can help them ... but they have to win it, the people of Vietnam.

Perhaps more than they realized, President Johnson, General Westmoreland, and most of their advisers had put these cautious words behind them. America was taking over the direction of the war—and most of the fighting.

LBJ and Premier Ky meet for the first time at Honolulu in February 1966. The summit was a public relations success for both men but elicited fewer concrete commitments from Ky than Johnson would have liked.

Pacification: A Village-Eye View

by Donald Kirk

A Revolutionary Development cadre distributes literature to children in the delta village of Tan An. This brochure asks the children to choose between communism and freedom.

In a rambling old house near Tan Son Nhut air base on the outskirts of Saigon, young field workers for the International Voluntary Service talked about their roles in Vietnam with missionary zeal. The year was 1965. Critics of the war did not understand, they said, what the U.S. could do to help the people in the countryside to improve their farms, build up the local economy, and stave off efforts by the Vietcong or National Liberation Front to win recruits and undermine lives. One of the IVS volunteers from a farming family in Kansas described the hours he had spent mulling over new ways of increasing production, squatting on the dikes by the rice fields with peasants whom he had come to know as well as his neighbors at home.

I had just arrived to write about what the Americans called "a new kind of war," to which pacification was as vital as the helicopters needed to provide air mobility for combat assaults. The IVS program epitomized an American dream for creating conditions in which a contented populace would no longer be responsive to Communist "lures." With the vast American build-up, however, IVS gradually became subordinate to a fast-proliferating organization called the United States Operations Mission (USOM), housed in a labyrinthine office building near the center of Saigon. More and more, IVS volunteers complained about "bureaucracy"—and the priority now given to military rather than civilian needs.

IVS volunteers gradually grew angry and frustrated with USOM's handling of pacification. IVS program director Don Luce quit, attacking the U.S. establishment for exacerbating the social problems it professed to want to cure. Luce, who wore black peasant garb and spoke Vietnamese, believed passionately that American forces were as much to blame as the North Vietnamese for expanding the war. He was also miffed by the requirement that IVS coordinate its activities with the new bureaucratic structure named CORDS, or Civil Operations and Revolutionary Development Support, which was set up in 1967 to direct the entire pacification effort. Within CORDS lines between civilian and military inter-

ests blurred as army officers were assigned to a single organization along with career diplomats and specialists from the Agency for International Development, the U.S. Information Agency, and the CIA.

The names of the new programs still reflected dreams once held by Luce and his colleagues. There would be no more "strategic hamlets," the late Ngo Dinh Diem's program to draw peasants into fortified bases. The accent now was on Revolutionary Development with "New Life" hamlets theoretically thriving on new fish ponds, new bridges, new roads, new schools, new whatever-they-needed to inspire trust in the Saigon regime. To minimize small-scale attacks and ambushes, U.S military officers from the district teams advised Regional and Popular Force units, dubbed "ruff puffs." The CIA exerted its influence through Revolutionary Development teams—villagers functioning as do-gooders, intelligence gatherers, and terrorists. Senior CORDS officials with large staffs in regional headquarters formed the links in a chain of civilian command that descended to provincial and district advisory teams.

From the outset, the problem with pacification on such a large scale was that the lofty plans so easily inscribed on briefing charts, in guidelines, and in propaganda pamphlets seemed strangely irrelevant in the field. Shortly after Luce had quit IVS I visited a village named Ninh Hung, some sixty miles northwest of Saigon, and chatted with members of a Revolutionary Development team charged with winning the people's loyalty in an area strongly influenced by the NLF.

"We're 'organizing the populace,'" said Nguyen Van Len, assistant leader of the fifty-nine-man team, quoting directly from a rule book supposedly put out by the South Vietnamese government but drafted by American advisers. "We hold meetings of the hamlet population and find out who has Vietcong inclinations and who is nationalist. We believe that 60 percent of the village is on our side." The RD slogans—"destruction of VC infrastructure," "eradication of corrupted elements"—rolled uneasily off his tongue in a setting of dirt roads, thatched-roof

huts, and lolling pigs and dogs.

"We are supposed to bring a better life for the people," said Len when pressed on what his team had been doing since arriving in the village a few months earlier, "but we do not yet have good results." The villagers, hesitant to say what they thought of the Saigon government, Revolutionary Development, or the NLF, confirmed his assessment. In a clay-walled house across the road, Van Teo, surrounded by his wife and six children, conceded that, yes, he had listened to little lectures from RD team members, who theoretically lived and worked in the village twenty-four hours a day. "They came to my house and said they wanted to help the people," said Teo. "They said they had a government program for the village. They promised to lend me money to grow a fruit tree, but up to now we have nothing." Teo's wife, holding a feverish little girl in her arms, was equally disillusioned with a government medical aid station, largely the responsibility of the RD team. "I will not take my daughter there," she said. "The woman who works there does not know what she's doing."

In the center of a nearby network of sandbagged bunkers surrounded by six rows of coiled barbed wire, a fresh-faced young U.S. Army lieutenant, adviser to a company of local Popular Force troops, spoke even more harshly of the RD team—and the village chief as well. "RD team members are supposed to meet with the people, discuss their problems and do something about them," said the lieutenant, who had majored in Far Eastern history at the University of Washington. "For some reason it's not working." In fact, he went on, "we're doing all the work of the RD while they're just sitting there having a good time. We're trying to get a school built, and we're out there every day bringing clothes to the kids and giving medical help. We have to show the villagers we can do the same things the VC can. As long as we're here, the village is for us."

The lieutenant's greatest complaint was that RD team members shared the bunkers with Popular Force troopers instead of living among the villagers. "They spend all their time sleeping, they're not a part of the village at all," he said. "They're as foreign to the villagers as we are." He—and other U.S. officials—estimated the village then was "two-thirds Vietcong." As for the village chief, the lieutenant said that "all he does is sit in his office and smile at everyone"—and sleep in the provincial capital rather than risk a night at home. Moreover, he strongly suspected that the chief, if he was not with the Vietcong, was at least an accomplished fence sitter. "We think that's one reason he got elected," he said. "He convinced the people he could keep them out of trouble from both sides." The lieutenant admitted, though, that he rarely if ever met with the chief or RD team members. "I'm not sure what's my relationship with them [sic]," he said. "Technically, I'm only advising the PF unit."

Indeed, life for Ninh Hung's two thousand inhabitants, who earned their livelihood mainly by working on rice and rubber plantations, resembled that of millions of South Vietnamese on the borderline between government and VC authority. They paid approximately 10 percent of their income in taxes to the VC and shared half their crops with landlords, who in turn also paid taxes to the VC. Many of the villagers, moreover, were afraid to work the fields more than half a mile from the outskirts for fear of attacks by guerrillas based in a rubber plantation another half a mile or so to the west.

The plight of the people of Ninh Hung, however, was far preferable to that of millions of others who had been forced to flee their homes as American troops, backed up by air power and artillery, fanned into the countryside in pursuit of the North Vietnamese. In the doorway of a long row of tin and concrete refugee huts in a village named Ninh Loi, not far from Ninh Hung, a tough-looking peasant named Tran Van Kein rather reluctantly discussed the nature of the pincers movement that had caught him and his family in the middle. "I could not support the injustices of both sides," said Kein when I arrived in Ninh Loi after visiting Ninh Hung. What kind of injustices? "There are only two reasons for leaving," he said, looking at the ground, as his twenty-eight-year-old wife nursed a baby in the shadows, "dropping bombs and injustice by the Vietcong."

In the presence of an American refugee adviser, Kein said the reason he had left his home was the bombing. "We could not keep living there," he said. "The bombs fell around my house. Part of my neighbor's home was destroyed." One of several hundred refugees living in the encampment, Kein laughed at the programs for caring for them and said cryptically that whoever had "the most tanks" would win the war. In fact, much of the "pacification" effort was attuned to caring for such refugees, whose presence in squalid camps in "secure" areas unrealistically raised the ratings of the Hamlet Evaluation Survey, a computerized scheme for grading every hamlet on a letter scale beginning with "A." Brain child of Robert Komer, who became deputy ambassador in charge of pacification seven months before the Tet offensive, the survey symbolized the naiveté of Americans intent on spreading their ideology of democracy.

Could anyone come up with valid statistics to show, say, that "56.2 percent" of the hamlets with "72.4 percent" of the populace were "pacified?" With Komer setting the pace, the accent had to be on the positive, and American officials habitually praised their Vietnamese "counterparts," who learned the American bureaucratic idiom and reveled in the benefits. The Americans, often petty power brokers heady with the glory of "running a province" (or district), tended to shrug off corruption endemic in a local elite enriched by a wartime economy bloated on American dollars. What the surveys never revealed was the total dependence of this structure on the U.S. not only for combat support but also for materiel and money.

Donald Kirk covered the Vietnam War for four years and has written numerous articles and two books about the conflict.

Three Battles

In 1964 during his election campaign, Lyndon Johnson had affirmed his conviction that "American boys" should not "do the fighting for Asian boys." By June 1966, two hundred eighty-five thousand American troops were on combat duty in South Vietnam, and another hundred thousand would be pouring in by the end of the year. With draft calls rapidly approaching forty-five thousand men per month, the largest quota since the Korean War, there seemed to be no end in sight.

Through 1966 and 1967, Americans would read newspaper accounts of American military operations, such as Masher-White Wing, Malheur, Attleboro, and Birmingham, to name only a few. Yet these would not be the dramatic, set-piece battles Americans were familiar with from World War II and Korea. For above all, Vietnam would be a war of no fronts. All of South Vietnam would eventually become the battlefield: the dense jungle and rugged hills near the DMZ, the wet-

lands and impenetrable forests north of Saigon, and the myriad waterways and rice fields of the Mekong Delta. In these diverse and hostile environments, General Westmoreland was calculating that his search and destroy tactics could work. The application of that strategy was demonstrated, in part, by three of MACV's efforts in South Vietnam: Operation Hastings near the DMZ, Operation Cedar Falls in the Iron Triangle northwest of Saigon, and Operation Coronado V, a "riverine" mission in the Mekong Delta.

The marines and Operation Hastings

May 17, 1966. After a three-hour truck ride and a night march from the North Vietnamese coastal town of Vinh Linh, two hundred NVA soldiers waded across a shallow section of the Ben Hai River, the demarcation line dividing North from South Vietnam. Once across, the soldiers followed a narrow jungle trail through the lower half of the six-mile-wide demilitarized zone. Their mission was not to fight but to reconnoiter four districts in central and eastern Quang Tri Province. And they knew something big was in the works: an invasion of Quang Tri in late May by the ten thousand men of NVA Division 324B to annihilate the ARVN 1st Division assigned to defend the province.

Division 324B, commanded by General Nguyen Vang, was a relatively new unit, untested in battle. It had been formed a year earlier, brought up to strength with draftees, and trained for combat. Despite the division's past inexperience, General Vang was confident his men would acquit themselves well against the South Vietnamese or, if need be, the Americans. Even after recent setbacks in South Vietnam, NVA morale was high. A song on Radio Hanoi summed up the soldiers' mood:

> Yankee, I swear to you
> With words sharp as knives
> Here in Vietnam, it is either you or me
> And I am already here
> So you must go!

The political and military crisis affecting Quang Tri and other northern provinces of South Vietnam in the spring of 1966 made them ripe for takeover. Since March, the hostilities between Buddhists and the government had paralyzed the military and weakened the defense of I Corps. Non-Communist areas of Quang Tri and Thua Thien had been held by dissident ARVN units in sympathy with Buddhist factions. The North Vietnamese proceeded with customary caution, organizing a complicated logistic effort to "prepare the battlefield." Lacking anything comparable

to U.S. air mobility to resupply troops already in the field, the NVA had to establish advance logistical bases with food and armaments for incoming troops.

The NVA relied primarily on their VC allies already in Quang Tri to collect and store rice. But General Vang, poised to cross the Ben Hai River in the last week of May, discovered that his VC supply unit had not done its job. Reconnaissance reported that rice depots were few in number and poorly stocked. As a result Division 324B's mission was delayed while several of its battalions shuttled back and forth to North Vietnam for rice. While 324B stood stalled in the DMZ, the American commanders monitored its activity and speculated about its intentions.

The unprecedented infiltration of the DMZ by an NVA division created a stir at MACV headquarters in Saigon. The specter of an invasion, Korean-style, across the DMZ had preoccupied American and South Vietnamese commanders since 1954. To General Westmoreland in the spring of 1966, such aggression appeared imminent. In February he had told President Johnson and Premier Ky that if he were NVA General Vo Nguyen Giap he "would strike into Quang Tri . . . to seek a quick victory."

In the ensuing months MACV, at the war rooms in Saigon, had compiled data on NVA activity near the DMZ indicating that an invasion was in the offing. By May, Vietnamese agents were tracking 324B's movements through the DMZ. Aerial observers spotted troops and trucks in the eastern sector of the zone, and infrared aerial photographs revealed nighttime fires in the jungle and probable encampments. A lucky break provided further evidence when an NVA soldier surrendered to an ARVN outpost and disclosed preparations for 324B's invasion.

Still, Westmoreland was unwilling to mobilize his forces and commit them to immediate counterattack. He later remarked, "I had to have more intelligence on what was going on up North, and there was no better way to get at it than by sending in reconnaissance elements in force."

The marines, whose tactical area of responsibility included Quang Tri, shared MACV's concern about the NVA build-up in the North. But they disagreed with MACV that the build-up constituted preparation for an all-out invasion of Quang Tri and Thua Thien. Some marine estimates suggested that an invasion was unlikely because of the insurmountable logistics and supply problems a division-size NVA force would incur. Several marine commanders also speculated that 324B was bait to lure the marines' limited forces away from their successful clear and hold pacification efforts near Da Nang and to bog them down indefinitely in a static defense of the DMZ. While acknowledging the marines' progress in pacification, Westmoreland was impatient with their stubborn devotion to it. To spur them to action, Westmoreland ordered General Walt's marines to conduct the reconnaissance needed to ascertain the purpose and scope of NVA infiltration into Quang Tri.

Preceding page. U.S. Marines scatter from a burning CH-46 helicopter shot down in Helicopter Valley near the DMZ on July 15, 1966, the first day of Operation Hastings. Thirteen marines died in the crash, and three were severely burned.

Testing the waters

July 1. A few minutes before nightfall, marine Lieutenant Terry Terrebone and about a dozen marines, their faces blackened with grease, carefully checked their gear and weapons on the airstrip at Dong Ha. After boarding two CH-46 helicopters, they headed in a northeasterly direction. Their destination: two miles south of the DMZ at a junction of two known infiltration trails. Their mission: to locate 324B.

As reported by Robert Shaplen in the *New Yorker*, Terrebone was not optimistic about contacting 324B in the thickly wooded foothills below the DMZ: "We intended to stay forty-eight hours" and "find out what we could." He and his men were in for a nasty surprise. They had been on the ground only twenty minutes when fifty NVA soldiers approached them from over a ridge. The NVA quickly moved to surround the marines. Scrambling back to the landing zone, Terrebone called for helicopter gunships and waited to be picked up while the NVA encircled the LZ only fifty yards away. Terrebone recalls: "They were holding their fire, which showed good discipline. Ten minutes later, two A-4 Skyhawks and another helicopter gunship arrived. They sprayed the area with heavy fire and received automatic weapons fire in return. Two CH-46's were right behind them, and they came down and lifted us off."

Terrebone's reconnaissance party checked out several other sites over the next two weeks. Besides spotting three hundred fifty NVA regulars, the marines sighted fortifications, including mortar pits, trench lines, and foxholes. General Walt of the marines concluded, "General Giap and Ho Chi Minh had decided to slug it out with us." Westmoreland was now "convinced that the better part of 324B had moved across the DMZ."

General Westmoreland swiftly ordered Walt to ready as many as seven marine infantry battalions (eight thousand men) to stop 324B. Reinforced by five ARVN infantry and airborne battalions (three thousand men), backed by artillery and aircraft, and covered by the long-range guns of the U.S. 7th Fleet, Walt's marines fanned out in mid-July toward the DMZ. Operation Hastings, the largest marine operation up to that time, was underway.

The marines had embarked on one of their first major operations near the DMZ. The conditions of the battlefield could not have been less favorable (see map, page 111). Mountains make up roughly half of Quang Tri, dropping off eastward into foothills separated from the sea by a thin stretch of paddy land and sandy beaches. The hill the marines called the Rockpile, with sheer cliffs straight up and down, dominates relatively flat terrain just north of the Cam Lo River. An almost impenetrable jungle blankets Quang Tri's razor-backed ridges with thick brush topped by a double canopy of deciduous trees, one thirty feet high and the other a hundred. So thick was the canopy that, according to one observer, "bombs explode harmlessly" on it.

Hastings was commanded by Brigadier General Lowell English, a combat veteran of World War II and Korea. His battle plan was to repulse NVA penetration by cutting their access to two key infiltration trails converging some four miles below the DMZ. He deemed control of the Rockpile, overlooking the entire operational area, a particularly important objective. Aggressiveness was the crux of English's plan to take "the enemy by surprise on his key trails and behind his own lines and to smash and destroy him before he had a chance to regain his balance and his momentum."

That the marines were coming after them, however, would be no secret to the North Vietnamese. For three days before Hastings, B-52s pounded the trails, hillsides, and ravines near the DMZ to "soften up" NVA entrenchments. Meanwhile, on a broad plain west of Dong Ha, the staging area for the operation, huge four-engine planes disgorged a million pounds of supplies and equipment. As the planes skimmed the runways, rose-colored dust clouds billowed into the sky, a portent surely not missed by the men of 324B.

D-day

On July 15 at first light, a squadron of CH-46 helicopters, resembling mammoth grasshoppers, lifted off from Dong Ha with members of the 3d Battalion, 4th Marines (3/4) of the 3d Marine Division. Their operational zone was the Song Ngan Valley, within rifle range of the DMZ. The first wave of helicopters set down in the river valley without incident. Sniper fire ended hope for a quiet landing as the second wave swooped toward the LZ. The third wave met disaster. In the LZ, choked by jungle, two helicopters collided and crashed. A third, trying to avoid them, rammed into a tree, killing two marines and injuring seven. Snipers downed one more. Lieutenant Colonel Sumner Vale, the battalion commander, remembers the grisly sight of several panicked marines being slashed to death "by the helicopter blades as they were getting out of the helicopter." The Song Ngan Valley earned that day an infamous place in marine lore as "Helicopter Valley." It was an ominous beginning.

Vale's 3d Battalion initiated a sweep through the valley, while the 2d Battalion landed at the other end about three miles to the northeast. The 3d was to serve as a blocking force on a suspected infiltration route. The 2d, commanded by Lieutenant Colonel Arnold Bench, moved southwest to take Hill 208 overlooking the 3d's position. The almost impassable jungle combined with oppressive heat slowed the 2d's progress to a crawl. By midafternoon it had covered barely two miles. Captain J.W. Hilgers vividly recalls the difficulty of negotiating the terrain particularly the thick vegetation: "Though we knew our location, we could not see where we were going, trusting only to our compasses. The heat with no breeze and unlimited humidity was devastating."

Delays erased whatever tactical surprise General English had counted on. And the marine battalions, now isolated behind NVA advance positions, were quickly thrown on the defensive. At four in the afternoon, after unsuccessfully trying to cross the Song Ngan, Vale radioed that his men were "under heavy fire" and were "in trouble." By seven-thirty the 3d was surrounded, awaiting the inevitable NVA night attack. It did not have to wait long. Shortly after eight an NVA company tried to overrun Company K's position, igniting a wild three-hour fire fight. "It was so dark," said Captain Robert Modrzejewski, "we couldn't see our hands in front of our faces, so we threw out trip flares and called for a flare plane overhead. We could hear and smell and occasionally see the NVA after that. When the firing stopped, we heard them dragging the bodies of their dead away, but in the morning, at the first light, we found twenty-five bodies. . . . On the basis of the dragging we had heard . . . we figured we got another thirty of them, which we listed as probably killed."

The 3d's problems were not over. The next evening, still unable to ford the river, the marines dug in while the NVA picked up where they had left off, lobbing mortars at their perimeter. At this point the 2d Battalion changed the direction of its advance to assist the 3d. When it finally did reach Vale's unit, the 2d too was pinned down by the intense mortar attacks. The marines returned fire, directing ear-shattering air and artillery strikes to within a few hundred yards of their own positions, and killed a hundred of the enemy, some at close range with pistols and even bayonets. After two more days of incessant bombardment, the 2d and 3d got new orders: pull out.

In the early afternoon of July 18, Vale and Bench moved their units toward the eastern end of the valley. Captain Modrzejewski's battle-weary Company K stayed behind to destroy the crippled helicopters at the LZ. Instead of pursuing the main body, the NVA massed to attack Company K. Around two-thirty, several hundred NVA infantrymen charged the LZ, blowing bugles and whistles and waving flags. Company K stubbornly held its ground. The 1st Platoon, cut off in the confusion, bore the full brunt of the assault. First Platoon Sergeant John McGinty and his rifle squads threw everything they had at the NVA force but it was not enough: "We started getting mortar fire, followed by automatic weapons fire from all sides. . . . [Charlie] moved in with small arms right behind the mortars. . . . We just couldn't kill them fast enough."

So close were the NVA to overrunning the company that Modrzejewski called air strikes virtually on top of the marines' position. One marine forward air controller, less than fifty feet from the enemy, had to plunge into a nearby stream to escape being burned by a napalm strike. The shower of bombs and napalm sent the enemy scurrying for cover. In three hours of close combat, the bloodiest of the entire operation, a beleaguered Company K suffered over fifty casualties, with some marines hit in five or six places. When reinforcements from Company L arrived to cover withdrawal, Modrzejewski's men "formed a column of walking wounded . . . and then proceeded upstream, where the wounded were evacuated that night." For their actions, Modrzejewski and McGinty each received the Medal of Honor.

The 2d and 3d Battalions had not seen their last of Helicopter Valley. General English, after evacuating the wounded, immediately sent these battalions back to the valley from the south to join the 1st Battalion of the 1st Marines commanded by Colonel Van Bell, in blocking NVA infiltration. All the battalions saw action in a deadly game of cat and mouse. A marine summed up NVA tactics: "a probe followed by an attack with mortars, automatic weapons and small arms, then disengagements and flight." What happened on Hill 362 is a classic example.

On July 17 Lieutenant Colonel Edward Bronars's 3d Battalion, 5th Marines, began patrolling south of Helicopter Valley. A week into the patrol, Bronars ordered Captain Samuel Glaize's Company I to establish a radio relay station atop Hill 362, three miles below the DMZ. After hacking its way to the crest with two-foot-long machetes, Glaize's 2d Platoon descended the other side of the hill to scout defenses. It had not gone far when it met a hail of mortar and machine-gun fire. "They had everything zeroed in on the trail," First Sergeant Bill Chapman recalled. Other platoons rushed to aid the 2d but were ambushed. Soon the entire company was trapped near the crest of the hill by a steady mortar barrage. "We could only dig small trenches," said Second Lieutenant Robert Williams. "We put a wounded man in with a man who could fight. Every third man was wounded, but they still tried to man the weapons."

It was a harrowing night for Company I as NVA soldiers probed to within fifteen to twenty feet of the marines' perimeter. Corporal Mack Whieley remembered, "The Commies were so close we could hear them breathing heavily and hear them talking." For Private First Class Michael Bednar, it was hell. Struck by a bullet, he fell near another wounded marine just as some NVA soldiers emerged from a clump of trees. Both marines played dead, but the NVA wanted to make sure. After the soldiers plunged a bayonet into the marine beside Bednar and he groaned, they shot him through the head. Three times the soldiers jabbed Bednar with bayonets but he refused to cry out. Leaving him for dead, the soldiers snatched Bednar's cigarettes and watch and moved on to other wounded marines. According to another wounded survivor, Corporal Raymond Powell, "it was damn near like a massacre."

The next day, U.S. artillery struck at NVA emplace-

A "tippy-toe" landing atop the Rock-pile, this one occurring during Operation Hastings, was a precarious maneuver. The pilot of this UH–34D supply helicopter had to keep his craft at full throttle while it was quickly unloaded.

Near Helicopter Valley, U.S. Marines hit the dirt to avoid knee-high NVA fire.

ments. Helicopters whirred in to remove the wounded, including Private Bednar, who had managed to crawl back to his lines "with his guts hanging out." Glaize's unit suffered a casualty rate of 45 percent—eighteen dead and sixty-five wounded. As for the force of NVA, the *New York Times* reported that it "vanished into the countryside."

The view from the Rockpile

Along with the assault on Helicopter Valley, General English launched a corollary offensive, the occupation of the Rockpile. There was not much to occupy, only a narrow ledge a few feet wide at the summit. With a lookout post perched on one of the region's highest peaks, English could monitor NVA infiltration trails for miles in all directions. Lieutenant James Hart of the 1st Force Reconnaissance Company got the mission. Hart and his men—trained as parachutists and scuba divers—faced a tricky drop by helicopter onto the Rockpile's tiny promontory. On July 16 two helicopters hovered above the Rockpile while Hart, twelve of his men, and a demolitions team made jumps of six to eight feet to the ledge. Just as Hart jumped, a gust of wind jerked the helicopter upward. He fell thirty feet to the ledge and was temporarily stunned.

Hart and his men were on the Rockpile an hour when they spied thirty-eight NVA on a trail below. A well-directed artillery strike killed all the NVA soldiers. Before lifting off the mountain two weeks later, their observations enabled artillery and air strikes to keep important trails free of further infiltration.

By month's end, it appeared that 324B had abandoned its offensive and was pulling back through the DMZ. Marine patrols discovered bodies, weapons, and ammunition left behind. The marines overran an NVA regimental base camp containing a 100-bed hospital and twelve hundred pounds of medical supplies. An account in *Time* magazine noted that "one North Vietnamese unit apparently pulled out so fast that 500 men abandoned their field packs and left their rice still cooking in open pots." As enemy contacts tapered off, General English terminated Hastings at noon on August 3.

In his after action report to MACV, General Walt was effusive in his praise for Hastings: "As a result of· the battle, the 324th NVA Division suffered a crushing defeat and enemy designs for capture of Quang Tri Province were thwarted. ... It was a significant victory for the United States and represents a tribute to the courage, skill, and resourcefulness of the personnel and units involved." General Westmoreland was no less pleased; he was convinced that the timely execution of Hastings had spoiled NVA strategy and foiled an invasion.

The marines exacted a stiff price from 324B for its incursion: 882 killed, 17 captured, and the seizure of two hundred weapons, three hundred pounds of documents, and over three hundred thousand rounds of ammunition.

The soldiers of 324B, described by General Walt as "well equipped, well trained, and aggressive to the point of fanaticism," also showed themselves a formidable foe. In all, 126 marines were killed and 448 wounded.

From a long-term perspective, Hastings demonstrated the problems faced by MACV forces fighting in the rugged hills of northern I Corps. Although its invasion fizzled in the jungles below the DMZ, 324B was able to withdraw successfully across it into North Vietnam, its offensive capability virtually intact. By exploiting their continuing ability to move across the DMZ into South Vietnam, 324B and other NVA divisions were able to control the tempo of combat in I Corps. Their options included full-scale invasion and hit-and-run attacks, in addition to attempting an increasing flow of infiltration to the south. These types of NVA offensive threats caused a steady build-up of U.S. Marines from 1966 to 1968 near the DMZ. Operation Prairie (see picture essay, page 153), which immediately followed Hastings, confirmed the trend the marines had feared, proving Walt and Westmoreland overconfident in their assessment of Hastings. This time, more marines—eleven thousand of them—would be reacting to renewed thrusts by NVA Division 324B and would become tied down to a string of defensive positions along the DMZ. As a result, one army report concluded, "General Walt, with his forces stretched to the limit and short of helicopter and logistical assets, was unable to do more than hold his own." NVA General Vo Nguyen Giap described the situation in I Corps this way: "The marines are being stretched as taut as a bowstring."

Stalking the Vietcong where he lives

"It's like defending a stockade in the days of the Indian wars," said air force Lieutenant Colonel Grove Johnson of Saigon's sprawling Tan Son Nhut air base. Charged with securing the multimillion dollar base, only a few miles from downtown Saigon, from VC attacks, Johnson installed barbed wire, round-the-clock patrols, and a network of booby traps. But no level of vigilance seemed able to deter daring raids by Vietcong guerrillas and saboteurs. On the evening of December 4, 1966, twenty-five VC breached Tan Son Nhut's defensive perimeter to within hand-grenade range of U.S. warplanes, parked unattended in an open field. Base security discovered and killed the VC before they accomplished their mission of destroying the aircraft. The incident confirmed evidence piling up at nearby MACV headquarters: VC activity in the Saigon area was reaching alarming proportions.

Tan Son Nhut was not the only target. Eight VC battalions, operating brazenly within a twenty-five-mile radius of Saigon, were slowly strangling the city's commercial, agricultural, and communications links with the rural population in thousands of villages. The VC controlled many of the roads and waterways surrounding Saigon and ex-

A young resident of Ben Suc is led out of his doomed village by an ARVN soldier, January 1967.

torted "tolls" for their use, imposing financial drain as well as political embarrassment on the GVN. Particularly galling was the ability of VC units to strike almost at will into the heart of South Vietnam's capital. When the VC sent a mortar barrage into a Saigon crowd celebrating South Vietnam's National Day on November 1, 1966, the top officers at MACV and the South Vietnamese government decided they had had enough.

General Westmoreland, impatient with GVN foot dragging in pacification and in the suppression of rampant VC terrorism in and around Saigon (incidents doubled in 1966), opted for an American solution: a hard-hitting search and destroy operation to eliminate the source of VC pressure on Saigon and its environs. He called it Cedar Falls, after the home town in Iowa of a young army lieutenant recently killed in action and posthumously awarded the Medal of Honor. Its target was the wedge of jungle and paddy fields northwest of Saigon known as the Iron Triangle (see map, page 110). MACV referred to the Triangle, long a VC sanctuary, as a "dagger pointed at

Saigon." It functioned as the nerve center for VC terrorism in the Saigon region, with a vast network of concrete bunkers, base camps, supply depots, and field hospitals connected by tunnels. Some American officers thought the Triangle served as headquarters for the VC Military Region IV, which controlled all the villages in the vicinity.

Operation Cedar Falls

For eighteen months prior to Cedar Falls, U.S. B–52s had been blasting VC installations in the Triangle, hoping to drive the guerrillas from their hide-out. The rain of more than a million pounds of bombs, however, yielded no tangible results: The VC's hold on the Triangle was unshaken. Now, in early 1967, his army bolstered by thousands of new troops to a total of three hundred eighty-five thousand, Westmoreland felt he had the muscle to go into the Triangle in force.

Cedar Falls was to employ a force of fifteen thousand men drawn from several American and South Vietnamese

Ben Suc villagers gather together bicycles, furniture, pigs, buffaloes—anything they can carry or herd—for loading onto trucks and barges by the ARVN soldiers in the background.

divisions, making it the largest operation yet in the war. Its principal objective was "the destruction of the enemy's Military Region IV headquarters" and the razing of enemy fortifications there once and for all. If Cedar Falls was as successful as MACV envisioned it, the VC would be finished in the Triangle.

The U.S. Army units involved were the 11th Armored Cavalry and the 173d Airborne Brigade as well as elements of the 25th Infantry Division, the 196th Light Infantry Brigade, and the 1st Infantry Division. Part of the ARVN 5th Infantry Division was also involved. Their mission: to seal off the Triangle's perimeter, using the standard hammer and anvil maneuver. One force—the hammer—would conduct a coordinated sweep across the Triangle, while a second—the anvil—would position itself to block the enemy's avenue of escape. To prevent intelligence leaks to the VC, MACV kept preparations for Cedar Falls exclusively American. Cedar Falls's commander, Lieutenant General Jonathan Seaman, commander of II Field Force, delayed briefing the ARVN III Corps commander and arranging for ARVN support troops until two days before the operation. Despite the unusual emphasis on surprise, General Seaman did not alter the practice of prepping the operation zone with air and artillery. No target in the Triangle was spared, except for one small village set in a loop of the Saigon River in the far northwestern corner of the Triangle.

Cedar Falls, with its air and artillery bombardment, troop maneuvers, and search and destroy tactics, bore many of the trappings of conventional warfare. Not so conventional, however, was what MACV had in store for the village of Ben Suc, the reputed hub of VC control of the Triangle. A U.S. Army history described it as a "fortified supply and political center" in which "the central organization for the Vietcong's secret base was located."

Ben Suc posed a serious dilemma for MACV. For almost a decade the village had been cooperating with and supporting the VC. An army representative complained that "we haven't even been able to get a census in there to find out who's there." If, according to Mao's aphorism, the people are the sea in which the guerrilla "fish" must swim, MACV concluded there was no option in the case of Ben Suc but to drain the sea by removing the people and destroying the village. As one American colonel remarked, "This is probably the only military or political solution for this place."

After a surprise helicopter assault into Ben Suc by units of the 1st Division, the village was to be sealed off and swept for VC. On the eve of Cedar Falls, Major Allen Dixon outlined the scenario to a group of six reporters: "The attack is going to go tomorrow morning and it's going to be a complete surprise. Five hundred men of the 1st Infantry Division's 2d Brigade are going to be lifted right into the village itself in sixty choppers.... We have learned that the perimeter of the village is heavily mined,

and that's why we'll be going into the village itself." Its people did not know it, but Ben Suc no longer had a future.

Zero hour at Ben Suc

On January 8, 1967, Cedar Falls got underway. Thirty miles from Ben Suc, sixty "slicks," troop-carrying helicopters, hovered above Dau Tieng airstrip, forming two giant Vs against the clear morning sky. Major Nick Primis, the mission's aviation officer from the 1st Aviation Battalion, had everything timed to the second. At precisely 7:45 A.M. the helicopters, traveling less than fifty feet apart, skimmed above the tree tops at eighty-five miles per hour. Within minutes the lead pilot spotted smoke from the colored smoke grenades exploded by the Pathfinders, specially trained soldiers put in ahead of the main body of troops to mark the landing zone. Suddenly the call came in over the radio of Major George Fish, piloting one of the ten gunships covering the landing: "Rebel 36, go in for the

Old woman and baby uprooted from their home, Ben Suc, a village with a recorded history going back to the late 18th century.

SAFE-CONDUCT PASS TO BE HONORED BY ALL VIETNAMESE GOVERNMENT AGENCIES AND ALLIED FORCES

Đây là một tấm Giấy Thông Hành có giá trị với tất cả cơ quan Quân Chính Việt - Nam Cộng - Hòa và lực lượng Đồng - Minh.

Nº 301289 E

An ARVN soldier "opens his arms" to an NLF soldier on one side of the leaflet.

ĐÂY TẤM GIẤY THÔNG HÀNH CÓ GIÁ TRỊ VỚI TẤT CẢ CƠ - QUAN QUÂN CHÍNH VIỆT-NAM CỘNG - HÒA VÀ LỰC - LƯỢNG ĐỒNG - MINH. SAFE-CONDUCT PASS TO BE HONORED BY ALL VIETNAMESE GOVERNMENT AGENCIES AND ALLIED FORCES

The other side assures safe passage to the pass holder.

Left. A leaflet dropped over Ben Suc and the Iron Triangle during Operation Cedar Falls invites the NLF soldier to turn himself in under the Chieu Hoi ("Open Arms") program. According to the U.S. Army, over seven hundred people did so during the operation. One "defector" told his experience to writer Jonathan Schell: "When the bombs started falling and the helicopter came, I ran into a bomb shelter under my house with my wife and children. Later, the government troops came to the mouth of the tunnel with a loud-speaker and told us to turn ourselves in or be shot. We were scared of being shot! We turned ourselves in and handed them American leaflets."

Below. A VC suspect who eventually died from wounds incurred during Operation Cedar Falls, which resulted in 720 enemy KIAs.

Right. ARVN soldiers excavate rice stored in underground tunnels in Ben Suc, January 1967. During Operation Cedar Falls allied forces uncovered huge caches of rice—food for the population of Ben Suc and the NLF soldiers headquartered in the area.

Below. The making of a free fire zone: U.S. soldiers of the 4th Cavalry, 1st Infantry Division, incinerate Iron Triangle jungle. The military's purpose in destroying Ben Suc and the surrounding jungle was to deprive the NLF of lodging and food in the area. "By making these paths in the jungle," explained one bulldozer operator, "we're going to be able to see them a lot more easily than before. From now on, anything that moves around here is automatically considered VC and bombed or fired on."

Orchards of mangoes, jackfruit, and grapefruit disappear as Ben Suc and its environs are stripped by bulldozers.

mark." Fish dove toward Ben Suc, taking fire from a bunker. His guns quickly silenced it. Fish then took a moment to admire the view: "You look out to see a whole bunch of choppers ... beautifully coordinated and planned." The landing was textbook perfect. "Our skids were almost in the water," recalled Major Donald Ice, "then we jumped a tree line, flared up, and popped into the landing zone." In less than ninety seconds, all the helicopters had touched down, deposited 420 soldiers, and headed back to Dau Tieng.

The people of Ben Suc were caught totally by surprise. Major Ice remembers having "to push Vietnamese out of the landing zone. They didn't know what was happening." The villagers remained strangely calm, almost in a state of shock, even as pandemonium erupted around them. Helicopters with public address systems circled above the village, and ARVN officers blared the same message: "Attention people of Ben Suc. You are surrounded. . . . Do not run away or you will be shot as VC. Stay in your homes and wait for further instructions." Most obeyed the warning. Those seeking to escape met a wall of fire in every direction. In addition to an artillery barrage, gunships fired rockets into the surrounding jungle, and jets screeched low over the village with loads of napalm. The messages broadcast by the loud-speakers could hardly be heard through the din. A distraught young woman later cried: "The loud-speakers came overhead, but how could I hear

A 1st Engineer Battalion bulldozer crushes a hut in Ben Suc.

Hastily erected canopies at Phu Loi shelter thousands of former inhabitants of Ben Suc. The Vietnamese army and government were given twenty hours notice of their assignment to provide for as many as ten thousand refugees.

Shelter for the Ben Suc villagers: Each family is assigned about ten square feet under the Phu Loi camp's red and white canopies.

them? The bombs were exploding everywhere. My father is deaf, so how could he hear the voices from the helicopter. . . . My father is very old. . . ."

Ben Suc had its own surprise for the Americans. Besides occasional sniper fire, resistance was much lighter than expected from a VC stronghold. Yet for the soldiers this offered not relief but frustration. For days they had anticipated combat with well-entrenched guerrillas, and the tons of captured food, medical supplies, and equipment seemed small return for the risk they had taken. It was eerie for the Americans to see the visible signs of an army whose soldiers, in spite of all efforts to envelop them, had disappeared like phantoms into the jungle.

The people of Ben Suc presented a quandary for Americans responsible for interrogating and evacuating them. The men, women, and children, though they wore no uniforms and carried no guns, were no less members of the local NLF infrastructure. Divided into four rear service companies, the villagers did everything from transporting rice and supplies to constructing village defenses. Even the children played a role by assisting their parents whenever possible. All this hindered efforts to isolate truly "hard-core" Vietcong among the villagers.

For the tense, battle-primed GIs ordered to seal off the village, the decision—VC or not VC—often had to be reached in a split second and was compounded by the language barrier. The consequences of any ambiguity sometimes proved fatal to Vietnamese villagers, as witnessed by writer Jonathan Schell. One unit of American soldiers crouching near a road leading out of Ben Suc was on the lookout for Vietcong. A Vietnamese man approached their position on a bicycle. He wore black pajamas, the peasant outfit adopted by the VC. As he rode twenty yards past the point where he first came into view,

The village of Ben Suc is no more.

a machine gun crackled some thirty yards in front of him. The man tumbled dead into a muddy ditch. One soldier grimly commented: "That's a VC for you. He's a VC all right. That's what they wear. He was leaving town. He had to have some reason." Major Charles Malloy later added: "What're you going to do when you spot a guy with black pajamas? Wait for him to get out his automatic weapon and start shooting? I'll tell you I'm not." The soldiers never found out whether the Vietnamese was Vietcong or not.

"Welcome to freedom and democracy"

At ten o'clock, two hours after the Americans had landed, it was already hot in Ben Suc. While interrogations went on in a schoolhouse, about a thousand people gathered in the center of the village clutching their bundles of possessions. Thousands more followed. By now shock had given way to resentment and hostility, expressed by the villagers' sullen stares. The evacuation and transporting of nearly six thousand villagers to the refugee camp at Phu Loi near Phu Cuong commenced immediately. This sign, near the camp entrance, greeted them: "Welcome to the reception center for refugees fleeing communism."

Conditions in Phu Loi were atrocious, frustrating the smooth relocation process sought by MACV. General Westmoreland observed that "for the first several days the families suffered unnecessary hardships." For a week the camp lacked latrines, wood and water for cooking, and tents for shelter. But even the construction of such facilities could not alleviate the pain of refugees separated from the family rice fields they had tilled for generations and the tombs of their ancestors. Despite the promise of new homes, the people of Ben Suc faced bleak days ahead as psychologically, as well as physically, "displaced persons." One refugee, an old man, lamented: "I was born in Ben Suc, and I have lived there for sixty years. My father was born there also, and so was his father. Now I will have to live here for the rest of my life."

While the refugees at Phu Loi pondered their future, the U.S. 1st Engineer Battalion of the 1st Infantry Division, commanded by Lieutenant Colonel Joseph Kiernan, entered Ben Suc with bulldozers, "tankdozers," and demolitions teams. Its mission was to destroy the "two" villages of Ben Suc, the structures above ground and the tunnel complex below. The engineers' powerful tankdozers, M48 medium tanks armored against mines, rolled over the villagers' homes and buildings.

Outside Ben Suc, massive Rome plows, called "jungle-eaters," gobbled up wide stretches of jungle. The Rome plow, a large tractor with a bulldozer blade, was specially developed for land-clearing operations. As Colonel Kiernan remembers, "I guess it was about twenty acres of scrub jungle. . . . The place was so infested with tunnels that as my dozers would knock over the stumps of

trees, the VC would pop out from behind the dozers. We captured about . . . six or eight VC one morning. We went through and methodically knocked down the houses. . . ." When it was all over, according to the army's account, "one of the major objectives of Operation Cedar Falls had been achieved: The village of Ben Suc no longer existed."

While Ben Suc was being flattened, the hammer forces of the 3d Brigade of the 1st Infantry Division swung into action with simultaneous attacks across the Iron Triangle and into the Thanh Dien Forest. Theirs was a tall order, entailing airmobile assaults into Thanh Dien, search and destroy operations, demolition of enemy installations, and evacuation of all civilians.

In Cedar Falls, it quickly became apparent that Vietcong Main Force units were evading the blow of the hammer. When sixty helicopters carrying troops of the "Big Red One" landed in an LZ that had been pounded by a preparatory air strike, one observer noted, "It's like a Cecil B. De Mille production." Not one VC was found at the LZ, dead or alive.

U.S. forces, however, chalked up impressive statistics in terms of enemy installations destroyed, food and supplies seized, and documents uncovered. During the nineteen-day span of Cedar Falls, U.S. and ARVN troops, operating throughout the Triangle, destroyed eleven hundred bunkers and five hundred tunnels. They captured enough rice to supply thirteen thousand VC for a year and a wide array of equipment and weapons. The credit for much of it belonged to members of the army 1st Infantry Division's 242d Chemical Detachment, nicknamed the "tunnel rats," volunteers accepted on the basis of their small stature, physical agility, and aggressiveness.

While Joe Kiernan's bulldozers and plows cleared over 8 percent of the sixty-three square miles of the Triangle, the tunnel rats explored the nearly twelve miles of tunnels exposed at various locations. Descending into the VC's dark, winding labyrinths was a hot, dirty, difficult job at best. The members of a six- to ten-man team had to squeeze their bodies through narrow openings and shallow corridors on all fours. The point man, armed with a pistol equipped with a silencer (to fire without one in a tunnel meant ruptured eardrums), a hand telephone, flashlight, and compass, never knew whether the tunnel might collapse or what might be waiting round the next turn in the way of mines, booby traps, bats, and scorpions—or even a Vietcong.

Exploring one major tunnel complex between the Ho Bo Woods and the Filhol Plantation in late January, the tunnel rats unearthed a valuable cache of documents belonging to VC intelligence. Said one American officer, Brigadier General Richard Knowles, "This is by far the most important one yet." The documents included detailed maps of the Saigon and Tan Son Nhut area, diagrams of U.S. billets in Saigon, and blueprints for future terrorist raids. The documents proved that the tunnel rats had found Military

Tunnel Rats

Left. An American ``tunnel rat'' squeezes out of a Vietcong tunnel after exploring its narrow, winding passages.

Right. PFC George Nagel of the 173d Airborne Brigade tries out a sewing machine found in a Vietcong tunnel complex.

Vietcong cadres seek protection from American troops and firepower in their elaborate tunnel and bunker system constructed below the jungle.

Region IV headquarters, one of Cedar Falls's principal objectives. One engineer said, "They've been working on this one a long time. It's going to kill them when we blow it all up."

When Cedar Falls ended on January 26, American commanders called it "an operation with a difference." Major General William DePuy, one of the principal architects of American strategy in Vietnam, declared it "a decisive turning point in the III Corps area; a tremendous boost to the morale of the Vietnamese government and army; and a blow from which the VC in this area may never recover." In addition to the number of VC killed, 775, the army's seizure of VC headquarters and the destruction of so many of their tunnels and fortifications dealt the enemy a substantial logistical setback.

The transformation of the Triangle into a "free-fire zone," in which artillery and air strikes could be made without prior approval of the GVN or warning to its inhabitants, did not deter the Vietcong from filtering back to reoccupy the jungle and rebuild their bases. Lieutenant General (later General) Bernard Rogers, army historian for Cedar Falls, has written: "It was not long before there was evidence of the enemy's return. Only two days after the termination of Cedar Falls, I was checking out the Iron Triangle by helicopter and saw many persons who appeared to be Vietcong riding bicycles or wandering around on foot." As for Ben Suc, the razing of the village amounted to a blatant admission that the GVN was not up to pacification even in an area so close to Saigon. In effect, all the government of South Vietnam acquired from Ben Suc was a devastated forest and a horde of hostile refugees. An American colonel summed up with regret: "To tell you the truth, I don't think we can afford any more Ben Sucs."

Search and destroy comes to the Mekong Delta

Lieutenant Commander Nguyen Thanh Chau of the South Vietnamese navy and his naval crew had been out in the Mekong Delta a hundred times, patrolling its maze of inland waterways ranging from manmade canals and irrigation ditches to flood-swollen rivers, creeks, and tidal bayous. The job of Chau and his 25th River Assault Group, a motley flotilla of junks, sampans, and old French patrol boats equipped with heavy armor, cannons, machine guns, and mortars, could have been cause for despair. Chau's assault group was part of a navy force of nine thousand officers and men and six hundred small vessels responsible for preventing some eighty-two thousand VC from using the Mekong's thirty-five hundred miles of waterway for transporting men and supplies and raids on rural outposts and villages.

Chau, born in the delta district, knew virtually every bridge, every bend in the waterways, every possible crossing point for VC guerrillas. His shrewd knowledge of the terrain and his tenacity in pursuing the Vietcong paid off in enemy casualties. In 1965, while losing only two boats, five killed, and eight wounded, Chau and his crew racked up hundreds of VC kills, thirty-three in one operation alone.

The effectiveness of Chau's assault group, however, was not typical of South Vietnamese naval operations in the Mekong Delta. Army dominance of the South Vietnamese General Staff left its sister service, the navy, a chronically poor relation. As a result, the Mekong's river assault force performed under a variety of handicaps: outdated vessels and inferior equipment, lack of funding, shoddy training, and a shortage of personnel. Mediocre leadership, internal corruption, and low status exacerbated the problem. Navy contingents, particularly in the high-risk environment of the delta, adopted a "stay-out-of-trouble" attitude toward the VC. Yet overly cautious and unproficient navy patrols were bushwhacked and mauled by well-trained and highly motivated VC guerrillas.

The GVN evinced concerns over increasing VC activity in the delta but had been resisting MACV's desire to engage U.S. forces there. With their wont for big sweeps and enormous firepower, large American units operating in the delta, Saigon feared, could result in heavy civilian casualties and economic damage. Five million people, a third of the country's population, crowded onto the delta's arable land to a density of more than three hundred per square mile. It was also South Vietnam's agricultural heartland and is one of the most fertile rice bowls in the world. But accepting the status quo in the delta could have amounted to political as well as economic suicide. The VC were taking a steadily larger "cut" of the delta's rich rice crop. After hitting a high of 4 million metric tons in 1963, the amount of rice reaching Saigon had declined in 1966 to 3 million, necessitating expensive importation from the United States. While the VC fed off Mekong rice, thousands in Saigon endured scarcity and higher prices.

Against deteriorating resistance, the VC consolidated and threatened to expand their hold on about one-third of the delta's population. In An Xuyen Province, government forces controlled less than 4 percent of the land. MACV also reported that 35 percent of all VC attacks on the GVN occurred in the delta's IV Corps tactical zone. To a worried American staff, it looked as if the VC, unless countered quickly, were going to wrest the delta from the GVN for good. By the end of 1966, the GVN's fear of losing the delta finally outweighed its reluctance. Americans were invited to the war in the delta.

The tactical and logistical limitations peculiar to the delta—a water-logged terrain of waterways interlacing paddies and swamps, few roads, and inadequate bridges—required a fresh approach to the use of American troops. Outside the delta, American ground forces had already experienced one innovation, search and de-

A crewman aboard a PBR Mark II loads (inset) and fires an M60 machine gun to return Vietcong ground fire. The craft came under attack in a narrow canal off the Bassac River while broadcasting "psychological operations" messages urging Vietcong soldiers to lay down their arms and come over to the South Vietnamese government.

stroy by helicopter. Now the combat units of the U.S. 9th Infantry Division, the first unit to be stationed permanently in the delta, were in for another—search and destroy by boat. MACV called this unusual marriage of army and navy the Mobile Riverine Force. While the navy operated the riverine vessels, the army was responsible for conducting onshore combat operations. Riverine warfare was not entirely new to the American military. The marines conducted riverine operations against the Seminole Indians in the Florida Everglades from 1837 to 1842, and the navy did the same along the Yangtze River in China from 1927 to 1932. The army and navy teamed up for riverine fighting along the Mississippi during the Civil War and again in the Philippines as recently as World War II. But the twenty-six-thousand-square-mile Mekong Delta was a monumental test for MACV's riverine concept.

The riverine force MACV deployed in early 1967 in-

corporated two chief components of General Westmoreland's search and destroy tactics: troop mobility and superior firepower. Two of the 9th Infantry Division's three brigades would be based at permanent shore facilities at Ben Cat, east of Saigon, and in the vicinity of My Tho, the capital of Dinh Tuong Province. The river base constructed near My Tho was itself a logistical triumph. Army engineers, under occasional enemy fire, excavated flooded rice fields as a basin for river craft, while hydraulic dredges sucked up sand from the river bottom to form six hundred forty acres of dry fill for the base site. Westmoreland personally selected the name for the base to symbolize American and South Vietnamese cooperation: *Dong Tam*, which is Vietnamese for "unite hearts and minds."

The 9th Division's 3d Brigade was housed offshore aboard U.S. Navy barracks ships and barges able to pull

Three Battlefields

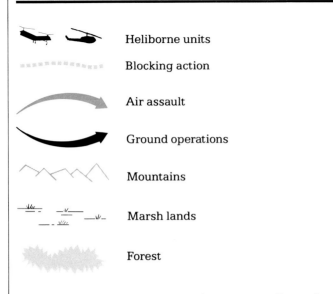

Heliborne units

Blocking action

Air assault

Ground operations

Mountains

Marsh lands

Forest

U.S. troop unit designations abbreviated in some cases. Except where noted all allied units in Operation Hastings are U.S. Marines under command of the 3d Marine Division; 2/4, for example, means 2d Battalion, 4th Marine Regiment. In Operation Coronado V, allied units are from U.S. Army and 3/60 means 3d Battalion, 60th Infantry. Units in Operation Cedar Falls are from U.S. Army.

Miles
0   100

Kilometers
0   100

Quang Tri
Hue

Da Nang

OPERATION
HASTINGS

THAILAND

LAOS

I CORPS

Quang Ngai

CAMBODIA

II CORPS

Qui Nhon

Nha Trang

War Zone C   War Zone D

Tay Ninh

III CORPS

Iron Triangle

Saigon

OPERATION
CEDAR FALLS

IV CORPS

OPERATION
CORONADO V

N
S

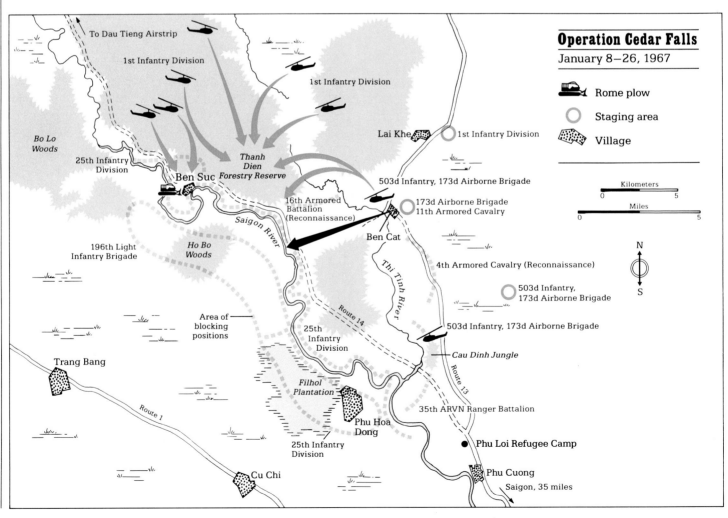

Operation Cedar Falls
January 8–26, 1967

Rome plow

Staging area

Village

Kilometers
0   5

Miles
0   5

N
S

To Dau Tieng Airstrip

1st Infantry Division

1st Infantry Division

Bo Lo Woods

Lai Khe   1st Infantry Division

25th Infantry Division

Ben Suc   Thanh Dien *Forestry Reserve*

503d Infantry, 173d Airborne Brigade

16th Armored Battalion (Reconnaissance)

173d Airborne Brigade
11th Armored Cavalry

Saigon River

Ben Cat

196th Light Infantry Brigade

Ho Bo Woods

4th Armored Cavalry (Reconnaissance)

Thi Tinh River

503d Infantry, 173d Airborne Brigade

Area of blocking positions

Route 14

25th Infantry Division

503d Infantry, 173d Airborne Brigade

Cau Dinh Jungle

Route 13

Trang Bang

Filhol Plantation

35th ARVN Ranger Battalion

Phu Hoa Dong

Route 1

25th Infantry Division

Phu Loi Refugee Camp

Cu Chi

Phu Cuong

Saigon, 35 miles

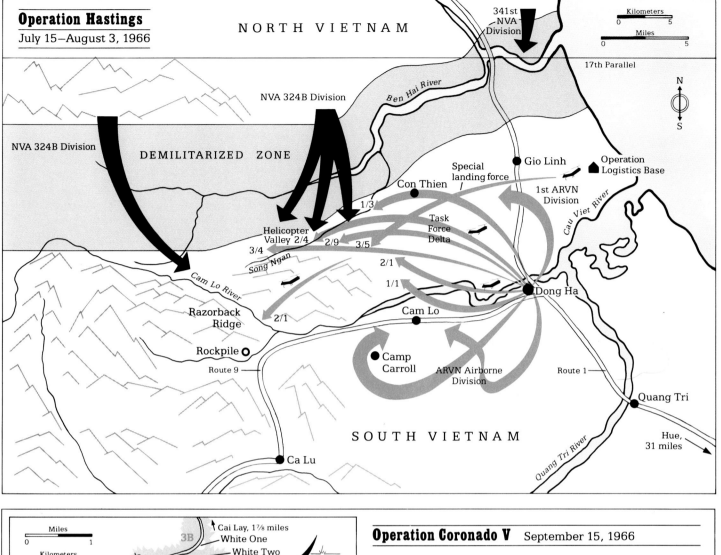

Operation Hastings
July 15–August 3, 1966

NORTH VIETNAM

341st NVA Division

17th Parallel

Kilometers
0   5

Miles
0   5

N

Ben Hai River

NVA 324B Division

DEMILITARIZED ZONE

NVA 324B Division

Gio Linh

Operation Logistics Base

Con Thien

Special landing force

1st ARVN Division

Cau Viet River

1/3

Task Force Delta

Helicopter Valley 2/4

3/4   2/9   3/5

Song Ngan

Cam Lo River

2/1

1/1

Dong Ha

Razorback Ridge

2/1

Cam Lo

Rockpile

Camp Carroll

ARVN Airborne Division

Route 9

Route 1

Quang Tri

SOUTH VIETNAM

Hue, 31 miles

Quang Tri River

Ca Lu

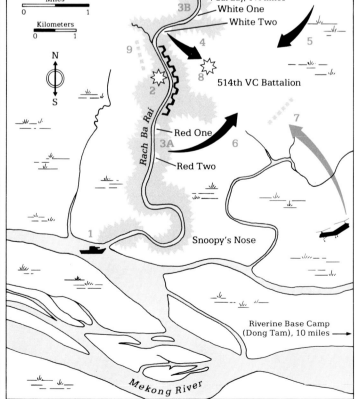

Miles
0   1

Kilometers
0   1

N

Cai Lay, 1⅞ miles

3B

White One

White Two

9

4

5

2

8

514th VC Battalion

Rach Ba Rai

Red One

3A

6

7

Red Two

Snoopy's Nose

1

Riverine Base Camp (Dong Tam), 10 miles

Mekong River

Operation Coronado V   September 15, 1966

〰〰   VC fortifications

☆   Major enemy contact

⛵   River assault squadron

〰   Beach

1. 3d Battalion, 60th Infantry starts up the Rach Ba Rai with the 11th River Assault Squadron.

2. 3/60 is ambushed by VC.

3A. The main section of the convoy is forced back to regroup at beaches Red One and Red Two.

3B. One boat forges on and reaches beach White One.

4. The remainder of 3/60 finally reaches White One and White Two on its second attempt.

5. 5/60 sweeps in from the north in an attempt to link up with 3/60.

6. 3/47 pushes north from beaches Red One and Red Two.

7. 2/60 is helilifted in and assumes a blocking position to the southeast.

8. 3/60 encounters heavy enemy resistance as it moves to link up with 5/60.

9. ARVN troops assume blocking positions on the western bank of the river.

Singing the Mekong Delta Blues

American soldiers called it "wading in oatmeal." Even during scorching days of the delta dry season, mud was everywhere. It fouled weapons, mired tanks, and crippled even amphibious tracked vehicles; it ruined leather and caused a near epidemic of "immersion foot," a sort of athlete's foot run wild. So serious was the health hazard from wading in the delta's swamps and rice fields that the men of the mobile riverine force could patrol "on land" no more than four to five days. Returning for a drying-out period aboard one of their floating barracks ships, the American riverine fighters enjoyed, by infantrymen's standards, special treatment in recognition of the special hazards they faced.

The headquarters of River Assault Flotilla One, the U.S.S. *Benewah*, was air conditioned, a luxury in South Vietnam's searing heat. Although the *Benewah* was a strange looking vessel, the more than one thousand army and navy personnel billeted there welcomed its amenities. In addition to air conditioning, there was fresh food, sometimes helilifted in, and a complete surgical suite able to handle many medical emergencies. Above all,

there was security: Peace and quiet could almost be taken for granted aboard the barracks ships. It was moored near the center of a river, and countermortar radar aboard ship provided coverage of the surrounding area, while army security forces reinforced by artillery patrolled the shore. Unlike life aboard the attacking craft, the monitors and amphibious armored troop carriers, there was little danger of a sudden barrage of fire for those recuperating back at "the base."

After several days of drying out and repairing equipment, troops assigned to riverine operations would be on the move again in the delta. Some brigades would conduct as many as four operations in a month, patrolling the rivers as well as engaging enemy troops hidden among the paddies and inland waterways. In their primary mission of providing security for commercial traffic and reducing VC access to population centers and the rice market, the riverine force encountered hazards that infantrymen near the DMZ were not likely to face. As Commander Sayre A. Swarztrauber recounts, while performing the routine, often unpleasant task of searching junks and sampans, a PBR crewman suddenly discovered "the latest in VC booby traps: opening a bilge compartment, he is met by a deadly—and very angry—tropical snake whose tail had been tacked to the keel board."

Enemy mines were an ever-present danger. Elaborate measures were taken to protect friendly commercial vessels and elements of the "brown water navy" against underwater explosions. Once more, the enemy's deceptiveness occasionally caused problems, as Swarztrauber recalls: "A river mine sweeper crewman, throwing a hand grenade at a suspicious C-ration box, is startled by a 150-foot geyser of cocoa-colored water; the box was a VC disguise for a floating mine."

When seeking out the enemy, away from the protection of their assault craft, members of the riverine forces encountered problems similar to those that afflicted American search and destroy missions elsewhere in the country. In addition to patrolling and interdiction, the mobile force employed a repertoire of offensive measures to encircle the VC and drive them against a blocking force, with the

Americans' flanks covered by helicopter gunships. But, as happened so often, when the enemy was not surprised and chose to withdraw, it took advantage of the concealment offered by dense foliage on the river banks, breaking into small groups and leaving the scene under cover of sniper teams.

The experience of the men of the army's 4th Battalion, 47th Infantry, 2d Brigade, on patrol in late June 1967 was a particularly dramatic example of the VC's ability to ambush an assault force disembarking to engage the enemy on his own ground. At midday, Captain Robert Reeves was leading his men from River Assault Force One across a stretch of water ten inches deep and bordered by mangroves. When they were about a hundred yards from the trees, in an open field, the VC cut loose. "During the initial contact," Reeves said, "I had approximately fifty men wounded. Some of them died almost instantly." "We had nowhere to go," added a private, "We just dove into the water."

Forced to keep their heads above water to breathe, and immobilized by heavy fire, the men were easy targets for VC snipers. River-based artillery and air support worked over the VC positions but could not stop the fire. Meanwhile the tide rolled in, placing the men neck deep in water and causing malfunctions in their M16 rifles. Four helicopters sent in to evacuate the wounded were shot down. Finally monitors accompanying the assault force were able to train their cannon and mortars on the forest and drive off the VC. "Their firepower saved us," Reeves recounted, "It was pretty bad." Although a force had been sent to try and locate the ambushers, none was found.

It was a harrowing case of enemy and environment combining to make life miserable for the riverine fighters. In the last analysis, it was not immersion foot, the dangers of mines, or even water snakes that most affected the Americans, but the VC's ability to set ambushes while evading the standard hammer and anvil movement. The delta was hotter, and wetter, than South Vietnam's other battlefields—the highlands, northern provinces, and central coast. But in this crucial respect—the elusiveness of the enemy—the delta war was still the Vietnam War.

Flame throwers of a Mobile Riverine Force monitor incinerate possible enemy ambush sites along a narrow stream in the Mekong Delta.

up anchor and move to other locations. To support riverine units aboard the floating base there was a squadron of repair, salvage, and supply ships. The tactical element of the mobile flotilla, the river assault squadron, included a variety of craft: troop carriers, command vessels, gunboats, and refuelers. The offensive flotilla was to be preceded by mine sweepers and escorted by armored boats, called monitors, which resembled the Civil War craft of the same name, and packed 81MM mortars, 20MM cannons, and M79 grenade launchers. Artillery barges, helicopters, and fixed-wing aircraft were available for fire support and air reconnaissance.

The riverine force proved its worth in the delta's intensifying guerrilla war. Previously inviolate VC bases in the Plain of Reeds, the Rung Sat Swamp, and the Ca Mau Peninsula, unapproachable by land, were now within striking distance of the riverine units. Hefty American river patrols also provided security for commercial traffic, reduced VC access to population centers and food-producing areas, and interrupted VC communications and supply routes. But even such a significant dent in VC activity did not break the guerrillas' grip on the countryside.

Cruising the delta

Operation Coronado V, launched September 15, 1967, demonstrated search and destroy "riverine style." Following reports that the Vietcong 514th Local Force Battalion was in the Cam Son area of Dinh Tuong Province, the riverine command devised a plan to trap the enemy and destroy its fortifications there. Colonel Bert David, in command of Coronado V, intended to crush the 514th between riverine forces—the 3d Battalion, 60th Infantry, with the 11th River Assault Squadron—landing on the Rach Ba Rai, a river in central Cam Son, and the 5th Battalion, 60th Infantry, moving overland from the northeast. So that the riverine force could reach the landing zones at beaches White One and Two without alerting the enemy, Colonel David ordered preparatory fire withheld until the riverine assault craft could pass a wide curve in the Rach Ba Rai known as Snoopy's Nose (see map, page 111).

On D-day, at 7:15 A.M., Lieutenant Colonel Mercer Doty's 3d Battalion, aboard the riverine flotilla, made its way swiftly up the Rach Ba Rai. Within minutes it was

Two Vietcong pose at their base camp in the Rung Sat Swamp, an enemy stronghold southeast of Saigon overrun by the Mobile Riverine Force during Operation Great Bend in June 1967.

past Snoopy's Nose, seemingly undetected. At 7:30, however, as the landing crafts approached White Two, the VC unleashed rocket, automatic-weapons, and small-arms fire from pointblank range on both sides of the river. With the heaviest fire coming from the east bank, the assault boats trained their cannons and machine guns in that direction. In the smoke and confusion, one boat, forging ahead of the mine sweepers, proceeded through a vicious crossfire to land at White Two.

Colonel Doty, observing from his command helicopter the mobility of the assault craft and the successful landing, wanted "full speed ahead." But just before 8:00, Doty's navy counterpart, Lieutenant Commander Francis "Dusty" Rhodes, aboard one of the support craft for Doty's unit, ordered all boats to turn back and reassemble down river at beaches Red One and Two. His order was prompted by

numerous casualties and damage to mine sweepers. Doty, the senior officer, eventually got word to Rhodes to reverse course and "send in the troops."

While the 5th Battalion swept overland toward White One from the northeast, Doty's battalion once more ventured upriver, again running a blazing gauntlet of VC recoilless rifles, grenades, and machine guns. This time, despite the volume of fire, the convoy reached White One and Two. Casualties ran high, Company A reporting eighteen wounded in one platoon. Once ashore, the 3d attacked in a southeasterly direction against tough enemy resistance, making contact with the 5th by early afternoon. To complete the encirclement of the VC 514th, another battalion pushed north from Red One and Two, while the 2d Battalion, 60th Infantry, was helilifted in to assume a blocking position on the southeast rim of the circle.

By nightfall Doty's battalion, unable to overcome VC resistance, dropped back to improve its defensive position. Riverine craft covered the enemy's escape route westward across the river, assisted by an ARVN battalion on the west bank. Although air and artillery illumination were maintained over likely enemy concentrations, it was a relatively uneventful night for the Americans camped in the mud of Cam Son. Except for a flurry of fire between 2:00 and 4:00 A.M., all was quiet by dawn and no more VC were sighted. The sweep continued throughout the day, meeting only token resistance. Many of the VC had slipped away during the night. Coronado V was over.

Coronado V was one of the sharpest actions yet for the riverine force, a relatively new factor in the Vietnam War. After two days of action, 213 Vietcong had been killed. The Americans and South Vietnamese suffered 16 killed and 146 wounded. The disturbing number of assault ship crewmen wounded by the Vietcong's B40 and B50 rockets emphasized the need for more protective armor. It was also an omen of things to come. In future operations, one of every three crewmen on the assault boats would be wounded at least once.

During its baptism by fire in 1967, the navy, like the marines in Operation Hastings and the army in Cedar Falls, was drawn into the battle against an elusive enemy, in this case, the Vietcong Main Force units and guerrillas fighting in the watery terrain of the Mekong Delta. The navy's joint participation with the army in the unique Mobile Riverine Force came to symbolize both the navy's substantial role in the war effort and the pressing need for the American military to adapt its resources and tactics to the diverse battlefields of South Vietnam.

The M16: Politics of a Rifle

In 1965 a new automatic weapon, the M16 rifle, was introduced and tested by the United States military in the jungles of Vietnam. At first only a few hundred rifles were issued to Special Forces and airborne units. But by 1967 the M16 was rapidly replacing the older and heavier M14 as the standard American military weapon.

A 1967 report in *Newsweek* praised the M16 as a major advance in small arms weaponry, "light enough," it said, "to lug through the thickest underbrush, fast enough to spray 700 rounds of .22-caliber bullets a minute, and powerful enough to tear off a foe's arm at 100 yards." Under combat conditions the M16, however, had a tendency to malfunction. On a disturbing number of occasions, it either jammed after firing several rounds or failed to extract spent cartridges.

Questions about the M16's reliability finally reached the attention of Congress and the American public in a dramatic way. In May 1967, after 160 American soldiers lost their lives and 746 were wounded in the battle for Hill 881 in Quang Tri Province, a marine who saw action there, irate over the performance of the M16, sent a bitter letter to Congress. "Believe it or not," he wrote, "do you know what killed most of us? Our own rifles. Practically every one of our dead was found with his rifle torn down next to him where he was trying to fix it."

Other letters poured into Congress from soldiers citing problems in combat experienced with the M16. One marine wrote,

the M16 rifle—it is a miserable piece—cheap and unreliable—we used it in every engagement since I returned from Okinawa. In every instance—Operation Bean-Diddle-Action at 881—Operation Hickory and now Operation Torch and Cimarron—the weapon has failed us at crucial moments when we need firepower most. Often ... as many as 50 percent of the rifles fail to work.

Another asserted:

Our M16s aren't worth much. If there's dust in them, they will jam. Half of us don't have cleaning rods to unjam them. Out of forty rounds I've fired, my rifle jammed about ten times. I pack as many grenades as I can plus bayonet and K bar (jungle knife) so I'll have something to fight with.

Charges like these elicited a chorus of denials from high-ranking military officials. General Lewis Walt, commander of the III Marine Amphibious Force, reacted with a press statement that included the results of a poll he had conducted with some two hundred soldiers in his division about the performance of the M16s. "At least 95 percent have been most favorable," he concluded, "the other 5 percent have complained about malfunction. Some of these have been due to improper cleaning of their weapons."

The army's experience with the rifle was also inconsistent. A commander of the 5th Battalion, 7th Cavalry, who served in Vietnam from August 1966 to January 1967 stated that

he did experience, in his unit, a couple of failures to extract the spent round. He said the weapon was more sensitive than the M1 and M14 .... Any malfunctions were normally caused by dirty ammunition or a bent magazine. This causes the gun to fail to extract the spent round or fail to feed the round into the chamber.

The M16 was, in fact, more delicate and required more careful cleaning and maintenance than previously used rifles.

The investigation

To investigate the charges in the aftermath of Hill 881 that the M16 was unfit for combat in Vietnam, a House of Representatives armed services subcommittee, chaired by Richard Ichord, Democrat from Missouri, interviewed thirty-five to forty soldiers at Fort Benning and conducted hearings on the history and manufacturing of the M16 rifle. They also visited Vietnam to check on the rifle's performance.

In the course of the subcommittee's investigation, problems in the design and procurement of the rifle came to light. The M16 rifle, originally designed as the AR15 Armalite by Eugene Stoner in 1957, was lighter (less than seven pounds loaded while the M14 weighed about eleven pounds) and packed a smaller bullet (.22 caliber, or 5.56mm) that could do more damage than the .30 caliber of the M14. In 1963, however, the army was skeptical of the rifle's suitability. Despite the favorable responses from military bases where the AR15 had been tested, the Army Materiel Command and the Ordnance Corps ran their own tests that year to compare the M16 to the older M14 and the Soviet AK47. Both the Materiel Command and Ordnance Corps concluded that "only the M14 is acceptable for general use in the U.S. Army. ... [The M16] is less reliable."

The Ichord committee heard testimony that these tests had, in part, been "rigged" because of the ordnance's desire to discredit the AR15 (M16). Moreover, the army had then used these 1963 "tests" to make modifications on the rifle without consulting Stoner, the original designer. A "twist" was put in the barrel, making the bullet spin faster, thus reducing its destructive power. A manual bolt closure device was added, in keeping with the tradition of previous rifles, the M1 and the M14. The Ordnance Corps changed the original design to conform to the "military standards" of the army. As Colonel Howard Yount, project manager at the Rock Island arsenal in 1968, said to the Congressional committee, the changes were made not because of tests or complaints but "on the basis of direction" from his superiors on the army staff.

In early 1964 the Colt Company, manufacturer of the now renamed M16 rifle, first tested its new weapon. For these tests they used IMR (improved military ribe) powder ammunition, which had been used for the original AR15. The military, on the other hand, had since decided to procure a ball propellant type of ammunition for the M16. The Ichord investigation found that, although the ball propellant increased the rate of fire from 700 to 1,000 rounds a minute, it left carbon deposits on the inside rifle chamber and increased the possibility of malfunctions. Colt used the finer IMR powder and did not encounter these problems in its tests.

As the build-up of American troops in Vietnam continued, the American military had sought a lightweight, small-caliber weapon that would enable the soldier to carry more ammunition. Westmoreland wanted it; so did the soldiers who had seen action using earlier models of the

original AR15. Based on the Colt Company and Army Ordnance Corps assessments, the army's Infantry Board procured the M16.

A battle against dirt

To most of the soldiers, who had trained with the M14, the M16 rifle was unfamiliar. The rifle was assigned to the troops as they arrived in Vietnam, and they had only a few days to become acquainted with it before entering combat. One army field manual informed the soldier that the M16 "requires the least maintenance of any type weapon within the army arsenal today." In the experience of many soldiers, however, this was not the case. The M16 rifle, less rugged than the M14, needed meticulous attention. As a result, soldiers constantly battled rust and dirt on their rifles. In addition, as General Westmoreland himself admitted in 1970, sweat could erode certain of the M16's aluminum parts.

Many military officers ascribed M16 malfunctions to the lack of proper rifle care. A captain with the 25th Infantry Division, for example, considered the M16 a solid weapon. The M16, he conceded, was "slightly more delicate. The problems of malfunctions," he concluded, "are caused by failure to keep the rifle clean." Poor planning on the part of the military had increased the difficulty of maintaining the precise standard of cleaning that the rifle required. For example, during 1967 platoons were frequently short of the necessary cleaning supplies and instruction manuals. Sometimes as many as ten soldiers had to make do with one cleaning rod or resort to using their toothbrushes to clean their weapons. (It was not until 1970 that a special brush, which closely resembled a toothbrush with bristles at either end, was designed for the M16.)

The Ichord committee, in its summary

report in the summer of 1967, concluded that "the greatest single malfunction was the failure to extract [spent cartridges]. This is caused by any number of things: 1, a dirty round; 2, the cartridge expands from being left in the chamber; or 3, the extractor doesn't get enough of the cartridge." On August 27, 1967, after the investigation had ended, Ichord conceded that there were more problems with the M16 rifle because of the use of faulty ammunition. Two days later, the Pentagon admitted that switching to the new firing powder, the ball propellant, for the weapon in January 1964 had "caused an increase in malfunctions."

Today, despite the earlier controversy, the M16 rifle is still the standard rifle in all U.S. military services. Because of the findings of the Ichord committee in 1967–68, the design was changed so that by 1968 soldiers equipped with modified M16s were reporting a marked decrease in malfunctions.

A fundamental question not addressed by the Congressional committee was the rifle's overall effectiveness for use in South Vietnam, given the combat conditions it would face there. Was the M16, which needed close attention and care, really suitable for I Corps, where fine, red clay blown into dust frequently clogged the marines' rifles? Or the rainy season that turned the Mekong Delta to mud? These questions, however, were never raised during the several years in the early 1960s that army bureaus haggled over the development of the M16. Through the slow, tangled process of military bureaucracy the pieces were not tied together. The tests, the modifications of the M16, the procurement of proper ammunition, even the development of cleaning instructions and sufficient training for soldiers had evolved separately, without sufficient attention to how the M16 would actually perform in a tropical climate like that of South Vietnam.

Small Arms

For all the big bombs, large guns, and deadly aircraft that made up American firepower in Vietnam, the weapons that meant the most to soldiers on the ground were their constant companions—rifles, pistols, machine guns, hand grenades, grenade launchers, and mines.

The principal weapon issued to an American infantryman was his rifle. In Vietnam, beginning in 1965, the newly developed M16 rifle was introduced to replace the older M14 automatic rifle, which had been adopted by the U.S. Army in 1957. The M16, part plastic, was an automatic weapon able to fire up to 700 rounds of .22–caliber bullets per minute. Its light weight compared to the M14's (8.4 pounds to 11.25 pounds, loaded) made it easier to handle. It also enabled an infantry soldier, without increasing his total load, to carry more than twice as much ammunition as a soldier equipped with the M14, thus significantly

increasing the firepower or "kill potential" of a rifle squad in combat.

The .45–caliber M1911 automatic pistol was and is still the standard infantry sidearm. It was issued only to company commanders, machine gunners, and grenadiers. Occasionally some officers and even enlisted men "unofficially" carried commercially manufactured "maverick" pistols. The most popular of these was the .357 magnum revolver, which, according to one American officer, "looked like a cowboy pistol and had a lot of guts," and the 9MM parabellum automatic that held thirteen shots to the seven in the M1911.

In addition to the rapid firing M16 automatic rifle, the M60 7.62 light machine gun was standard issue to infantry platoons. Gas operated and air cooled, the M60 was normally used with 100–round belts of ammunition. Standing on a tripod, its maximum effective range is nearly a mile and its cyclic rate of fire 550 rounds per minute.

Also part of the infantry's basic arsenal was the M26 fragmentation grenade, which the average soldier could throw up to forty yards. Others included smoke grenades to mark landing zones for helicopters and tear gas grenades to clear enemy bunkers and tunnels. The most lethal grenade available to the infantry was the M8, or White Phosphorous gre-

nade, an antipersonnel weapon. When exploding it emitted particles of white phosphorous that burned through the skin and deep into the bodies of its victims. Since it was effective over a wider area than other grenades, the M8 could inflict substantially heavier casualties. But it was also dangerous to handle, so soldiers tended to carry it infrequently.

Not all grenades were hand thrown. Infantrymen also fired grenades with a weapon unique to the American army: the 40MM M79 grenade launcher. The M79 was designed to give an infantryman the capability to deliver accurate fire to more distant targets (over 300 yards) than with the older conventional rifle grenade. A single shot weapon fired from the shoulder of a grenadier, the M79 could fire five rounds per minute. A variety of ammunition could be used with the grenade launcher, including grenades loaded with high explosives or CS gas, a kind of tear gas.

One of the most common explosive devices carried by the infantry was the claymore directional mine. It was so named because the swath its projectile cut recalled the destructive sweep of the Scottish broadsword called the claymore. Infantry units often set claymore mines around their defensive positions at night or at ambush sites. The mines were deto-

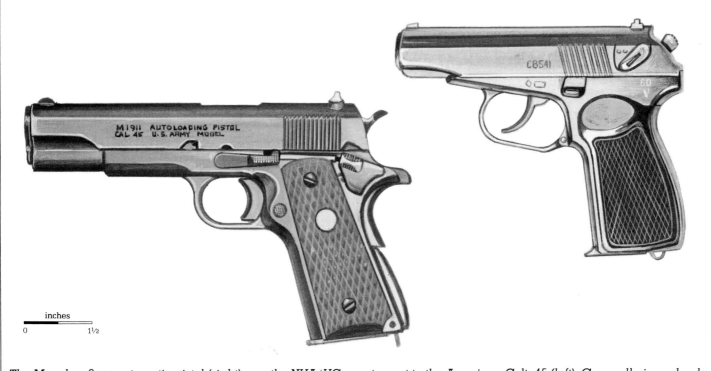

inches
0   1½

The Marakov 9MM automatic pistol (right) was the NVA/VC counterpart to the American Colt .45 (left). Generally issued only to high–ranking enemy officers, the Marakov was a rare and highly prized combat trophy.

nated electronically. If not fired they could be recovered and used again.

A remarkable feature of American infantry weapons was their uniformity among combat units. There was virtually no variation in the weapons carried by an infantry patrol of the 1st Infantry Division, the 1st Air Cavalry Division, or the 199th Light Infantry Brigade. That American infantrymen from Quang Tri to Can Tho were similarly equipped attests to the efficiency of the U.S. logistics system.

NVA and VC small arms

The North Vietnamese and Vietcong logistics system was not nearly as effective. Although NVA and VC soldiers fought with a variety of weapons—rifles, pistols, machine guns, grenades, mines, and antitank rockets—there was much less uniformity in the weapons' source and type. The primary sources of NVA weapons were the Soviet Union and China. As long as the North had a steady supply of Russian and Chinese weapons, their infantry soldiers were able to maintain a modest degree of uniformity in the type and quality of their firepower. The VC, however, had to rely on three different sources: old French weapons, captured South Vietnamese weapons (mostly World War II-vintage American equipment), and those of Russian and Chinese manufacture smuggled down from the North.

The standard NVA rifle, replacing the SKS semiautomatic clip-fed rifle, was a 7.62MM-caliber automatic rifle usually equipped with a folding bayonet. This legendary weapon—the Russian AK47 assault rifle, simple, rugged, and reliable—was well suited for use by NVA combat infantry units. Fully automatic, the AK47 has less accuracy and a shorter range than its American counterpart, the M16. But it was prized by the NVA since it was durable, simple to handle, and easy to field strip. Unlike the M16, the AK47 was easy to clean even under the harshest battle conditions. Its tumbling bullet was devastating, capable of mangling a leg or arm or tearing up internal organs.

Some Main Force VC units were equipped with AK47s but, in general, VC guerrillas carried whatever weapons they could procure or capture. The VC even organized weapons factories to produce copies of older Communist-bloc weapons. But the VC's so-called "zip gun guerrilla force" gradually obtained more standard Russian- and Chinese-made rifles as the war progressed.

Like the Americans, NVA and VC infantry units also carried light machine guns. Theirs were of several types, but the most common was the Degtrayev (RPD) 7.62MM, which replaced the DP light machine gun. The biggest boost to their firepower, however, was provided by two Russian-made weapons, the RPG-2 and RPG-7 antitank rocket launchers. The RPG-2 fired a rocket with an 82MM diameter warhead to an accurate range of 492 feet. The RPG-7, which had greater range, accurate to about 1,500 feet, earned great respect from American soldiers. Its warhead was powerful enough to blow a five-to-ten-inch hole in the aluminum armor of U.S. armored personnel carriers.

The NVA and VC employed a variety of hand grenades. Among the VC, homemade types that used explosive fillings scooped from "dud" U.S. ordnance were common. These included cast-iron "stick grenades" and cast-iron grenades similar to the U.S. MK2 "pineapple." Also available were Russian and Chinese antitank hand grenades (the RPG-43, RPG-6, and PKG-3), as well as RG-Y2 and RGD-5 fragmentation grenades. NVA and VC infantry troops generally did not carry other explosive devices, such as mines and booby traps. But the soldiers often improvised, as they did with grenades, expertly fashioning several kinds of mines from unexploded mortar and artillery shells, bombs, M26 hand grenades, and even from U.S. claymores.

inches
0   4

The opposing rifles. Life or death, victory or defeat often hinged on the basic component of the soldier's arsenal. For U.S. and South Vietnamese forces, it was the M16 (below); for the other side it was the AK47 (above).

A soldier stands guard with his M60. Introduced in 1960, the M60 replaced the heavier, classic World War II Browning automatic rifle as the standard infantry-squad machine gun. While it often overheated, the M60's light weight (23.1 pounds) allowed it to be fired from the hip.

A Vietcong Youth Volunteer poses with his Chinese-made copy of the RPD light machine gun (Roschnoi Pulemet Degrayeva: "Degtrayev light machine gun"). It had a range of 900 yards and was capable of firing 700 rounds per minute, although if it were fired faster than 150 rpms for more than two or three minutes the gun would burn up.

Crying out a warning to his buddies, a marine fires his M79 grenade launcher at a hill near Khe Sanh in 1968. Because of the excellent balance of the M79, most grenadiers in Vietnam could hit a foxhole up to 200 yards away without using the sight.

Workers at this open-air Vietcong grenade factory produce a pile of stick grenades using hollow wooden cylinders, string cast-iron fragmentation sleeves, and friction fuses.

The International Front

June 29, 1966, was a typical workday in Haiphong, North Vietnam's second largest city. Factories, docks, and storage facilities teemed with the usual activity of the country's biggest and busiest port. Certainly no one that day expected to see and hear the squadron of American A-4 Skyhawk bombers streaking across the sky toward Haiphong's vital oil tanks and pipelines only two miles north of the city. In just eight minutes the bombers had gone, leaving much of North Vietnam's precious oil supplies consumed by fire. Smoke rose five miles high, visible one hundred fifty miles offshore. Commander Charles Smith, a reconnaissance pilot who photographed the destruction of 75 percent of Haiphong's fuel capacity, reported: "It looked as if we had wiped out the world's entire supply of oil."

The first bombing of North Vietnam's hitherto sacrosanct industrial-petroleum complexes in the Haiphong and Hanoi areas introduced a new phase of the war. In Washington President John-

son exulted at the mission's success, relieved that months of painstaking planning had come off without a hitch. The bombing was carried out, said a White House aide, "because the president felt Hanoi was making a serious miscalculation that might prolong the war" by "interpreting dissension in this country as weakening the president's position.... Now he has told them, emphatically, that there will be no change in U.S. policy for the next two-and-a-half years." Johnson was convinced that he had the broad support of the American people for his bombing policy and that it would continue through the "next two-and-a-half years." Long-term support from America's allies, however, appeared much less likely.

While smoke still blackened the sky above Haiphong, Washington was jolted by protests from the United States' European allies. French President Charles de Gaulle expressed "alarm" over the bombing raid, calling it a reckless escalation of the Vietnam conflict. In London, British Prime Minister Harold Wilson felt compelled to "disassociate ourselves from the bombings." West Germany's pointed silence following an event the United States deemed so sensitive and significant added to President Johnson's discomfiture. From all Europe the message was identical: Washington's conduct of the war, dramatized by the unprecedented June 29 bombing of Haiphong, was alarming some of its most important allies.

The harsh tenor of allied criticism was a bitter disappointment to President Johnson. From the outset he and his advisers tended to view diplomatic and political backing by the allies for America's Vietnam policy as a sort of extension of the administration's domestic consensus. They soon learned, however, that it would not be easy to build, much less preserve, even a semblance of unity abroad.

The administration's first attempt at an allied consensus came in the spring of 1964 when President Johnson launched an international appeal known as "more flags in Vietnam." For a time the goal of more flags was confined to technical and economic aid. U.S. ambassadors traveled throughout Europe, Asia, and Latin America to persuade host countries to pitch in and help South Vietnam with development funds, medical and engineering advisers, and food. Many promises but very few weighty commitments resulted. Nevertheless, Washington periodically published a list of contributions: a shipload of coffee from Latin America, an x-ray unit from Europe, and sundry other such items.

As the war escalated, so did Johnson's calls for allied

assistance. In 1965 he began pulling every lever at his command—the SEATO treaty, diplomatic pressure, personal entreaties, and the disposition of U.S. foreign aid—to broaden the allies' involvement in South Vietnam. More flags had come to mean troops, not just economic and technical assistance. With nearly twenty years of allied "containment policy" against communism on the line in South Vietnam, the president was understandably eager to avoid going it alone. The resistance he encountered among the allies emphasized the extent to which South Vietnam since 1954 had become almost solely an American burden.

De Gaulle: "I told you so."

Charles de Gaulle's caustic response to the June 29 air strike did not come as much of a surprise to the Johnson administration. Since U.S. Marines had landed at Da Nang in 1965 the haughty French president had been lashing out at Washington's "misguided" escalation of the war. American diplomats, miffed at de Gaulle's strident criticism, attributed his hostility to a French national ego still bruised by defeat in the French Indochina War. But in ascribing de Gaulle's verbal assaults simply to "sour grapes," Washington glossed over long-lasting French-American disputes over Vietnam dating back to 1954.

De Gaulle was never averse to reciting the litany of French complaints against American "meddling" in Vietnam: The refusal of Ngo Dinh Diem, with U.S. encouragement, to hold reunification elections, thus prolonging the division of North and South; Diem's anti-French crusade that precipitated France's decline in South Vietnam and the ascendance of the Americans; and most offensive in French eyes, America's bankrolling of Diem's corrupt government, which drove North Vietnam to seek closer ties to Communist China and the Soviet Union and encouraged the insurgency in the South (where the French themselves after 1954 paid funds to a stable of French agents, many of them officials of the Saigon government).

As the Vietnam War intensified in 1966, America and France had a complete parting of the ways over Vietnam. The final rift occurred when French Foreign Minister Couve de Murville aired de Gaulle's rejection of the very bottom line of U.S. policy: that Communist aggression, instigated and directed by Hanoi, was responsible for the turmoil in South Vietnam. First and foremost, said de Murville, "what is happening in South Vietnam is a civil war." From the French perspective, "communism" and "democracy" were no more than slogans in a predominantly nationalist uprising against an oppressive military junta and foreign occupation. In effect, the French were joining the Communists in branding the United States a "neocolonial aggressor" in Southeast Asia. Besides denouncing U.S. objectives in South Vietnam, de Gaulle, drawing on France's own Vietnam experience, was also not reticent

Smoke billows to thirty-five thousand feet over a POL site three and a half miles from Hanoi, which was struck by American F-105s on June 29, 1966. The same day, POL sites outside Haiphong were also destroyed.

about forecasting doom for Americans fighting a war he believed was futile. His prediction was often repeated by the French ambassador to the United States, Jean de Chauvel: "They [the Americans] cannot win this war. No matter how far they push it in the future, they will lose it."

Lyndon Johnson did not take de Gaulle's scathing criticism lightly. He interpreted the French president's persistent harping on Vietnam as but one aspect of his campaign to restore France's leadership in Europe and influence in Southeast Asia at the expense of the United States. De Gaulle had already rocked the European alliance with France's unilateral withdrawal from NATO. Johnson and his top advisers fretted that de Gaulle's NATO decision, coming as it did on the heels of his formal recognition of the People's Republic of China, would undermine the western allies' carefully constructed containment barriers against Communist expansion both in Europe and Asia.

The antagonism between the Johnson and de Gaulle administrations became so intense that French recommendations on Vietnam, whatever their merit, were likely to be ignored just because they were French. Thus when Undersecretary of State George Ball, an intrepid critic of de Gaulle, suggested that the administration consider undertaking peace negotiations along lines proposed by de Gaulle, he specifically recommended that the French be left out of the process. Ball told the president: "Certainly de Gaulle's policy will be to try to bring about maximum, rather than minimum, cost to United States prestige." Johnson, in despair of ever bringing de Gaulle around, could only hope that, for a once-close ally's sake, he would at least be silent on Vietnam. De Gaulle would not oblige.

The doubts of old friends

If President Johnson might have expected de Gaulle's negative reaction to the bombing raid on Haiphong, he was not prepared for the negative responses of Britain and West Germany. With no chance of swaying the intractable de Gaulle, the president had been lobbying vigorously to bring Britain and West Germany, America's two most powerful NATO partners, into the fold. For a while, President Johnson got something of what he wanted.

Until the bombing raid, official statements from London were generally supportive of American aims in Vietnam. But this was more because of Britain's interest in strengthening Anglo-American bonds than any strategic importance it accorded to South Vietnam. In fact, prior to U.S. military intervention there, British Prime Minister Wilson had characterized the Vietcong insurgency as a "spontaneous national uprising." Yet soon after American moves in 1964 to bolster the sagging British pound, observers detected a shift in Wilson's Vietnam position. President

Johnson's additional promise of cordial cooperation on issues important to Wilson's government—the doomed proposal for an allied Multilateral Nuclear Force, revision of NATO strategy, and coordination of Indian Ocean defense—also served to attract official British support for American objectives in Southeast Asia.

Thus, in June 1965 British Foreign Secretary Michael Stewart announced that Wilson's Labour government shared U.S. determination to save South Vietnam from falling victim to aggression. "An abandonment," he said, "would be a plain indication that Communist aggression had succeeded and it would be profoundly unwelcome to every non-Communist country in Asia." Moral support and agreement in principle were one thing, but money and troops were another. In anticipation of Wilson's 1965 Washington visit, President Johnson told two British correspondents that he wanted more flags in Vietnam to avoid any suggestion that the U.S. was waging a "colonial war." He declared that there should be a contingent of three to four hundred Britons in Vietnam and a British aircraft squadron or two. He even informed Wilson a few days later that he would settle for a "company of bagpipers."

Wilson's answer was a polite but emphatic "no." In fact, Wilson would have found it difficult to say otherwise. As cochairman with the Russians in overseeing the Geneva Agreements of 1954 and 1962, Britain considered itself obliged to maintain at least technical neutrality even though it might support American policy within the bounds of its role as cochairman.

Despite his increasing dissatisfaction with the U.S. involvement in Vietnam, Wilson had no desire to cause a rupture with the Johnson administration by embarrassing or humiliating the United States. He was always careful to soften his criticism by echoing Washington's assertion that "the opportunity for bringing all the fighting in Vietnam to an end is open to Hanoi, and the onus for continuing it rests there also." More than anything, the British government feared that it was America's obsession with Vietnam, not allied criticism, that posed the most serious threat to its international prestige and leadership. While watching the United States mire itself ever deeper in Vietnam in the name of upholding the credibility of its worldwide defense commitments, the British worried that the Johnson administration was being distracted from more important commitments elsewhere, particularly in Europe.

As antiwar sentiment grew in Britain, Wilson found himself in a severe bind. Because of his official support for the U.S. in Vietnam, he saw his own foreign policy consensus begin slowly to unravel. One member of Parliament from his Labour party warned that "the government must realize they have been wrong all along to support the self-defeating policy of the United States, particularly in view of [Britain's] cochairmanship of the Geneva Conference." Yet for Wilson to speak out completely candidly on Vietnam, even to try to save the United States from its

According to North Vietnamese sources, this nine-year-old girl died from wounds received during the June 29 bombing. Concern over bombing raids so close to densely populated areas stirred international criticism of American war policy.

"folly," ran the risk of driving a permanent wedge between London and Washington. Since President Johnson, short of support for the war, did not want candor, Wilson was backed into a corner, whipsawed between Washington's insistence on unity and a parliamentary revolt by his own party. To a harassed and ultimately embittered prime minister Vietnam would prove to be, as for President Lyndon Johnson, a political albatross.

West Germany, unlike France and Britain, had no history of colonial or military involvement in Vietnam or Southeast Asia. Nor had it ever developed significant economic or political connections there. For Germans in the 1960s Vietnam was still as remote a land as it had once been to Americans. Yet the West German government not only exhibited a rare official enthusiasm for an allied consensus on Vietnam but backed it up with generous contributions to the American aid program. In 1966, Karl-Günther Von Hase, a government spokesman, announced a grant of $40 million in West German aid for

South Vietnam, emphasizing "our political and moral support for United States policy in Vietnam."

There was a schizophrenic quality, however, to the opinions of West German leaders on Vietnam. While publicly applauding Washington's effort to stave off a Communist victory, West Germany's political leaders were privately haunted by the specter of an America so debilitated by its snowballing commitment to South Vietnam that it would become impotent to fulfill its European defense obligations. When U.S. Deputy Secretary of Defense Cyrus Vance, during a visit to West Germany in July 1966, made a plea to the U.S. 7th Army stationed there for volunteers for Vietnam, the West German government was alarmed. Reassignment of 7th Army troops to Vietnam suggested to anxious German officials the eventual depletion of U.S. troops and resources in Europe to satisfy the spiraling demands of the war. Budding controversy in the U.S. Congress over Vietnam's drain on America's defense capabilities in Europe only magnified this apprehension.

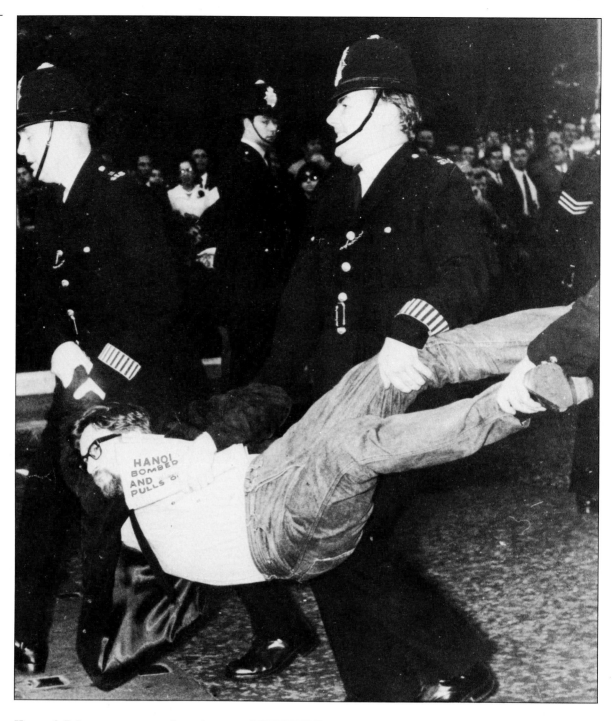

Outside the American Embassy in Grosvenor Square, London, a demonstrator is carried off from a rally protesting the June 29 U.S. bombing of North Vietnam.

Former Chancellor Konrad Adenauer summed up, for a beleaguered Johnson administration, the fears of Germans living in the psychological shadow of "the Wall": "If you ignore us there is a chance Russia will succeed in gaining control over both Germany and France. Then we shall all be lost."

West German Chancellors Ludwig Erhard and Kurt Kiesinger kept an official lid on simmering discontent over the "perils" of America's Vietnam policy. Although West Germany's silence after the June 29 air strike reflected tacit disapproval, the West German government as far as Vietnam was concerned generally adopted, like British Prime Minister Wilson, the old expedient of getting along by seeming to go along.

One Asian to another

To rally the moral support and troops his European allies held back, President Johnson campaigned hard among America's Asian and Pacific friends. The members of the U.S.-sponsored Southeast Asia Treaty Organization at first seemed logical allies for Washington's more flags effort in South Vietnam. SEATO called for a joint response by all members in the event that any country covered by the treaty, including South Vietnam, was "affected or threatened by any fact or situation which might endanger the peace. . . ." The lack of support, however, from France and Britain, two of SEATO's principal members, severely weakened the organization's collective military capability. Other member nations—Pakistan, Thailand, the Philippines, Australia, and New Zealand—were either lukewarm to a call for more flags or too strapped for economic and military resources to make much of a difference.

Thailand, the Philippines, Australia, and New Zealand did agree to make a modest number of troops available for deployment in South Vietnam. The Thais had been closely monitoring the war in South Vietnam, aware that the violence there could spill over into their own country by way of Cambodia. In 1964 Thailand decided to dispatch a sixteen-man Royal Thai Air Force contingent to South Vietnam. But President Johnson was not satisfied with the gesture and wrote to Thai Prime Minister Thanom Kittikachorn with the request that Thailand "find ways of increasing the scale and scope of its assistance to Vietnam." For the Johnson administration the presence of Thai troops in South Vietnam had both political and military import. Washington concluded that Americans would not continue to tolerate U.S. troop increases unless another Southeast Asian nation accepted a larger role in South Vietnam's defense. Secretary of Defense Robert McNamara said as much when he stated that a beefed-up Thai troop contribution was "mandatory" to persuade the American public that more flags was not a political charade. Militarily, a rise in Thai and other foreign contingents in South Vietnam could also help partially to offset General Westmoreland's mushrooming requests for additional U.S. forces.

On December 30, 1966, four Bangkok newspapers carried front-page stories that the Thai government was contemplating sending a seven- to eight-hundred-man combat battalion to South Vietnam. The public response was overwhelming, especially in light of the traditional enmity between Thais and Vietnamese. More than five thousand men volunteered, including thirty Buddhist monks and the prime minister's son. Despite this show of patriotic fervor, the Thai government was unwilling to fund, supply, or equip the battalion or any of the other eleven thousand volunteers it eventually put "on loan" to South Vietnam. For the United States, the principal and interest on that loan were high: approximately $50 million annually to train, equip, base, and supply the Thai units.

Washington's experience with the Thais was repeated when it tried to coax the Philippine flag to South Vietnam. The Philippines offered a fifteen-hundred-man engineering unit. Philippines' President Ferdinand Marcos's motives had as much to do with financial gain for his country as with concern for South Vietnam's welfare. The Philippine force cost the United States $39 million between 1967 and 1969, about $26,000 per man deployed in South Vietnam. There was more. In return for Philippine support, the U.S. military assistance program granted Marcos several types of military aid, some of it for use in the Philippines. Included were four river patrol craft, M14 rifles and machine guns, and equipment for three engineer battalions. This and other "Vietnam-related aid" would soon approximate 10 percent of the Philippines' foreign exchange in-

A British cartoon depicts Prime Minister Harold Wilson as a lackey to LBJ and his Vietnam policy.

129

Australian soldiers prepare to set out on patrol in Vietnam. The Australian commitment was one of President Johnson's few successes in his effort to internationalize the American cause in Vietnam.

come. Marcos had struck his "bargain" with the United States despite some criticism by the Philippine public and press over "trading soldiers for the hope of dollars." But the protests were to no avail. The United States had added one more flag in South Vietnam.

Australia, New Zealand, and South Korea send troops

The other SEATO members who sent their flags to South Vietnam were Australia and New Zealand. Actually, since 1962, before Washington's more flags appeal, Australia had been furnishing military assistance to South Vietnam in the form of thirty jungle warfare specialists to advise ARVN. During the international uproar following the Tonkin Gulf incident and Washington's military escalation in

response to it, Australia's military detachment in South Vietnam jumped to thirteen hundred men with the addition of a combat battalion stationed at Bien Hoa. In the spring of 1966, renewed overtures from Washington spurred the Australian government to reinforce the one battalion with another. Accompanying it were a headquarters staff, a special air-service squadron, and artillery, engineer, and supply units, raising the total Australian strength to forty-five hundred men. Squadrons of Iroquois helicopters, RAAF Hercules air transports, and further troop increments swelled the Australian military presence in South Vietnam to its peak in October 1967 of over eight thousand troops. New Zealand's total contribution amounted to approximately one thousand combat and artillery support troops. Both Australia and New Zealand bore the costs themselves. The Australian government even introduced conscription to fulfill its commitment.

Why did Australia and New Zealand, countries separated from Southeast Asia by over two thousand miles of ocean, answer America's call? For the same reason the Johnson administration gave for sending Americans to fight a war twelve thousand miles from home: to avert the "domino effect" they feared a Communist victory would inflict on the rest of Southeast Asia and the western Pacific. Prime Minister Keith Holyoake of New Zealand defined the threat in these terms: "South Vietnam is something of a test case in Asia. If the Communists have their way there, they will move on to probe elsewhere, in Thailand, Malaysia, and farther west. Every Communist step forward is a step closer to Australia and New Zealand." Australian Prime Minister Harold Holt was more succinct in his support: "All the way with LBJ."

Outside of SEATO, the only major troop contribution to South Vietnam was the Republic of Korea. President Chiang Kai-shek of the Republic of China did broach with President Johnson the subject of sending combat troops from Taiwan to South Vietnam, but the State Department raised two objections: traditional Vietnamese antipathy toward the Chinese and the possibility of Chinese Communist retaliation. Japan, with no army or extensive military resources, was able to proffer no military aid and made no pretensions that it would do so even if it could. Because of Japan's smoldering domestic opposition to the war in Vietnam, the United States, content with access to Japan's port and air facilities, never pressed the issue.

South Korea's contribution was the strongest boost to President Johnson's more flags campaign. It brought to the side of South Vietnamese and American soldiers some forty-seven thousand troops from an Asian nation that itself had earlier repulsed aggression with international assistance. South Korean President Chung Hee Park proudly explained that his country's engagement in South Vietnam "would not only solidify our national security but also contribute toward strengthening the anti-Communist front of the Free World."

The material cost of South Korean participation in the war was paid by the United States. It amounted to nearly $1 billion from 1965 to 1970, plus other benefits to President

A dying Korean marine is carried off the battlefield. Forty-seven thousand South Korean troops served in Vietnam.

毛主席和胡志明主席亲切握手。

越南南方人民反对美国-吴庭艳集团的爱
国正义斗争，不論在政治上或者軍事上，都取
得了重大的胜利。我們中国人民是坚决支持越
南南方人民的正义斗争的。

毛泽东

A Chinese poster shows Ho Chi Minh and Mao Tse-tung shaking hands to demonstrate North Vietnamese-Chinese unity in the "struggle against imperialists."

Park's government that included $150 million in development loans and perhaps $600 million in profits from military procurement, contracts for services, and construction projects.

General Westmoreland praised the Koreans' combat effectiveness, ranking them the equal of U.S. troops. And captured Vietcong documents showed the enemy's respect for them, stipulating that "contact with the Koreans is to be avoided at all costs unless a [Vietcong] victory is 100 percent certain." Some western observers charged that the Korean "effectiveness" sometimes bordered on "atrocities," one more problem for Washington in a war already steeped in moral controversy.

While President Johnson assiduously courted allies to help fight the war, the South Vietnamese government took a casual approach to the whole matter. They did little to encourage more flags in the form of foreign combat troops. Puzzled and occasionally annoyed Americans correctly diagnosed South Vietnam's attitude as xenophobia. But they never recognized how naturally this grew out of the country's history and culture, out of the thousand-year struggle of the Vietnamese to repel foreign invaders and to carve a national identity for themselves among the diverse peoples of the Indochina Peninsula. Nevertheless, South Vietnamese xenophobia, in all its political and social manifestations, was destined to have enormous reper-

QUYẾT ĐÁNH THẮNG
GIẶC MỸ XÂM LƯỢC !

Giôn xơn

ĐẾ QUỐC MỸ
LÀ KẺ THÙ
KHÔNG ĐỘI TRỜI CHUNG
CỦA CHÚNG TA !

A North Vietnamese poster (bottom) declares: "Imperial America is the enemy with whom we cannot live under the same sky" as the fingers of the world point accusingly at President Johnson. The top slogan says, "We are determined to defeat the American aggressors."

cussions for South Vietnam and its American allies. As the war build-up progressed it is no wonder that the South Vietnamese government felt that with almost five hundred thousand American soldiers on its soil, one ally was enough.

South Vietnam's generals had additional reasons for their indifference to the more flags campaign. Intent more on political jockeying and internal power plays than on the war, they also considered President Johnson's proposals to broaden the alliance to be a public relations campaign directed primarily at the American people. Thus Saigon was willing to leave to Washington the role of supplicant for support.

North Vietnam's allies

While Washington's escalating military commitment to South Vietnam engendered disunity among its allies, it enhanced Hanoi's ability to garner international support. In dealing with North Vietnam the Johnson administration had always hoped to avoid drawing other Communist countries, particularly the Soviet Union and the People's Republic of China, into the fray. When orchestrating the momentous air strike on Haiphong's petroleum complex, for instance, the president and the Defense Department had taken every precaution against hitting any Russian tankers or Chinese ships that might have been docked in the harbor.

That of course did not forestall response by the two Communist superpowers. Moscow vehemently denounced that attack and countered that its aid to North Vietnam would "keep growing." Peking issued a stern warning to the United States that the latest escalation of the war freed China from "any bounds or restrictions." Peking went on to affirm its resolution to match U.S. escalation with an equivalent rise in economic and military assistance to Hanoi: "Wherever you extend the war and however heavy the price, we will unswervingly support the . . . Vietnamese people . . . to the end."

For the Soviet Union the bombing marked a turning point in its gradual transition from a spectator offering primarily moral support to an active participant supplying a huge chunk of the economic and military aid to Ho Chi Minh's regime. Since 1960 a chill had characterized Soviet-North Vietnamese relations, the result of shifting trends in international Communist politics and widening fissures in the Sino–Soviet alliance. In late 1960, when Ho Chi Minh contemplated accelerating the anti-Diem insurgency in the South, the Soviets, pursuing a line of peaceful coexistence with the West and engrossed with cold war tensions in Europe, did not share his revolutionary zeal. Hanoi also interpreted Soviet willingness to compromise in the 1962 Geneva settlement guaranteeing a "neutral, sovereign, and independent" Laos as undercutting the doctrine of "wars of national liberation." What apparently irked Ho the most was Russian Premier Nikita Khrushchev's merely tepid endorsement, in a speech on January 6, 1961, of the Maoist–type national liberation movements favored by Hanoi and its ally in South Vietnam, the National Liberation Front. Temporarily, therefore, China became "in" among high-level North Vietnamese policy makers, the Soviet Union "out."

Being in for the Chinese entailed not only giving official encouragement to the Hanoi-backed insurgency in South Vietnam but also picking up the Soviet slack in military and economic aid. The Chinese supplied a vast array of basic construction materials for North Vietnam's essential irrigation and dike systems and for its burgeoning light industries. Ho announced in 1964 the arrival of the first group of a stream of fifty thousand Chinese technicians to supervise the building of roads and railways (and later the repair of bombed facilities). These freed many North Vietnamese soldiers for specifically military duties. In addition to large deliveries of rice and other foodstuffs, the Chinese gave tens of millions of dollars worth of military hardware, mostly small arms and ammunition.

In return for close ties with North Vietnam during the early 1960s, Peking acquired "bragging rights" in its competition with the Soviet Union for leadership among the Communist nations of Asia and Southeast Asia. To Peking, North Vietnam was also valuable as the agent, or so it hoped, of a Chinese-sponsored, worldwide crusade against "the imperialist camp." In addition, the threat of Chinese intervention on behalf of its Communist ally could serve Hanoi as a potent restraint upon America's willingness to invade North Vietnam. The testing ground would be South Vietnam; the method, the National Liberation Front's war of liberation; and the "imperialist" target, the United States.

Despite the presence of an ardent and influential pro-Chinese faction in Ho's ruling politburo, foreign combat troops, whether Russians or Chinese, were the last thing he wanted. He was unwavering in his conviction that in wars of liberation "nationalism" and "communism" were inseparable forces. To the Vietnamese, as Ho well knew, foreign troops, allies or not, would discredit the movement's strongest claim to popular support, namely, commitment to national unity and independence.

As the war grew, China, in the throes of its cultural revolution, was unable to meet all Hanoi's needs for economic and military aid. Moreover, long experience had taught Ho that too great a reliance upon one ally could diminish North Vietnam's freedom to conduct its own affairs, especially its handling of the war. Rejecting rigid alignment with the Chinese, or anyone else, he sought support instead from a diversity of sources. This involved warming relations with the Soviet Union. To accomplish this required dealing with the bitter Sino–Soviet split without losing either ally's support or restricting North Vietnam's freedom of action.

Ho was up to the challenge. He set about cautiously wooing the Soviets in 1964 with a delegation to Moscow headed by Le Duan, the first secretary of the North Vietnamese Lao Dong (Communist) party. Khrushchev granted them a cordial reception but was cool to Vietnamese proposals for more Russian support for their "war of liberation" in South Vietnam. A change of leadership from Khrushchev to Leonid Brezhnev in late 1964, however, heightened prospects for a rapprochement between the Soviet Union and North Vietnam. With Brezhnev at the helm, the Russian leadership was readying itself to reverse Khrushchev's concession of Southeast Asia to the Chinese sphere of influence and to play a more energetic role in Asian and Pacific affairs.

Although not eager to embroil itself in the Vietnam conflict and thus risk confrontation with the United States, the Soviet Union, soon after Brezhnev's accession, began sending signals to Hanoi that it was prepared to offer substantial assistance. But it was the American bombing of North Vietnam in the first week of February 1965, during a state visit by Soviet Premier Aleksei Kosygin, that officially thawed relations between Moscow and Hanoi. One American official called the timing of the bombing "bad manners." Another remarked, "I think it was a mistake." In any event, Kosygin expressed fury over the U.S. action and promptly negotiated an economic and military aid

Soviet-supplied MIGs with their North Vietnamese pilots on alert. Increased Soviet aid after the June 1966 Hanoi-Haiphong bombing gave North Vietnam an air force of 110 to 115 MIGs in early 1967.

agreement with the North Vietnamese. Although modest in proportions, the agreement promised Hanoi "necessary aid and support."

Not until after the Haiphong-Hanoi raid in June 1966 did the Soviet aid program really shift into high gear with a promise of more than $500 million in military and economic aid for North Vietnam. The aid included stepped-up deliveries of Soviet jet fighters and surface-to-air missiles. Many more shipments would follow, of rocket launching equipment, antiaircraft guns, airplanes, tanks, and gunboats. The Chinese, not to be outdone by their Soviet rivals, hiked their aid to almost $200 million annually.

By 1966 Ho Chi Minh had succeeded, even in the face of deep divisions within the Communist camp, in winning and maintaining the solid support of two major allies. While steering clear of excessive influence by the Soviet Union or China but preserving friendship with both, Ho's government found it possible to extract from them the means to pursue its objectives in the war against the South.

A world in search of peace

While President Johnson's campaign for more flags in Vietnam failed to achieve the broad allied support he sought, search for a peaceful settlement found the allies united. America's principal allies in Europe—France, Britain, and Germany—and in Asia—Japan and later Australia—either publicly or privately urged the U.S. to explore a solution for Vietnam at the negotiating table instead of at war. But as the U.S. raised the military stakes in South Vietnam, it appeared to some allies that Washington was not genuinely interested in peace short of total victory in its war against the Vietcong and North Vietnamese. President Johnson, stung by even the hint that his policy was blocking the road to peace, set out in late 1965 to silence his critics by launching an international "peace offensive." In December he declared a pause in the bombing of the North and initiated what he called "one of the most widespread diplomatic campaigns of my presidency." Johnson's peace ambassadors—including Averell

135

Harriman, United Nations Ambassador Arthur Goldberg, Vice President Hubert Humphrey, Assistant Secretary for African Affairs G. Mennen Williams, Thomas Mann ("our top man in Latin American affairs"), and the president's national security adviser McGeorge Bundy—embarked on diplomatic missions to forty countries in the Far East, Middle East, Africa, Europe, and South America.

The rationale for his offensive, as Johnson saw it, was that "we wanted to overlook no opportunity for peace, and we wanted the world to be informed." His administration also did not overlook the opportunity to erase the doubt of critics, at home and abroad, about its commitment to peace. After all, hadn't LBJ repeatedly pledged that "we will meet at any conference table; we will discuss any proposals—four points or fourteen or forty; we will work for a cease-fire now or once discussions have begun."

Yet the impression lingered within the international community that the United States was not intent on peace, not doing enough. As a result, the president's peace offensive, like his more flags drive, was ridiculed in some circles as "fandangle diplomacy," fandangle being a popular term in Texas for a "big to-do" involving singing, dancing, eating, and fireworks. The French press billed it as "an American diplomatic ballet." And it ended, like so many others to follow, with more violence in Vietnam.

The president more than once answered these reflections on his sincerity with characteristically earthy remarks: "I keep trying to get Ho to the negotiating table. I try writing him, calling him, going through the Russians and the Chinese, and all I hear back is 'Fuck you, Lyndon.'"

The fact was, however, that whenever either Washington or Hanoi extended a peace feeler, neither side handled matters very adroitly. Hostility, stubbornness, distrust, and confusion always seemed to get in the way. American and North Vietnamese peace formulas were frequently encumbered by many qualifications, ambiguous terminology, and fine distinctions. A simple change of tense, deletion of a word, or shade of phrasing could alter a proposal's entire meaning and scuttle it. The fate of the American peace initiative of January 1967, code-named Sunflower, was typical. President Johnson sent Chester Cooper, a State Department official, to London with a confidential message for Prime Minister Harold Wilson stating that the U.S. would institute a bombing halt if the North would reciprocate by agreeing to stop further infiltration. Wilson interpreted the proposal as a possible breakthrough toward a cease-fire and conveyed it to Russian Premier Kosygin, then in London for talks.

Just before Kosygin's departure from London, however, Washington changed the wording of the message Wilson had passed on to Kosygin. According to the amended version, the president would halt the bombing after, not before, infiltration had stopped. Wilson rushed the message to Kosygin, but its tougher language dimmed hopes for a favorable response from Hanoi. Wilson was embarrassed and angry. Hanoi dismissed the message. The bombing continued. The United States and North Vietnam were back where they had started.

Both Washington and Hanoi wanted peace and an end to the fighting. But each adversary tended to equate peace with what amounted to defeat from the standpoint of the other. The United States conceived of peace in terms of a halt to North Vietnamese infiltration, the cessation of the Vietcong insurgency, and the preservation of a free, non-Communist government in South Vietnam. To the North Vietnamese these U.S. demands were an insurmountable obstacle to the kind of peace they envisioned: recognition of the political program of the NLF as the legitimate basis to settle the internal affairs of South Vietnam, the unconditional withdrawal of all foreign troops from the country, and the eventual unification of North and South as mandated by the Geneva accords. As long as the Johnson administration believed victory and peace were within its grasp on the battlefield, it had little impetus to negotiate seriously. For the only alternatives it perceived to military victory, aside from North Vietnamese capitulation, were either hopeless stalemate—neither victory nor peace—or defeat and withdrawal.

In its approach to negotiations, North Vietnam also acted on a narrow interpretation of its acceptable options. In light of what they considered the American and South Vietnamese betrayal of the Geneva accords, the North Vietnamese were wary of the negotiation process itself. Moreover, since Hanoi and the NLF never abandoned hope of military victory, both rejected the resort to any compromise. Ho and his advisers also had other motives for spurning compromise. While it was becoming more likely that the American public would not tolerate stalemate or a drawn-out war, the North Vietnamese leaders believed that they could move their countrymen to wait out the United States and fight for as long as it might take. In the opinion of North Vietnamese Prime Minister Pham Van Dong, Hanoi had the "momentum" of history behind it: "We have been fighting for our independence for four thousand years. We have defeated the Mongols three times. The United States Army, strong as it is, is not as terrifying as Genghis Khan."

In a contest of wills with the United States, the North Vietnamese could also point to two more advantages: the loyalty of their allies and the obvious dissension within the ranks of America's friends. Ho Chi Minh, ever sensitive to the impact of world opinion on the conflict in Vietnam, found considerable cause for optimism in all this. "The American imperialists," he said, "see that their isolation is increasing with each passing day. They are subjected to ever-sharper criticism throughout the world, and even in the United States."

Although throughout the period 1965 to 1968 Washington and Hanoi frustrated each other in the negotiation

Two views of Ho and LBJ in the power "game" of peace negotiations: (Left) Ho plays "hulahoop" with the Pentagon; (right) LBJ uses Ho Chi Minh as a whipping boy.

process, the endless search for peace attracted heads of state, diplomats, academics, and clergymen from many parts of the world. According to Chester Cooper, "some were skilled diplomats, others were fumbling fools; many were highly motivated, others were simply eager for publicity and the Nobel Peace Prize." Whatever their motives, these volunteer intermediaries employed every means to open a dialogue between Washington and Hanoi: diplo-

matic contacts, televised appeals, telegrams and telephone calls, secret messages, clandestine meetings, cloak-and-dagger intrigue, and public petitions. Some of their peace initiatives became important enough to receive official code names from Washington like Marigold, Kelly, and Ohio. Yet for all the skill and good intentions of so many would-be peacemakers, their efforts went for naught. The war lurched on.

The War Comes Home

Norman Morrison had been thinking about killing himself for months. On November 2, 1965, the thirty-two-year-old Quaker, father of three, decided to do it. Under the late afternoon shadow of the Pentagon and within view of Defense Secretary Robert McNamara's third-floor office, Morrison poured kerosene from a gallon jug over his body and set himself afire. According to Major Richard Lundquist, a witness to the incident, Morrison managed to climb on top of a concrete wall and cry out before a burst of flame, shooting seven feet high, consumed his body. "He was a torch," Lundquist said. Pentagon guards called a military ambulance that rushed Morrison to nearby Fort Myer Hospital. He was pronounced dead on arrival. Following her husband's self-immolation, Morrison's wife, Ann, issued this statement: "Norman Morrison has given his life today to express his concern over the great loss of life and human suffering caused by the war in Vietnam. He was protesting our government's in-

volvement in this war. He felt that all citizens must speak their convictions about our country's action.''

To Americans, aghast at Morrison's fiery suicide, it seemed a macabre replay of an incident that had made headlines and shocked the world a couple of years earlier. The day was June 11, 1963; the place, Saigon. A Buddhist monk, Thich Quang Duc, had immolated himself on a downtown street to protest the oppressive regime of South Vietnamese President Ngo Dinh Diem. More than any incident up to that time, the monk's dramatic suicide brought Vietnam into the consciousness of the American people. But the emotional impact of that strange episode in the continuing crisis of South Vietnam was short-lived. The suicide, like the Buddhists, and like the country itself, remained a distant phenomenon. Until, that is, the bizarre act of protest by Norman Morrison. Vietnam was beginning to affect the life and mood of America.

Rumblings of discontent

Even as the first contingents of U.S. Marines in Vietnam were digging in at Da Nang, discontent was brewing on the home front. In 1965 the country witnessed numerous acts of protest against America's role in South Vietnam, which, though not so extreme as Morrison's, were unmistakable signs that the war was arousing passionate opposition among various segments of the American public. Students and young people generated much of the initial criticism of Johnson's Vietnam policy. After the marines landed, hundreds of students at the University of Michigan held a "teach-in," a one-day moratorium on classes in favor of a mass forum to discuss the war.

Student opposition to the war accelerated to a national movement by the fall of that year. An organization calling itself the National Coordinating Committee To End the War in Vietnam promoted two "International Days of Protest," a series of demonstrations against U.S. involvement in South Vietnam. In large cities—Detroit, Chicago, Oakland, and New York—and on campuses across the country, thousands of demonstrators marched, chanted, carried placards, and cheered speeches demanding an end to U.S. participation in the hostilities in South Vietnam.

At Detroit's Wayne State University, Al Harrison, a young black organizer, cried: "You all got me and my kind in chains! We got no business fighting a yellow man's war to save the white man." Harrison's complaint was echoed by several black leaders and activists who feared that President Johnson's Great Society and civil rights programs and the billions to fund them would be swallowed up by the far-off war in Southeast Asia. For black activ-

ists, some veterans of the long struggle against segregation and racism, the incipient antiwar movement represented not only a logical continuation of the fight for civil rights, equality, and social reform in America but also a means of dramatizing the disproportionate number of black draftees being inducted for combat in Vietnam. At another rally, in lower Manhattan, a young Catholic burned his draft card, citing religious grounds for his defiant act of civil disobedience: "Christ would not have carried this card. Neither will I.''

In this beginning stage of protest, some two hundred thousand people turned to various forms of demonstration. News coverage played up the presence of so many college students, many of them favoring long hair, beards, and jeans. *Time* magazine, for example, described the youthful demonstrators as a "ragtag collection of the unshaven and unscrubbed," and dubbed them "Vietniks," an allusion to the earlier dropout, nonconformist "beatniks" of the 1950s. A Senate internal security subcommittee report viewed the demonstrators and their activities from a sinister perspective. While most protesters are "loyal" Americans, it said, control of the movement has clearly passed "into the hands of Communists and extremist elements who are openly sympathetic to the Vietcong."

The characterization of student antiwar protesters as dupes of a Communist conspiracy was unfounded and distorted their motives. The antiwar movement was a grassroots expression of protest too diffuse to succumb to the direction and control of any centralized authority. For instance, the National Coordinating Committee To End the War in Vietnam began as little more than a shoestring operation, acting as an information clearing-house for a number of independent local end-the-war groups. At its headquarters near the University of Wisconsin at Madison, the committee primarily produced a newsletter and disseminated literature about the war. The chairman of the organization's forty-five-member steering committee, Frank Emspak, was typical in many respects of the students and young people whose commitment to stop the war led them to activism. Only twenty-two years old, Emspak had just received his zoology degree at Wisconsin. His deputy, Ray Robinson, was a civil rights worker recently out of the navy. The Central Intelligence Agency, in a 1967 report recently declassified at the Johnson Presidential Library in Austin, Texas, informed President Johnson that there was no Communist-controlled or foreign-inspired connection to the antiwar protests. But according to Charles DeBenedetti, the historian who made public the report, President Johnson "refused to believe it.''

The voices of students were joined by those of a diverse mix of respected academics, politicians, journalists, and clergymen and of more traditional antiwar dissenters like Quakers, pacifists, and other conscientious objectors. Yale history Professor Staughton Lynd shared the students' concern that "the United States has violated the principles of self-determination in Vietnam because of a fear that free elections would favor Communists." The influential journalist Walter Lippmann advocated negotiations to end a conflict to which "there is no military solution." Union Theological Seminary President John Bennett, novelist John Hersey, and Harvard's eminent historian of China, John Fairbank, among others, formed an antiwar group seeking a "moderate solution that is not pro-Vietcong, does not involve bombing and burning of villages, and does not involve wholesale support of the military regime of South Vietnam." Twenty-five hundred ministers, priests, and rabbis, on April 4, 1965, took a more direct approach, running a full-page ad in the *New York Times* entreating the president: "In the name of God, STOP IT!"

President Johnson, infuriated by what he called the "unpatriotic" behavior of Americans publicly opposing the war, assailed them as "nervous Nellies, who break ranks under the strain and turn on their leaders, their own country, and their own fighting men." But resisting war had a heritage reaching back to the Revolutionary War. In 1846 many Americans, including Abraham Lincoln, bitterly protested the Mexican War. During the Civil War, thousands of draft protesters rioted in Manhattan. Even draft card burning was nothing new: The noted writer and pacifist Dwight Macdonald had ignited his in 1947.

Still, in 1965, those speaking out against the war were a distinct minority. Most surveys showed that some 80 percent of the American people approved of the government's broadest objectives in Vietnam. But the statistics were far from decisive. A substantial number of Americans, while in agreement with the administration's overall goals of thwarting Communist aggression and preserving an independent South Vietnam, did not necessarily assent to waging a major ground war in South Vietnam to achieve them. Johnson's vaunted domestic consensus was a fragile one, and many in Washington knew it. The ostensible national support for an expanded American presence in South Vietnam came from a public basically uninformed and confused over what their government intended to do there or even how far it was willing to go. As a result, by 1966 the American people would find themselves wondering how the country had gotten into South Vietnam and where that commitment was taking them. The U.S. Congress, which during the furor over the Tonkin Gulf crisis had opened the way for the country's military commitment to South Vietnam, found itself in a similar predicament.

A war on trial

They were such basic questions. Why had the United States become involved in Vietnam? How long would the U.S. stay in Vietnam? How many soldiers might have to be sent to fight there? How many Americans would die? What right had the U.S. to be fighting there? What is a "war of national liberation?" And, most important of all, why were all these questions not answered, or at least asked, before America escalated its commitment to the war? As far as Congress was concerned, in February 1966, during a lull in the bombing of North Vietnam, the time had come to ask them.

The forum for Congress's version of a national teach-in was the chamber of the Senate Foreign Relations Committee chaired by Democratic Senator J. William Fulbright of Arkansas. On January 29 Senator Wayne Morse, one of two senators who had voted against the Southeast Asia (Tonkin Gulf) Resolution, had presented a resolution requesting the Foreign Relations Committee to conduct a "full and complete investigation of all aspects" of U.S. Vietnam policy. Later that day, on a television panel discussion, Senator Fulbright said he thought hearings of the sort proposed by Morse might be a good idea. "There is an abysmal lack of information on this matter," he said.

Fulbright was a logical choice to conduct such hearings, and not simply because he headed the Foreign Relations Committee. In August 1964 he had been instrumental in steering through Congress the Tonkin Gulf resolution which empowered the Johnson administration "to take all necessary steps, including the use of armed force, to assist any member or protocol state of The Southeast Asia Collective Defense Treaty requesting assistance in defense of its freedom." It was an act Fulbright came to rue more than any other of his political career. As American involvement in the war steadily escalated, President Johnson and his advisers seemed to be interpreting the resolution, to the dismay of Fulbright and many others in Congress, as carte blanche for whatever actions they deemed important. With his "Congressional consensus" officially in hand, the president was shutting out the legislative branch from the decision-making process regarding bombing, troop levels, strategy, and peace negotiations. This led a group of senators to complain that "while President Johnson wants their consent on any moves he may decide to make, he does not want their advice."

The administration's handling of the 1965 Christmas bombing pause was the catalyst that finally moved Fulbright and his committee to action. When on December 24, 1965, Washington initiated a bombing pause in the hope that Hanoi might become more receptive to negotiations, the president agreed to continue the bombing pause so long as he thought diplomatic progress was being made. On January 24, while Secretary of State Dean Rusk was testifying before the Senate Foreign Relations Committee, members had "pressed him for assurances that the committee would be consulted before the bombing pause was ended." Fulbright and his colleagues were increasingly irritated by the fact that President Johnson had hardly consulted them on matters related to his bombing policy. But the president, for all his fixation on consensus, was evidently not interested in debating the issue. After informing Congressional leaders of his conclusion that the North

"Hell No..."

Above left. Protesters from universities across the country throng to the steps of the Capitol on April 17, 1965, for the first mass protest in Washington, part of a nationwide protest organized by the Students for a Democratic Society.

Right. Among the Washington demonstration's fifteen thousand protesters was the Bread-and-Puppet Theater, a group using street theater as a form of protest.

Below left. Splashed with red paint thrown by a heckler, Dave Dellinger, Staughton Lynd, and Robert Parris Moses (left to right) lead the "Assembly of Unrepresented People" to the Capitol on August 9, 1965, to protest U.S. involvement in Vietnam.

The symbol of protest: a draft card in flames.

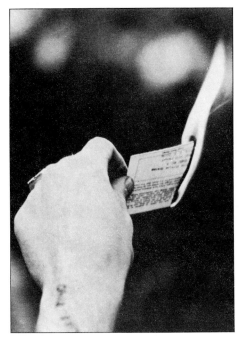

Vietnamese were taking military advantage of the bombing halt, the administration simply announced on January 31 that the bombing of North Vietnam had been resumed. Fulbright had taken enough. On February 3, the word went out that his Senate Foreign Relations Committee would "conduct a broad inquiry into Vietnam policy."

News of the committee's decision struck like a bombshell at the White House. One official recalled that "everything was quiet when he [Johnson] left the White House for lunch at 12:30, Thursday [February 3]; when he returned there was chaos." The president's response to the news was to resort to a political ploy, one in which he excelled, to "steal the headlines" by holding the hastily arranged summit with South Vietnamese leaders in Honolulu. So hurried were the plans for the impromptu conference, in fact, that the White House even failed to notify the South Vietnamese ambassador.

Inevitably, the president's well-publicized departure grabbed headlines and there was no shortage of news photos showing Johnson with his arm around Premier Nguyen Cao Ky's shoulders, the two vowing to launch a "social revolution" in South Vietnam. The suave Ky, always at home in front of the camera, played his part well, promising to make good on his pledge to hold national elections. Nestled in amid all the hoopla and back-slapping was the president's announcement of an American troop increase in South Vietnam to 383,500 by the end of the year and a further goal of 425,000 by mid-1967.

Lyndon Johnson, however, could not stay out of town for long. When he returned to Washington on February 7 the hearings were in full swing, covered by the nation's leading newspapers, magazines, and television networks.

Taking a good look around

In the aftermath of the Senate hearings, J. William Fulbright would emerge as one of the most outspoken opponents of LBJ's Vietnam policy. At the time of those hearings, he was not yet the famous dove he would become. Fulbright's main purpose in initiating the hearings was educational, "to get a clarification." The American people, he told reporters, should be able to decide "whether what they are fighting for is worthwhile."

Nevertheless, hostility had been building in the Senate toward the administration's almost single-handed running of the war, and inevitably the questioning of White House advocates of the government's Vietnam policy took on an adversarial tone. The reticent, even grudging, attitude of the president's advisers further tightened the tense atmosphere. During the hearings' first session, Fulbright revealed that Defense Secretary Robert McNamara was refusing to testify. According to McNamara, he and Joint Chiefs of Staff Chairman General Earle Wheeler had decided that it was "not in the public interest to appear in a public session." Senator Wayne Morse angrily cited

McNamara's stance as another example of how "the people of the Pentagon and the State Department have already led the American people down the road toward government by secrecy." Fulbright was not to be denied an opportunity to scrutinize the administration's intervention in South Vietnam. The hearings would go on even if McNamara and other top officials would not testify. "If they don't wish to come," he asserted, "there are other sources of information."

Those "other sources of information" would prove both embarrassing and damaging to the administration. Lieutenant General James Gavin was the first important non-administration witness to face the committee. Gavin had impressive credentials to add weight to his testimony. After joining the army as a private in 1924, he went from the ranks into West Point—a rare occurrence—and he rose to the rank of brigadier general as commander of the famed 82nd Airborne Division in World War II. Before retiring in 1958 he held several important positions, including chief of plans and operations for the army, and later became President Kennedy's ambassador to France. General Gavin was also widely respected for his expertise in military tactics, particularly for his tactical concept of the "sky cavalry" that later resulted in the formation of the 1st Air Cavalry Division.

In his testimony, Gavin immediately raised an issue on the minds of many senators by charging that the president's policy of continued escalation in Vietnam could lead to war with China. The government, he said, had become so "mesmerized" with Vietnam that it had permitted the commitment there to become "alarmingly out of balance." The general added, "we have been escalating at the will of our opponents rather than on our own judgment."

The testimony of such a distinguished career officer and war veteran carried considerable clout with the senators and the press. And the White House could not write him off as a dove. Gavin told the committee U.S. troops should remain in South Vietnam but not for the aggressive purpose General Westmoreland and the administration had in mind. He explained an "enclave strategy" he had recently advocated in *Harper's* magazine. It called for halting further troop increases and employing U.S. forces already in South Vietnam to hold areas under allied control while military and political alternatives to the escalation of offensive operations were considered. "I felt that the time had come," he said, "to take a reappraisal of where we were . . . look at what we now have there, what we can do with what we have, and see if we can't find another solution to this problem." The administration's strategy of escalation, Gavin concluded, was a bottomless pit: "In doing this . . . we have to match every commitment he [the enemy] makes, every man he sends, [until] we finally get our involvement so out of balance with all our other global commitments we are losing."

Before he was through, Gavin took aim at one of the

An early and vocal opponent of the war, Senator Wayne Morse, shown here in 1963 with President Johnson, predicted that many of the senators who voted for the Tonkin Gulf resolution would "live to regret it."

administration's "sacred cows," its strategic bombing of North Vietnam. Gavin argued forcefully that "the bombing of Hanoi would accomplish very little." He also referred to the U.S. Strategic Study after World War II, which indicated that strategic bombing had not achieved either its military or strategic objectives.

While Gavin cast doubt on the wisdom and effectiveness of the administration's military strategy, the committee's next witness, George Kennan, questioned the very basis of the Johnson administration's rationale for intervening in South Vietnam: that North Vietnamese aggression there represented a deliberate test and threat to long-standing Free World containment barriers against Communist expansion. Kennan, who under the pseudonym "X" had written the "containment" thesis that had guided U.S. foreign policy in the 1950s and early 1960s, asserted that such a strategy bore no relevance to the conflict in Southeast Asia, that it was out of date with contem-

porary world conditions. He informed the committee that the containment policy had been conceived "when there was only one center of Communist power [Moscow]" and that it had been adopted to protect Western Europe, a great industrial complex that had the resources to contribute to its own protection. "Today there is more than one [Communist power]," he added, "and that makes a great deal of difference." Kennan affirmed that he had never intended containment to be applied in Asia and asserted that the situation involving China and Vietnam was quite different from that of Europe in 1947.

Kennan said that the United States could not enforce containment everywhere, that it could not do everything. "I don't believe we can determine," he warned, "what kind of political conditions are going to prevail there [South Vietnam]. There are limits to our duties and capabilities." Kennan went one step further, daring to propose what to the administration and even to Fulbright himself at the

Ridgway's Boys

When the day comes for me to face my Maker and account for my actions, the thing I would be most humbly proud of was the fact that I fought against, and perhaps contributed to preventing, the carrying out of some harebrained tactical schemes which would have cost the lives of thousands of men. To that list of tragic accidents that fortunately never happened I would add the Indochina intervention.

—General Matthew B. Ridgway, ret. (1956)

Twice in the midfifties "Big Matt" Ridgway argued against and helped to prevent U.S. intervention in Indochina. In 1954 he advised President Dwight D. Eisenhower against bombing Vietminh forces around Dien Bien Phu. Later that year, during the negotiations at Geneva, he headed off increasing pressure from other U.S. military leaders for the U.S. to assume the burden of the war the French were finally relinquishing.

In a very thorough and detailed report the outspoken general outlined for Eisenhower the costs and the difficulties of entering the war: a minimum of five to ten combat divisions and fifty-five engineering battalions plus the seizure of Chinese air bases on Hainan Island that would inevitably lead to Chinese intervention including—possibly—the reopening of the Korean front. In short, Ridgway concluded, the costs both in men and materiel would be enormous.

Ridgway's opposition to fighting a land war in Asia stemmed from his experiences in Korea as head of the United Nations forces there, a post he took over from General Douglas MacArthur in December 1950. He believed that any Asian land war included the danger of Chinese involvement, in which the U.S. would again face the dilemma of confronting the overwhelming manpower superiority of the Asian enemy on the battlefield or relying on nuclear weapons. His views gave rise to a school of military thought aptly dubbed in the press the "Never Again Club." Concisely stated, the belief of members of this club was that America should never again fight a land war in Asia.

Along with Ridgway the group included two rising young generals: Maxwell Taylor and James Gavin. Both Taylor and Gavin had served under Ridgway for several years. Gavin first joined Ridgway in early 1942 as commander of the 505th Parachute Infantry Regiment in Ridgway's 82nd Airborne Division. Several months later Taylor was reunited with Ridgway, who had been his Spanish instructor at West Point, and under whom Taylor had served briefly in 1940. He served the 82nd, first as chief of staff and then as commander of division artillery. Both Gavin and Taylor were young (Gavin was thirty-five and Taylor forty-one), but by war's end they had become generals and heroes. Gavin returned to the U.S. leading the victorious 82nd in the ticker-tape parade down Fifth Avenue, while Max Taylor came home to assume the prestigious position of superintendent of West Point.

Taylor received his initiation into the "Never Again Club" in 1952 through combat. Again serving under Ridgway, he commanded the 8th Army in Korea and saw firsthand the problems of fighting an Asian land war. Gavin joined two years later in 1954 while serving as deputy chief of staff for plans and operations for the army. In this position Gavin oversaw the preparation of the army survey that Ridgway (now Eisenhower's army chief of staff) commissioned to study the problems and requirements of fighting a land war in Indochina. He learned only too well the difficulties of fighting such a war.

The knowledge Gavin accumulated during this period was instrumental in his early and continuing opposition to America's commitment in Vietnam. Scrupulously avoiding comment on the political wisdom of America's actions, Gavin publicly criticized Westmoreland's deployment of U.S. forces. He was a star witness in the Senate Foreign Relations Committee hearings on Vietnam in February 1966, in which he testified about the impracticalities of conducting a land war in Asia. That same month, writing in *Harper's* magazine, he called for a return to the "enclave strategy" employed in early 1965, as an alternative to escalation. Ironically, it was a position his fellow "Never Again Club" member, Maxwell Taylor, had earlier recommended but then discarded as events overtook his principled objection to an Asian land war and eventually made him one of its leading defenders.

Taylor's participation in Vietnam began in 1961. At President Kennedy's request he traveled to Vietnam in October with presidential adviser Walt W. Rostow

to assess the situation. In 1954 Ridgway's survey team, which had included a large staff of military experts, had been given the time and freedom by the French to conduct its own in-depth study of the situation. In 1961, however, Taylor was forced to conduct his study in the short span of six days with a staff consisting of himself, Rostow, and a handful of Washington agency representatives. Moreover, he had to rely primarily upon information gathered from often unreliable official Vietnamese sources.

His conclusions, like his working conditions, differed markedly from those reached by Ridgway. Whereas Ridgway had found Vietnam uniquely unsuited to U.S. tactics and forces, Taylor thought it to be "not an excessively difficult or unpleasant place to operate." He recom-

mended the introduction of around eight thousand American troops, not to be used for combat purposes, but rather "to raise the national morale and show U.S. determination." Taylor came later to realize that escalation, as Ridgway predicted, could not be controlled.

Torn by conflicting loyalties and beliefs, Taylor was, as David Halberstam observed, "at once committed to winning the war (or saving South Vietnam), remaining a player in good standing with the other players, loyalty to the tradition of the U.S. Army, and at the same time keeping the U.S. ground forces out and preventing a repeat of the French experience."

Thus while Gavin, the straightforward maverick, could openly criticize the growing U.S. commitment, Taylor found that

Lieutenant General James Gavin, a critic of the war, testifies at the Senate Foreign Relations Committee's hearings on Vietnam.

the price of fulfilling his political role was to compromise his beliefs. Late in November 1964, as massive U.S. escalation became imminent, Taylor was finally faced with the choice of standing by his beliefs and opposing an inevitable Americanization of the war in Vietnam or of joining Johnson's proescalation consensus. Taylor summoned his staff together in Saigon. "I am going to see the president," he announced, "and I am going to advise that ... we will need American troops here."

The "Never Again Club" had failed in its mission.

The author of the policy of containment, George Kennan, tells the Senate Foreign Relations Subcommittee that he knows of "no reason why we should wish to become involved [in Vietnam], and I could think of several good reasons why we would wish not to."

time seemed unthinkable: withdrawal from Vietnam. "I would submit," he affirmed, "there is more to be won in the opinion of the world by a resolute and courageous liquidation of unsound positions than in the most stubborn pursuit of extravagant or unpromising objectives."

After several days recess, hearings reopened on February 17 with the administration's two star witnesses, former U.S. Ambassador to South Vietnam Maxwell Taylor and Secretary of State Dean Rusk. Taylor appeared as an in-

dependent witness but was generally understood to be a proponent of the administration's case. General Taylor could claim much authority on Vietnam-related issues. As one of the primary advocates of the "limited war theory" in the Kennedy administration, he had proposed introducing combat forces into South Vietnam in 1961 "if that should become necessary for success." Later, as ambassador to South Vietnam from July 1964 to July 1965, Taylor had resisted but then acquiesced to the deployment there of large numbers of American combat troops.

"A rare blend of soldier-scholar"

Under questioning, Taylor reiterated his conviction that the administration was interested only in pursuing a limited war. "Our four-point strategy," he declared, "consists of a complex but coherent package of measures designed to improve the effectiveness of our forces on the ground in South Vietnam, to exploit our air superiority by attacking military targets in North Vietnam, to stabilize the political, social, and economic systems in South Vietnam, and to seek an honorable negotiated settlement of the conflict. It is limited as to objective, as to geographical scope, as to weapons and forces employed, and as to targets attacked." Taylor added, "All parts of it are interrelated; all parts are indispensable; we must be successful on all fronts."

But when asked about the "limit that the administration intended to put on the investment of United States ground forces," Taylor could not be specific. He did try to disprove Montana Senator Mike Mansfield's contention that the conflict could escalate almost indefinitely. The North Vietnamese, he reasoned, could only infiltrate so many troops to support the Vietcong and would some day run out of replacements: "The point is that there are factors which tend to keep our troop requirement finite and limit the capability of Hanoi to support large numbers of additional forces in the South." Still, Taylor wondered, "I wish I knew exactly where that ceiling is."

Among so many discussions of policies, theories, and strategies, the subject of what the American people actually thought about the war finally came up. After touching upon the French home front during the French Indochina War, Senator Wayne Morse queried Taylor about the role of public opinion in formulating Vietnam policy. "When the people of a country demonstrate an opposition to a foreign policy of that country and make clear that they want the Indochina war stopped," he asked, "do you interpret that as a weakness on the home front?" Taylor replied, "It certainly is a legitimate act on the part of any people to change the policy of their government."

Morse persisted, and one of the sharpest exchanges of the hearings then ensued. The senator, visibly agitated, declared: "You know we are engaged in a historic debate in this country, where there are honest differences of opin-

Secretary of State Dean Rusk and Senator William Fulbright, chairman of the Foreign Relations Subcommittee, confront each other during a break at the Vietnam hearings.

ion. I happen to hold to the point of view that it isn't going to be too long before the American people as a people will repudiate our war in Southeast Asia." "Senator," Taylor curtly remarked, "that, of course, is good news to Hanoi." Morse shot back: "All I am asking is if the people decided that this war should be stopped in Southeast Asia, are you going to take the position that is weakness on the home front of a democracy?" The general's only comment was, "I would feel that our people were badly misguided and did not understand the consequences of such a disaster." But Morse had the last word, "Well, we agree on one thing, that they have been badly misguided, and you and the president . . . have been misguiding them for a long time in this war."

Last to appear was Secretary of State Dean Rusk. Rusk had sparred with the Senate Foreign Relations Committee

over Vietnam before, especially with Senator Fulbright. This time, however, as Rusk and Fulbright squared off once more, the gloves were off.

They were formidable opponents. The *New York Times* described Rusk as "the picture of a decent, dignified, circumspect, self-controlled and self-effacing person. . . . He doodled, he played with his dark-rimmed glasses . . . but for the most part he doggedly defended the widely known positions of the administration." The description would have pleased Rusk. Modesty, self-control, and determination were his personal trademarks, the result of long cultivation. Growing up in a poor, southern family that lived by the Bible had taught him patience, endurance, and a subdued pride in both virtues. "We were rather a quiet family about expressing our emotions under any circumstances," he once recalled. "I think this was part of the reticence. Perhaps it goes with the Calvinism ... perhaps it comes from the tough battle ... in the family that has to wrest a living out of not too productive soil."

But his Calvinist upbringing also bred in him a belief "that any obstacle could be overcome, that hard work made no challenges insurmountable." That was certainly true for Dean Rusk, always moving forward: Rhodes Scholar, up-and-comer in government service where he gained expertise in Asian aspects of U.S. foreign affairs, then the pinnacle of his career, appointment as secretary of state by John Kennedy. Success without flash, an unusual accomplishment.

By 1966 Rusk had held office for five years and had loyally and self-effacingly served two presidents. He was uncommonly devoted to the responsibilities of his office and took pride in being one of the longest-serving secretaries of state in history. Above all, he had faith in the might and decency of the country he served, that it would never willingly dishonor itself and that with strength it would triumph in every good cause. When Vietnam came along, his conviction was never seen to waver. When friends or colleagues confided their doubts to him about Vietnam, Rusk would say, over and over again, "When a great nation like the United States of America puts its shoulder to the wheel, something has to give: Yes, I know that the French were there and the political situation is bad, and it may be worse than you say, but I can't believe that when a great nation like the United States puts its shoulder to the wheel...." On Friday, February 18, Dean Rusk appeared before the Senate Foreign Relations Committee to say it once again.

Chairman Fulbright

J. William Fulbright had some things in common with Dean Rusk: He, too, was a southerner and had been a Rhodes Scholar. There were many important differences. Fulbright was a public official, publicly elected, a man at home in the limelight and the pressure-cooker atmosphere of the Senate. He was a fashionable and adept, if somewhat languid, politician and moved comfortably in the elitist circles of Georgetown and the Metropolitan Club. His soft-spoken elegance combined with his intelligence earned him a reputation as the resident intellectual of the Senate. J. William Fulbright was not in awe of power, liked wielding influence, and worked comfortably in the spotlight.

Both Rusk and Fulbright could call Lyndon Johnson friend. But Rusk's relationship with the president was circumspect and lacked the sense of senatorial fellowship that once existed between Johnson and Fulbright. Lyndon Johnson, while majority leader of the Senate, had often consulted Fulbright on foreign policy. "See Bill," he would say, "he's my secretary of state." He even tried to make it a reality. It was no secret in Washington that Fulbright was the man Johnson wanted to become secretary of state in 1961.

Then foreign policy, Vietnam in particular, came between the two former political cronies. The administration's use of the Tonkin Gulf resolution cooled their relationship. When Fulbright bitterly attacked Johnson's dispatch of twenty-four thousand troops into the Dominican Republic in April 1965, their friendship was strained even more. The Senate hearings on Vietnam finally made them confirmed enemies. In February 1966, Rusk therefore was Johnson's secretary of state and Fulbright, ironically, LBJ's would-be nemesis.

In his verbal bout with Dean Rusk, Fulbright struck the first blow, challenging the cornerstone of the administration's policy in Vietnam: that it had intervened specifically to counter overt North Vietnamese aggression against the South. "If one reviews the development of this war," he postulated, "it clearly began in my opinion as a war of liberation from colonial rule. Now, after 1956, the struggle then became a civil war between the Diem government and the Vietcong ... I think this ... does explain the apathy ... or the indifference, of [America's] friends and allies. In short, I think it is an oversimplification ... to say that this is a clear-cut aggression by North Vietnam." Rusk countered by emphasizing North Vietnam's "appetite to take over South Vietnam by force." He maintained that the United States was simply asking, and in a restrained way at that, for the North Vietnamese and the Vietcong to stop what they were doing. If they would not, Rusk warned, "There are some moments ... when toughness is absolutely essential for peace."

Speaking slowly and tentatively, Fulbright probed the secretary of state on the administration's definition and conditions of "peace." "I get the impression that we are in an unlimited war, and the only kind of settlement is unconditional surrender. Therefore, there is nothing to negotiate about." Rusk retorted, "But the unconditional surrender of what?"

Toward the end of Rusk's seven-hour marathon in the witness chair, an exchange occurred that not only highlighted Rusk's and Fulbright's differing views of the war but those standing, as well, between the U.S. and North Vietnam, between North Vietnam and South Vietnam, and even between Washington and the antiwar protesters:

Rusk: Mr. Chairman ... some of the things you said

Three political cartoonists' views of President Johnson's Vietnam policy and the Senate hearings mirror the country's growing skepticism about the war.

'For Political Reasons We Should Spare Hanoi, Haiphong And The Senate Foreign Relations Committee!'

Escalation

"A Senator Fulbright to see you, sire. Seems he can't reconcile himself to your infallibility."

suggested that we should abandon the effort in South Vietnam.

Fulbright: After all, Vietnam is their country. It is not our country. . . . It seems to be the trigger that may result in world war.

Rusk: And none of us want it to happen. . . . But when you say this is their country. . . .

Fulbright: It is their country, with all its difficulties, even if they want to be Communists. . . . Just like the Yugoslavs. I do not know why we should object to it.

On this note the hearings ended.

The jury is out

The Fulbright hearings were an event of significance. *Newsweek* hailed them as "the most searching public review of U.S. wartime policy since the 1951 hearings on Capitol Hill prompted by Harry Truman's firing of General Douglas MacArthur." One of the committee members, Senator Frank Church, was convinced that the proceedings were a resounding success because of their educational function of airing the issues on Vietnam. We accomplished, he said, what we had set out to do: "To inquire both behind and beyond Vietnam, to try to determine where we are, how we got there, and where we are going."

The Foreign Relations Committee received some twenty thousand letters and telegrams, most of which thanked the committee for exploring the tangle of questions surrounding America's commitment to South Vietnam. Several letters expressed disappointment that Secretary of Defense McNamara had not testified. One commented: "If American boys die in South Vietnam, McNamara should explain in public."

Lyndon Johnson, who from the start had sought to drown out the hearings with presidential fanfare, was unimpressed with the outcome of the proceedings. "From what I read," he told a press conference, "I don't see that they have done any harm to anybody." If by "harm" the president meant inciting greater opposition to his Vietnam policy, he was right. In terms of eroding public support for the war, the hearings had a negligible effect. Although mail to the committee ran thirty to one against escalation of the war, new polls showed 53 percent of Americans favoring "more offensive ground war."

The hearings had focused on international relations, military strategy, "cold war" political theories, counterinsurgency and wars of national liberation, and global confrontations, topics generally unfamiliar to the "folks at home." Not surprisingly, a lot of viewers in the television audience thought the hearings were uninteresting, a bore. One woman from Cleveland wrote the committee advising it to "conduct any further inquiry in private, or between 4:30 P.M. and 7:30 P.M. Interference of regular daytime tele-

vision programming is losing you the support of the housewives." One of the networks televising the hearings, CBS, judged likewise and decided to broadcast a rerun of "I Love Lucy" instead of George Kennan's testimony.

In the Senate itself, the hearings seemed to exert no immediate negative impact on the president's consensus. Despite much criticism in the hearings directed at the administration's policy, few senators were ready to lessen their support of the White House. When Senator Morse introduced a bill a few days later to repeal the Tonkin Gulf resolution, his measure was defeated, ninety-two to five. The Senate then went on to approve a $12 billion military appropriation for the war.

From a longer-term perspective, however, the hearings did "harm" the administration. They gave the American press an opportunity to give broad, in-depth coverage to basic questions about the nation's involvement in Vietnam and to broach subjects previously ignored or superficially treated. They served to legitimize public debate on the war and established a framework for future inquiry. Some members of Congress also noticed something special about the hearings. Said Democratic Senator Joseph Clark of Pennsylvania, "Between Jim Gavin and George Kennan, we've broken the sound barrier. The policy of nonescalation has now become respectable." For antiwar activists and the small group of dissidents in Congress, the testimony of Gavin and Kennan helped them shed somewhat the image of being on the radical fringe of American public opinion about the war and would inspire them to redouble their efforts to end the war in South Vietnam.

The Congress, and the populace as a whole, were beginning to divide into "hawks" and "doves," words that became prominent in the national vocabulary to describe those supporting President Johnson's war policy and those opposing it. The years 1966 and 1967 belonged to the hawks, but the discord was to grow and to confront the country with severe political and social trials.

Operation Prairie

Heavily laden marines patrol near the DMZ during Operation Prairie. Their objective: to seek out and destroy invading enemy units from NVA Division 324B.

An aerial view of the "Rockpile," which the NVA tried unsuccessfully to take from U.S. Marines during Operation Prairie. Seven-hundred-foot-high sheer cliffs limited resupply of the marine squad atop the promontory to helicopter drops.

During Operation Hastings in July 1966, the U.S. Marines repelled NVA Division 324B's invasion of Quang Tri Province and forced the division to withdraw into the DMZ. But in the first week of August American intelligence discovered that 324B was moving back into Quang Tri and establishing fortified positions in the jungle-covered western mountains. The enemy's goal was to capture the Rockpile and launch an assault on Quang Tri's populous coastal region.

The marines immediately responded to the threat. On August 3, the day he ended Hastings, Brigadier General Lowell English, commander of the 3d Marine Division, launched Operation Prairie. In Prairie eleven marine battalions (nearly eleven thousand men) would face the same opposition and the same kind of combat as they had in Hastings. Their objective was also unchanged: preventing 324B from gaining a foothold below the DMZ for an attack on South Vietnam's northernmost provinces.

General English ordered marine reconnaissance teams to explore trail areas for signs of enemy reinfiltration and to call in artillery from Cam Lo and helicopter gunships and air power from Da Nang and Chu Lai for support. One top marine planner explained the marines' strategy: "If we sat back in defensive positions along the coast, the enemy would mass very large forces and make it difficult for us. But we are not sitting back, we are moving all the time, searching him out and hitting him before he can become set."

But, as in many large U.S. operations in Vietnam, the marines spent most of their time searching out the enemy. NVA units were, for the most part, well concealed, often revealing themselves only when certain they had superior numbers. Reconnaissance units endured long, uneventful marches through some of the densest jungle encountered by Americans in Vietnam.

When the marines were able to "fix" the NVA, the fighting proved bloody and intense. Most of Prairie's major action took part in the early going. In one fight, later called the Groucho Marx battle, thirty-two marines held off assaults by some 300 NVA for two days in early August, killing 37 enemy while suffering only five deaths of their own. Contact was regular throughout August and included heavy U.S. tank assaults of NVA positions as well as an appearance by "Puff the Magic Dragon"—the AC-47 gunship—over Razorback Ridge.

During a fire fight for Mutter Ridge, four marines recover the body of a comrade near Hill 484. "We were in the opening approaching a forty-foot rise," said photographer Larry Burrows. "Our point man ran to the top of the hill and was shot dead."

155

The battle for Mutter Ridge

The longest, fiercest fight in Prairie took place in mid-September, when General English decided to attack the elaborate fortifications being constructed by 324B along a ridge near Razorback. Hills 400 and 484 were the marines' objectives in the battle for Mutter Ridge, named after the radio call signal of the 3d Battalion, 4th Marines, engaged in the battle. Resupplied each night by helicopter so they would be unencumbered by food and camp gear, the marines began their assault on September 22. They had to move through undergrowth in murky darkness—almost no light filtered through the one-hundred-foot-high double canopy of trees and sometimes bombs had to be used to cut a path through the jungle.

On the morning of September 23, as the 3d Battalion's lead elements approached Hill 400, one marine captain recalled "moving along some of the lower hills [where] we saw more and more enemy positions, including enough huts in the ravines to harbor a regiment, and piles and piles of ammunition. NVA bodies lying about and hastily dug graves were signs that we were moving in right behind them." Company K pushed forward to Hill 400 but encountered NVA troops in heavily reinforced bunkers. The enemy counterattacked, assisted by spotters in the trees who directed fire. Yet, at a cost of six marines and fifty enemy, the marines controlled Hill 400 by that afternoon.

On Hill 484 NVA resistance was even stiffer. A frontal assault by the marines on October 4 was thrown back by NVA soldiers tossing grenades from the upper slope. The marines pulled back while air and artillery pounded the hill. The next morning, following another air strike, the 2d Platoon of the 3d Battalion's Company M gained the crest at noon. Fleeing into the jungle, the enemy left behind ten bodies and numerous blood trails that marked the evacuation of many wounded. The battle for the ridge was over. The 3d Battalion, 4th Marines, had driven NVA Division 324B back into the DMZ, in the process losing twenty dead but killing one hundred enemy.

A bloodied marine reaches out to a comrade-at-arms near Hill 484.

Left and above. The faces of American marines reflect the bitterness of Operation Prairie.

Above right. A marine gunner shoulders his rocket launcher during the fight against the enemy and the elements south of the DMZ.

Right. A wounded marine awaits medical evacuation to a base hospital.

Photographing the War

Larry Burrows, who took several of the photographs shown here of Operation Prairie for *Life* magazine, was one of the best of the photographers who covered the Vietnam War and a man beloved by his colleagues and the troops whose risks and hardships he shared. "You can't photograph bullets flying through the air," he once said. "So it must be the wounded, or people running loaded with ammunition, and the expressions on their faces." Burrows covered the war for nine years, surviving repeated exposures to danger—until one day in February of 1971 when a helicopter in which he was flying over Laos was shot down by the North Vietnamese. There were no survivors.

A marine mortarman at Con Thien digs up the base plate for his 81MM after night action in support of Operation Prairie. Monsoon rains caused the base plate to sink deeper into the mud with the firing of each round.

A marine leaves his foxhole on Hill 484 after NVA division 324B has been driven from Mutter Ridge by the 3/4 Marines.

Following Mutter Ridge, the action in Prairie tailed off, with a few intense skirmishes in October as the monsoon brought the first heavy rains. The last major fighting of the operation took place in November in the Caubretviet Valley, five miles southwest of Dong Ha, when U.S. Marines contacted a reinforced NVA company of two hundred. By January 1966 Prairie became, as the marine history described it, "no longer an operation but rather an area of operations."

Prairie had solved the immediate problem of 324B's reinfiltration. The marines held the Rockpile and forced the NVA to postpone their invasion of Quang Tri for another year. The 1,297 known enemy dead (at a cost of over 200 Americans killed) convinced the enemy to shift temporarily from Main Force warfare to guerrilla tactics. But if American firepower proved decisive, the enemy, despite their heavy losses, was already preparing for future incursions into Quang Tri. General English summed up: "I'm sure of one thing. Although we've definitely killed more than 2,000 in Hastings and Prairie combined, and probably a lot more, they haven't quit."

Men of Company H and S of the 3d Battalion, 4th Marines, prepare for a patrol near Con Thien in November 1966. Although Prairie lasted until January 1967, encounters with the enemy were infrequent during the operation's last two months.

A Year of Momentum?

"Nation building," the Americans called it, "rice-roots democracy." In September 1966, after years of authoritarian government by the military, free elections for South Vietnam's constitutional assembly were about to take place. Throughout the country 541 candidates campaigned for 108 seats in the assembly amid a blaze of red and yellow Vietnamese flags and the blare of political slogans from sound trucks. Banners and placards posted all over Saigon carried the message: "TO VOTE IS TO BEGIN BUILDING DEMOCRACY."

Despite Vietcong threats "to smash the election farce of the U.S. aggressors and their henchmen in Saigon," 81 percent of the country's 5,280,000 registered voters turned out on September 11 for the first national election since 1963. The newly elected members of the constituent assembly would face a formidable task: writing a constitution, the country's second in a decade, and formulating guidelines for the presidential elec-

One of Saigon's hundreds of street vendors displays his wares. Many consumer items, especially appliances, American clothing, and luxury items like jewelry and perfume, were available only through the city's flourishing black market.

tions scheduled for September 1967. These efforts were hampered, however, by the two generals presiding over South Vietnam's military junta, Nguyen Cao Ky and Nguyen Van Thieu.

When the Central Election Council refused to approve the Thieu and Ky military ticket for the scheduled presidential contest because the generals would not resign from office before the elections as the new constitution re-

quired, the junta decided to extort a "change of heart" from the assembly. First came intimidation: the murder of Tran Van Van, one of the assembly's most outspoken proponents of civilian rule. Tran's widow blamed his assassination on General Nguyen Ngoc Loan, a close lieutenant of Ky and head of the National Police. The evidence pointed that way, and many western correspondents agreed with her. While General Loan strode on the balcony with two armed guards and troops stationed themselves outside the building, the assembly backed down. Thieu and Ky did not have to resign from the junta after all. The presidential elections, the climax of South Vietnam's "experiment in freedom," were next on the agenda.

Preceding page. During a vicious twelve-day fight for the Khe Sanh Valley in May 1967, U.S. Marines under fire charge heavily fortified NVA positions on artillery-torn Hill 881 North.

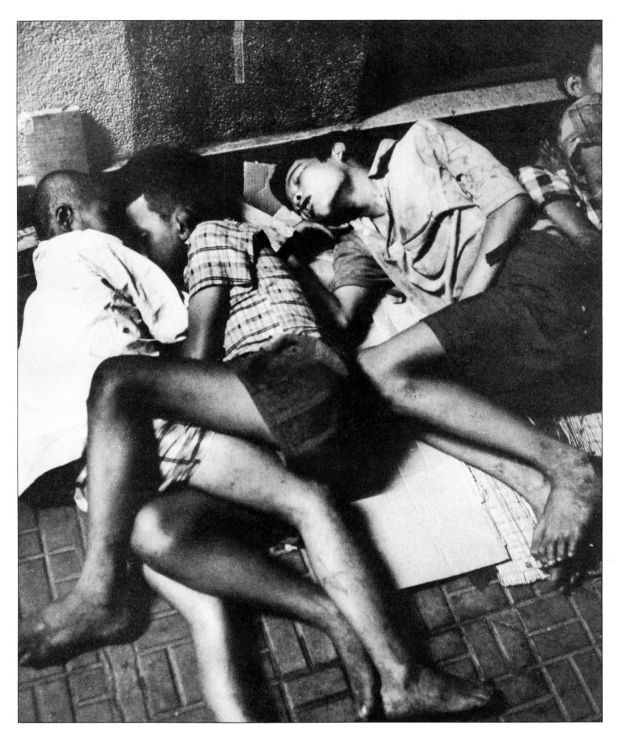

Homeless boys asleep on a Saigon street where they live.

Democracy at work

August 6, 1967, was the opening of South Vietnam's presidential candidates' twenty-two-province campaign tour. The ten civilian candidates and their running mates waited an hour and a half at Saigon's Tan Son Nhut Airport for a representative from the ticket of Thieu and Ky. According to election procedures mandated by the junta, the military candidates were supposed to travel with the other candidates, and the government was to provide transportation, distribute campaign funds, and arrange all speaking engagements. When no government repre-

sentative showed up, the frustrated candidates then boarded a plane and left for Quang Tri Province.

At Dong Ha, the provincial airport seven miles outside Quang Tri City, the candidates found themselves stranded once more: no government escort, no official welcome, no transportation. After cooling their heels for forty-five minutes, they flew to Da Nang, where they vented their fury. The leader of the Dai Viet party said, "Ky and Thieu agreed in advance to play this trick on us." The government, in the person of Premier Ky, responded with disdain. "What did they expect," said Ky, the military candidate for vice president, "a Mercedes? They are not presidents yet, but already they are acting like bosses."

Despite the fiasco at Quang Tri, the campaign continued. So did the incessant bickering. At almost every stop on the month-long campaign tour, the civilian candidates spent much of their time denouncing government "sabotage" of the election. A number of civilian candidates issued a joint communiqué alleging that "government authorities have taken measures to prevent voters from contacting candidates [and] have given instructions to civil servants and plainclothes men to occupy all the seats in the theater where the public talks by candidates will be held." One candidate, Tran Van Huong, leveled the accusation that "There are organized bands of hooligans charged not only with insulting our campaign workers, but also with mistreating and beating them up."

Thieu and Ky, to mollify the American Embassy, gave public assurances that "campaign procedures" would be improved. Thieu, disclaiming any connection with harassment of civilian candidates, indicated that "a couple of months ago I had a meeting with all the chiefs of police from all the provinces. And I told them not to intimidate or use their authority to crush the people. Until now, I have heard nothing about this." Public statements like these seemed to reassure the U.S. Embassy, or so Thieu and Ky thought. Ky confided to reporters, "The Americans come to see me and they tell me they want a free election. I promise I'll give them one and they smile. Then they say they believe me and then I smile."

Because of the haggling over campaign details, the presidential race quickly degenerated into a comic opera. A *New York Times* correspondent, R. W. Apple, wrote, "The Vietnamese are acting like Vietnamese. The politicians and the generals are showing the world, at a moment of crisis, just how sentimental, prideful, suspicious, conspiratorial, and stiff-necked they can be." It was not as if the candidates had no serious, substantial issues to debate. The most obvious was that of war and peace.

But the generals of the junta had seen to it that peace, in any context, would not be an issue in the campaign. After much arm twisting by the government, the National Assembly had disqualified the two most prominent "peace candidates," An Truong Thanh, a former minister for economic affairs in Ky's own cabinet, and former General Duong Van Minh, then exiled in Bangkok. The National Police branded Thanh, who advocated a cease-fire, a "Marxist." Ky dispensed with Minh simply by not allowing his return to South Vietnam.

Other serious problems, the sort that Americans would have found familiar issues in an election, afflicted the country but were ignored in the campaign: inflation and the economy, crime and corruption. The year 1966 had certainly been a bad one for South Vietnam's economy. Inflation had soared to 30 percent. The money supply in piasters had risen by 72 percent, fueling a brisk black market in American dollars. Unbridled inflation hit particularly hard at working-class city dwellers forced to pay skyrocketing prices for food and housing. The cost of living index for urban residents rose by 92 percent for 1966 alone. And with the war in rural areas depressing domestic rice production, they faced exorbitant prices for imported rice as well as periodic shortages.

U.S. Ambassador Henry Cabot Lodge was quick to recognize the political ramifications of South Vietnam's "wildcat inflation," which "could be an even more pressing danger—even more so than defeat in battle." Premier Ky, with his customary bravado, offered nothing more to cope with an economy careening out of control than outrageous threats. *Time* magazine reported Ky as saying, "I'll govern this country like a military command. If I say the price of rice should drop, what I want to see is a price drop. Even if I have to . . ." cocking his thumb and forefinger like a pistol, "twenty or thirty people."

U.S. officials had been endeavoring to alleviate the inflationary effects of so many American troops and dollars in South Vietnam by reviving the Commercial Import Program used there in the 1950s. The U.S. purchased consumer goods for import by South Vietnam with foreign aid dollars which it paid directly to exporters. South Vietnamese importers then bought these goods with piasters that went into a fund from which the GVN could finance its operations. The goal was to prevent an influx of American dollars that would put inflationary pressure on the piaster and prices for goods. Although the program kept the inflation rate between 25 and 30 percent, compared to the 2,700 percent rise in prices in South Korea during the Korean War, only a minority of Vietnamese—mostly wealthy urban consumers—benefited from the goods it made available. In part, this was because of poor transportation and shipping connections between the cities and rural villages.

The bulk of the problem stemmed from endemic corruption among South Vietnamese military authorities and civilian officials who cut for themselves a huge chunk of the U.S. aid. American refrigerators meant for hospitals, for instance, found their way to the homes and villas of army generals. Military commanders in the field developed their own racket, collecting the pay of "phantom soldiers," men who had been killed but whose deaths were not reported to Saigon. One trick in favor with some province chiefs was to blow up a bridge within their jurisdiction, blame the Vietcong, and win a fat contract from Saigon to replace it.

The government's administration of the aid program was so lax that even the Vietcong had little trouble taking "a piece of the action." U.S. soldiers discovered in captured VC camps entrenchments reinforced by imported American metal plates, as well as homemade mortars constructed from U.S.-made steel pipe; and a brand-new metal-working lathe, imported through the Commercial Import plan, was found buried under a pile of manure being transported aboard a VC sampan.

Financial and political corruption were twin ravagers

Three fashionably dressed Vietnamese women stroll past a public execution site (behind sandbag wall) in downtown Saigon, 1966.

in South Vietnam. While government officials enriched themselves off American aid, the general public—the poor, laborers, and lower middle classes—was left, in many cases, to fend for itself. Nevertheless, all these conditions remained nonissues in South Vietnam's rancorous 1967 presidential debate.

Watching the show

The American establishment in South Vietnam took a keen interest in the junta's version of democratic change. As one American reporter commented, "This election and all the trappings have excited the Americans a lot more than the Vietnamese." Washington had been clamoring for elections for two years, and the job of making sure they would happen had been assigned to a variety of U.S. in-country representatives: the embassy, the CIA, the U.S. Information Agency, and several "election experts" called in to consult.

Throughout the months preceding the elections in the fall of 1967, the United States had adopted an official neutrality toward the presidential candidates, but it was convinced that the military junta offered the best base for stability in South Vietnam. Washington employed diplomatic pressure to insure that the generals would not squabble but cooperate in choosing a mutually acceptable military ticket. Intense rivalry between Thieu and Ky for the top spot in the government during the late spring and early

summer, however, had threatened to throw the junta into turmoil and upset the elections.

Following the constituent assembly elections in 1966, it had looked to Americans in Saigon as if General Thieu had the presidential spot on the military ticket all wrapped up. Ky had publicly announced that he would not run for president in 1967. "I'm sure they [the people] would love me more as an airman," he had quipped. But then the notoriously unpredictable young premier changed his mind. American officials were in a dither in May 1967 when Ky, as well as Thieu, declared himself a candidate for president. Ky, ever the deft calculator, felt that he had much in his favor. Because he already held the country's number one job—the office of premier—Ky thought that he would appear, at least in the eyes of the Vietnamese public, as the natural front runner. He strove to reinforce the impression. His campaign symbol, a flying black dragon, was shown nightly on the state-owned television channel. Billboards plastered the countryside with Ky's message to woo villagers and peasants: THE GOVERNMENT OF NGUYEN CAO KY IS THE GOVERNMENT OF THE POOR.

What Ky banked on most in his race for the presidency was his reputation as a favorite of the Americans. The premier's public relations triumph with President Johnson at Honolulu in February 1966 had bolstered his ego. "Ky came back from Honolulu," one Vietnamese politician noted, "acting as if he were an adopted son of President

"Ky," a caricaturist's view.

The making of a president

September 3, 1967, 4:00 P.M. Election day in South Vietnam. The polls in the country's forty-four provinces and municipalities were closing. It had been a busy day. In nine hours, 4,868,266 people out of 5,853,251 registered voters had visited thousands of polling stations to cast their votes for president, an 83 percent turnout. Two days later the results were announced: Nguyen Van Thieu would be the president and Nguyen Cao Ky the vice president of South Vietnam. The American establishment in Washington and Saigon was pleased. A State Department spokesman acclaimed the election as a "major step forward." "It is an important and heartening fact," he stated, "that 83 percent who registered actually voted—a much higher percentage than in our presidential election of 1964."

President Johnson's hand-picked team of American election observers in South Vietnam—senators, governors, and respected citizens—was positive in its assessment of the fairness of the election. Senator George Murphy of California ventured to call the elections not "unlike an election in Beverly Hills." Democratic Governor Richard J. Hughes of New Jersey dismissed the possibility that the South Vietnamese might have hoodwinked the observers: "We could all possibly have been bamboozled, but it would have taken a minimum of 25,000 character actors and about 11,000 stagehands to put on the production we have seen."

Many Vietnamese had doubts about the fairness of the election. One Vietnamese businessman commented, "Ninety-nine percent of the people think it's a fraudulent election, but they are voting because it is the proper thing to do." There were also indications that the heavy turnout had much to do with government coercion and fears of retaliation against those not showing up at the polls. Since election officials stamped each voter's identification card, it was widely suspected that lacking this "symbol of loyalty" to the government would lead to trouble later, perhaps even charges of being VC.

In the wake of the elections, President Johnson sought to justify American involvement in Vietnam as a sacrifice in support of a "legitimate," elected government representing the will of the South Vietnamese people. But the will of how many South Vietnamese people? By official U.S. estimates about one-third of South Vietnam's population of nearly 17 million was in VC-controlled territory and so could not vote. The government itself disqualified tens of thousands of voters, and many Buddhists, the victims of harsh treatment by the junta, boycotted the election. Furthermore, the military ticket of Thieu and Ky received only 35 percent of the votes cast, hardly a popular mandate. Election rules mandated by the junta stipulated that no matter how low the percentage of votes secured by a winning candidate, there would be no run-off election, for that

Johnson." The fact that U.S. Ambassador Henry Cabot Lodge had shown him partiality seemed to further enhance his chances.

By late June 1967, however, the political winds in South Vietnam were blowing against Ky. General Thieu had not been idle. Despite Ky's premiership, his public appeal, and his obvious rapport with many Americans, Thieu had quietly risen to dominance among the other generals of the junta. From the junta's point of view, Thieu was an ideal candidate. Whereas Ky was a northerner, Thieu was a native southerner and married to a woman from the delta. In a land that reveres age and experience, that Thieu was seven years older than Ky—forty-four to Ky's thirty-seven—gave him an added advantage. Most important, Thieu, shrewd, patient, and unobtrusive, commanded more respect, both as a military man and a political leader, than his rival Ky, whom many resented for his cockiness and volatile temper.

On June 29, 1967, the day before the deadline for filing official candidacy for the presidential campaign, the generals of the junta decided to resolve the Thieu-Ky crisis. At a meeting of fifty high-ranking officers in a smoke-filled room at Tan Son Nhut air base, Ky and Thieu were allowed to make their cases. Charges flew back and forth: Ky called Thieu corrupt, Thieu returned the accusation. But it was quickly apparent to Ky that Thieu had done his spade work among the other generals, leaving the premier with little support for his candidacy. A dispirited Ky finally conceded. When he emerged from the military enclave on the morning of the thirtieth, the premier announced that he would be Nguyen Van Thieu's vice-presidential running mate.

might have allowed civilian candidates the opportunity to join forces on a second ballot.

Most Vietnamese, wrote Robert Shaplen in a dispatch to the *New Yorker*, felt that American-style elections were forced on them, with little relevance to their own political dynamics and conditions, that the elections were "simply an American-directed performance with a Vietnamese cast." As long as many Vietnamese believed the Thieu-Ky regime was not the majority's choice, it did not matter how hard the GVN would try to make it appear that way or how sincerely the Americans believed it. Meanwhile, the war went on.

1967: a year of momentum?

General William Westmoreland, in his "Report on the War in Vietnam" to CINCPAC Admiral Ulysses S. Grant Sharp, described 1967 as a year of "momentum" for U.S. forces fighting in South Vietnam: "Additional troops enabled the scope and pace of our offensive operations to in-

crease steadily throughout the year. U.S. strength increased from 385,000 to 486,000. The number of maneuver battalions available to allied forces rose from 256 to 278. By year's end twenty-eight tactical fighter squadrons were on hand to provide close in [air] support and assist in the interdiction campaign [against NVA infiltration]."

Westmoreland was convinced that U.S. "spoiling attacks" in 1966, like Operation Abilene in April and Hawthorne in June, against Main Force enemy units mobilizing to strike at densely inhabited coastal areas and cities had been effective. The net effect on the strategic situation in 1967, as he saw it, was that VC "Main Force units were almost exclusively employed in remote border areas and along the DMZ or in difficult mountain or jungle terrain . . . . The commander of enemy forces in the south thought that he could not afford to engage his growing Main Force units at greater distance from their border sanctuaries without exposing them to destruction by the firepower of the highly mobile allied forces." Westmoreland decided it was time to go out after them.

A South Vietnamese army veteran, wounded in the hand during combat, casts his vote at the Dong Hoa army hospital in IV Corps during the constituent assembly elections of September 1966.

A remote-control camera outside the door of a C-130 photographs men of the 2d Battalion, 503d Infantry, 173d Airborne Brigade, during Operation Junction City, making the first of five U.S. combat parachute assaults made during the Vietnam War.

MACV outlined its 1967 campaign to penetrate enemy sanctuaries in outlying border provinces and near the demilitarized zone in its annual campaign plan. The plan fused both military and pacification operations, assigning most of the military half of the campaign to American forces. They would shift their tactical focus from sweeping populated coastal provinces, as they had in past operations like Starlite, Piranha, and Thayer, to attacking suspected enemy enclaves in border regions and along the DMZ.

Behind the shield of American offensives, designed to clear areas of VC and NVA units, MACV expected ARVN to secure and pacify them. Pacification and the Main Force war, Westmoreland stressed, "were essentially inseparable—opposite sides of the same coin." In the previous two years, ARVN commanders had balked at being relegated to what they deemed the subordinate role of pacification. But Westmoreland wanted ARVN in the villages. ARVN soldiers, he reasoned, understand "the language, customs, problems, and aspirations of the Vietnamese people [and are] much better suited to measures requiring some degree of population control than U.S. Marines." Thus MACV's campaign plan posed a critical test of its dual strategy of search and destroy and pacification. It was on to War Zone C and an army exercise called

Junction City (see map, page 175).

Strategy for victory

Paratroopers of the 2d Battalion, 503d Infantry, attached to the 173d, were tense and quiet aboard the fleet of sixteen C-130s making its ascent from Bien Hoa air base on February 22, 1967, toward War Zone C, an approximately thirty-by-fifty-mile stretch of jungle adjacent to Cambodia. Sergeant Leon Hostake, jumpmaster on the seventh plane in line, had been in action before and knew the feeling. He had once dodged sniper fire on a jump in Korea. "Don't sweat it," he told his men. "After those B-52 strikes, if there are any [VC] in the drop zone, they'll be dead ones."

The jump had been Lieutenant Colonel Robert Sigholtz's idea. He had persuaded the brass to go along by emphasizing the difficulty of putting his battalion into the landing zone swiftly enough by helicopter. A couple of hours and 120 helicopter loads would be necessary to get the battalion on the ground and fighting. But with paratroopers and a handful of C-130s, Sigholtz argued, he could have the whole group of 845 men down in an open field amid the thickly wooded terrain of War Zone C and combat ready in ten minutes. MACV, intent on the element of surprise, gave its approval. When the light aboard the C-130 flashed "Go," Sigholtz and his men made the first combat parachute assault of the Vietnam War.

On the ground, things were going almost exactly according to plan. The 25th Infantry Division, controlling five brigades, had been airlifted in by helicopters to form a horseshoe-shaped cordon in the western half of War Zone C. They were to act as a blocking force along the Cambodian border. One of the operation's principal objectives was to capture Vietcong headquarters thought to be in the area and to engage, if possible, the Vietcong 9th Division. The next day, February 23, forces including the U.S. Army 1st Infantry Division, positioned at the southern edge of the horseshoe, would attack north, conducting search and destroy operations. Simultaneously, the paratroopers of the 503d Airborne would sweep west from their blocking position along the Saigon River. A Special Forces and CIDG camp was also to be established at Prek Klok to maintain surveillance of possible enemy reinfiltration after the de-

parture of main U.S. invasion forces. In addition, extensive clearing by Rome plows and bulldozers would strip tracts of jungle to deprive the enemy of concealment. Almost 30,000 American troops would be involved.

By February 24, all sweep maneuvers were underway. Resistance was light and scattered. One observer attributed this to the difficulty of locating the enemy in the dense jungle and to the noise and confusion of American air strikes, artillery, motorized units, and clearing equipment:

Typically, the three mechanized units bringing up the right side of the horseshoe sent out two columns apiece, but each was so far out of sight of the other that they left wide gaps for the Vietcong to slip through. For the foot soldiers, it was much the same. . . . Bravo Company of the 1st Battalion, 27th Infantry, 25th Infantry Division, walked through a tangled teak forest to within fifteen yards of a Vietcong base camp before the men realized they had almost stumbled into it. Then it was too late. The VC opened up from their trenches and the Americans had to pull back. Only after the air force pummeled the area for an hour did

One of thousands of documents uncovered in a VC tunnel complex during Operation Junction City, this photo shows what U.S. intelligence thought to be a meeting of Vietcong battalion commanders. Since only officers carried revolvers, the weapons suspended above the heads of the Vietcong signify their high rank.

A soldier of the 1st Infantry Division dodges enemy fire during Operation Junction City.

the infantrymen enter the camp—which was now completely deserted.

Three days into the operation, the sweep had killed only forty-two Vietcong, with fourteen American dead and ninety-three wounded. As one American official explained: "It was a classic military operation and it worked as it was scheduled to work. But the Vietcong—so far—have pulled a perfect countersweep [to evade the American sweep]." In succeeding days, the $25 million operation continued to be disappointing, prompting *Newsweek* correspondents at the end of March to ask "Whatever happened to Junction City?"

Pacification problems

In his evaluation of Junction City, General Westmoreland discounted North Vietnamese General Vo Nguyen Giap's claim that the operation represented a "big victory for the Vietcong," calling it "exaggeration." In his account Giap had erroneously reported American KIAs as 13,500, over forty-six times the actual number. Westmoreland was also guilty of exaggeration when he portrayed Junction City as a "disaster" for the enemy. "War Zone C," the American commander boasted, "an inviolate stronghold for many years was now vulnerable to allied forces any time we choose to enter." But Lieutenant General Bernard Rogers in his history of Junction City, written seven years later, noted that "reconnaissance flights over War Zone C fol-

lowing Junction City revealed that the enemy was returning." Rogers wrote that "One of the discouraging features of ... Junction City was the fact that we had insufficient forces ... to permit us to continue to operate [in War Zone C] and thereby prevent the Vietcong from returning."

What was happening with pacification, "the other side of the coin" of General Westmoreland's main force strategy? Operation Junction City did not include plans for pacification either during or after the operation. MACV considered War Zone C, like the Iron Triangle, a Vietcong stronghold outside the reach, for the time being, of pacification. That such large tracts of territory so close to Saigon had to be excluded from the pacification program, however, was a disturbing reminder of the GVN's lack of progress in this crucial aspect of the war.

On paper, the South Vietnamese had the resources to follow through on pacification. The Saigon government's Revolutionary Development (RD) program, employing an "army" of fifty-nine-member pacification teams, was due to be fully implemented by 1967. As many as fifty ARVN infantry battalions, as well as three ranger, one marine, and three airborne battalions, were made available to provide back-up for the teams. Regional and Popular Forces units could also act as support for pacification.

But despite impressive resources, the South Vietnamese pacification effort lagged dismally. MACV's search and destroy oriented strategy was partly at fault. One frustrated American officer defined the problem after Junction City: "If they [the enemy] don't want to stand and fight, if they break down into groups of two or three or five, it's almost impossible to throw a net they can't exfiltrate through." Consequently, search and destroy offensives did not effectively clear a highly mobile enemy force from areas of operation, making pacification a very difficult task for the South Vietnamese.

In I Corps pacification was in a chaotic state. After Premier Ky had crushed the Buddhist political organization there in 1966, the Vietcong had extended its influence by capitalizing on hostility toward the government. As a result, in January 1967 in Quang Nam Province, according to U.S. Marine estimates, out of a total of 549 hamlets only 18 could be classified "secure." Some 246 hamlets, with a total population of 171,241, were considered to be under undisputed Vietcong control, while the rest were designated as "contested."

Even provinces in the vicinity of Saigon itself showed little progress in pacification. In Long An, just south of the capital, American pacification advisers reckoned that of almost 600 hamlets there the government controlled fewer than 90, control of a hamlet being measured by the willingness of government officials to spend the night there.

Indiscriminate application of American artillery and air power often complicated ARVN's job of rooting out the political infrastructure of the NLF within the civilian population. The resultant disruption of civilian life—casualties, bombed villages, and destroyed crops—directed resentment not at the NLF but at South Vietnamese pacification workers. The inflicting of civilian casualties in particular (estimated by a U.S. Congressional committee at the end of 1967 to be one hundred fifty thousand, perhaps two hundred thousand) frequently produced more enemies for Saigon than friends. After a field study in 1967, a report by Senator Edward Kennedy's Senate Subcommittee on Refugees stated that over 80 percent of the refugees interviewed for the study "claimed that they were either deposited in [refugee] camps by the Americans or fled to camps in fear of American airplanes and artillery."

While in the spring of 1967 the lack of a workable pacification program received much attention from American officials trying to devise a solution, MACV reports of the progress of Westmoreland's handling of the American military offensive—the war of attrition—buoyed President Johnson as he confronted mounting criticism of his Vietnam policy. The president asked the general to come home and, in the wake of Operation Junction City, give a report to the American public on the state of the war.

Westmoreland reports to America

On the morning of April 28, 1967, the members of Congress jammed the chamber of the U.S. House of Representatives, and the galleries overflowed with journalists, photographers, dignitaries, and ordinary citizens. Television cameras conveyed the scene to millions around the country. In the sudden silence of the chamber, House

After marking a landing zone with a smoke grenade, GIs fighting in Junction City wave in a medical evacuation helicopter to remove their wounded.

Liftoff into Battle

by Robert Frost

Our company, a unit of the 52d Aviation Battalion, was on the coast north of Qui Nhon in the third week of February 1967 when the word about Junction City arrived. Major Joseph "Uncle Joe" Parlas, our company commander, had flown over from Pleiku to brief us on the mission. Late that afternoon Captain Norm Gustitus, company operations officer, called us together and said something about going "down south" for an operation. There would be just enough time to make one of our laundry stops in Ban Me Thuot and take off early the next morning for the operation staging area at Bien Hoa. This sort of briefing was typical. Rarely were we told how long the stay would be, who would be supported, or what would be done. The details, as usual, were received on arrival. So in the late afternoon, in the hot sun, sand, and whipping dust of Qui Nhon, the company broke camp. Twenty-six helicopters, all equipment, and over one hundred thirty men were gone in less than forty-five minutes, headed west at 1,000 feet. In the moment after liftoff I imagined the flies, the sand fleas, the centipedes, the scorpions, and the mites all moving back in before dark. I knew the urchins, scavengers, and the VC would.

Back in the corral at Ban Me Thuot each pilot showered, changed clothes, relaxed for a moment, and immediately started preparing for tomorrow. Uncle Joe opened up the clubs for two hours so everyone could get some beer—but no whiskey—since we had been dry for over a week up at Qui Nhon. The crews didn't bother unloading the tents and operational gear from the Qui Nhon mission. They just loaded up a supply truck and drove down the flight line stopping at each bird to bring the basic load of ammo, smoke grenades, batteries, radios, oil, hydraulic fluid, and C-rations up to snuff. By 10:00 P.M. the company was refitted, ready to go, and dog tired.

Before Morning Nautical Twilight (BMNT) was an insidious invention of the army; it meant you always got up too damn early. Silhouettes in the darkness before a rat fuck (combat assault) have a kind of fatalistic presence. Each man moved in silence, buried in his own thoughts, and readied himself and his bird for war. Few words were spoken. There was a sense that Junction City would be no piece of cake.

Uncle Joe took off for Bien Hoa ahead of us with the maintenance unit to act as the advance party. We then cranked our slicks and lifted off for the dash to Bien Hoa. On approach into Bien Hoa each of us realized our suspicion. This was to be a huge operation. Our helicopters were part of at least ten other chopper companies trying to land at Bien Hoa, all at the same time. Landing smoke pots dotted the periphery of the runway, where some two hundred helicopters landed while air force F-4 and Thud fighter-bombers were landing and taking off in formation. Around us in other open fields, more hives were gathering in their bees.

After landing, the key officers gravitated to Uncle Joe for the operation details and marking of maps. The roar and activity around the staging area was deafening. Against this backdrop, under the morning sun, we learned what Junction City was to accomplish. Our unit would carry in four combat assault groups, two of Australians and two of Americans. Our departure was in one hour. We briefed our crews, refueled, and ate cold C-rations, all at the same time.

Lifting off in staggered formation the company went for the Australians first. The approach to the pickup site brought with it the smell of cordite. The ground was pockmarked with smoldering artillery and bomb craters. The Aussies were ready, all queued up in lines of eight. On touchdown they jumped aboard and in less than ten seconds we were off, jockeying into a large V formation headed straight for War Zone C. More companies in similar Vs followed, in front, behind, and alongside us. The sky was a blanket of warbirds full of infantry, each covey protected by its gunships and roaring forward, formations within formations. It was an awesome sight, an unstoppable juggernaut closing with the enemy. Surrounded in this aerial charge, I cried, "My God, this is history. It looks like a thousand helicopters!"

As the LZ came into sight it seemed a ball of erupting carnage, flame, trees, chunks of earth, and death. The endless staccato of small arms and machine-gun fire from the VC awaited us. Our door-gunners returned the fire while gunships fired their pairs of rockets. Suddenly, as if from nowhere, appeared two Skyraiders strafing with their .50-caliber machine guns and dropping bombs just seconds before we landed. The shock waves from those bombs made our birds vibrate. We quickly landed, all guns blazing. The Australians jumped out and hit the ground in prone combat fire and maneuver formation. Our Vs were up and gone in less than eight seconds, headed back for our second lift and the return to a different LZ. Each of our assaults was a repeat of the first. All this time the intensity never abated; the ground was one endless state of shock of odor, a mix of shells and cut grass.

Back at Bien Hoa about noon there was a refueling pause while the ground situation developed. More than ten thousand troops were now fighting their way through the jungle while we waited to bring in reserves and reinforcements. In that pause, while waiting in the sun, I sat on the skid of my bird, flak vest open, chickenplate loosened, so the sweat could pour out. With my elbows on my knees, leaning slightly forward holding the flight helmet by the chin strap so it would swing below my folded hands, I slowly lifted my head, my mind reeling from what had just been wrought. In that moment, I drank in the jubilation of victory, and I knew we were going to win this war.

Robert Frost served three tours of duty as a U.S. Army pilot in Vietnam. He now works with the Department of Environmental Quality Engineering of Massachusetts.

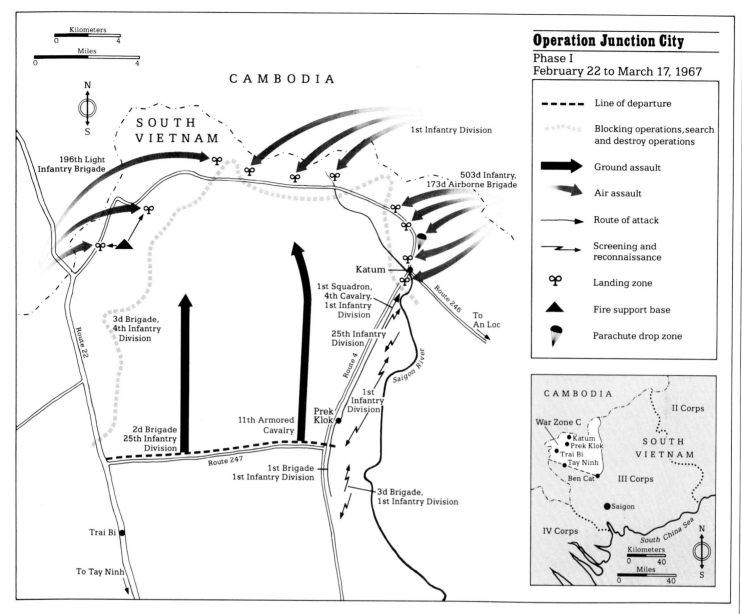

Operation Junction City

Phase I
February 22 to March 17, 1967

- - - - -   Line of departure

·········   Blocking operations, search and destroy operations

➤   Ground assault

➤   Air assault

→   Route of attack

⚡   Screening and reconnaissance

♈   Landing zone

▲   Fire support base

⛱   Parachute drop zone

Doorkeeper William Miller proceeded down the center aisle of the hushed chamber and announced, in his broad southern accent, "Mistah Speakah, Gen'ral William C. Westmoreland."

General Westmoreland's appearance before the Congress was unprecedented. General Eisenhower had stood before Congress to celebrate victory after World War II, and General MacArthur after his dismissal by President Truman, but no military leader had ever addressed such a joint meeting while directing an ongoing war. "I stand in the shadow of military men who have been here before me," Westmoreland began, "but none of them could have had more pride than is mine in representing the gallant men fighting in Vietnam today." He was not reporting imminent victory. He had come back to Washington with the message that the outcome of the war was as yet uncertain and the worst of the fighting was still to come. At a luncheon with Associated Press executives in New York City four days earlier, Westmoreland had warned, "I foresee, in the months ahead, some of the bitterest fighting of the war [with] no end in sight." In his twenty-eight-minute speech to Congress, Westmoreland praised the troops fighting in Vietnam and emphasized the progress made in thwarting the enemy's offensives. He also touched on the subject of antiwar activism. "In evaluating the enemy strategy," he said, "it is evident to me that our Achilles' heel is our resolve." Toward the close of his speech he roused his audience to its feet by declaring that, "Backed at home by resolve, confidence, patience, determination, and continued support, we will prevail in Vietnam over the Communist aggressor!"

Not everyone in Congress joined in the applause. Senator William Fulbright, among others, felt that President Johnson had summoned Westmoreland to Washington to "shut up" growing dissent on the war. The *New York Post* called his trip a "search and destroy" mission against antiwar groups. Minnesota Democratic Senator Eugene McCarthy expressed "grave reservations about using a field commander on active duty as an instrument to make a case which is not only military but also political."

Addressing the packed chamber of the House of Representatives on April 28, 1967, General William Westmoreland received a standing ovation after pledging that the American forces under his command would "prevail in Vietnam over the Communist aggressor."

There were also important military reasons for Westmoreland's return. Before coming home, he had submitted two proposals for additional U.S. troops beyond the ceiling of 470,000 approved for 1967. One called for a "minimum essential" force of 80,500 more troops to a total of 550,500 and the other for an "optimum" force of 200,000 for a maximum strength of 670,000. Westmoreland characterized the minimum essential force as "necessary to continue and expand operations within South Vietnam." The optimum force could support "an even greater step-up of operations within South Vietnam plus an ability to take the war to the enemy in Laos and Cambodia." In answer to the recurring question of President Johnson and his advisers, "How much longer will the war go on?" the general responded that with a minimum essential force, "the war could well go on for three [more] years." Pushing for optimum force, he offered the optimistic appraisal that the war would end in "two years."

General Westmoreland's optimum force request would be reviewed by Defense Secretary Robert McNamara and his staff of systems analysis specialists, known in Washington as the "whiz kids." If his request was to be approved, Westmoreland's numbers would have to jibe with their analytical projections. Systems analysis was a relatively new management and research process at the Pentagon, an outgrowth of the computer age dawning in American industry and business. An infinite variety of statistics and other information could be fed into the Pentagon's sophisticated computer system to be analyzed and applied to almost any military purpose, from maintaining cost efficiency to developing logistical data to making projections of future defense needs in terms of men, equipment, and funds.

The man who brought systems analysis to the Pentagon and to the Vietnam War was the former president of the Ford Motor Company, Robert McNamara (see sidebar, page 44). He had risen to be "commander in chief" of Ford's giant industrial complex by the brilliant application of numbers to achieve the highest quality product in the most efficient way possible at the lowest cost. After John Kennedy appointed him secretary of defense in 1961, McNamara applied the same approach to produce the highest quality and most efficient components of America's military defense at the least cost to the American taxpayer. For this purpose, he immediately established the Systems Analysis Office to devise the most efficient budget analysis procedures.

When the Vietnam War escalated into his most formidable managerial challenge, McNamara measured progress or lack of it by the criterion he knew best: quantification. After returning from his first trip to Saigon in April 1962, for example, he offered the positive assessment that "every quantitative measurement we have shows we are winning this war." After the introduction of Rolling Thunder bombing raids in 1965 and the deployment of American combat troops the following year, McNamara had calculated that the "right" number of bombs dropped on North Vietnamese military and industrial facilities and the input of sufficient military forces should in the end produce victory.

His initially firm belief in the administration's graduated bombing policy, intended to "get North Vietnam to cease its support of Vietcong aggression," was shaken in 1966, however, when the first major results of Rolling Thunder were collated. The numbers—statistics on North Vietnamese military and economic resources and on the quickening pace of infiltration—told a discouraging story. After studying Rolling Thunder for the Defense Department, an eminent group of scientists concluded in a report issued in August of that year that the bombing program "had not substantially affected the ability of North Vietnam to support the military operations in the South" and that "despite the bombing, the flow of aid from North to South had accelerated."

McNamara's public image as a man "who, above all, revered facts," was reflected in his response to the disappointing statistics on Rolling Thunder. Faced with the failure of the bombing as a political weapon to break North Vietnamese resolve to continue the war, McNamara advocated a change in policy to one of restricting the bombing of the North "to interdict the lines of communication and military traffic. Anything beyond that," he said, "short of the destruction of the North Vietnamese nation, is not likely to make a significant military difference so long as Hanoi believes that in South Vietnam the war can be won."

McNamara's proposal embodied his growing conviction that the war could not be won in South Vietnam by bombing Hanoi into submission. While bombing could help to cut infiltration, the burden of defeating the enemy, both the NVA and the VC, rested, as McNamara saw it, on the outcome of General Westmoreland's war of attrition.

As with the bombing, McNamara had been an advocate of the introduction of American ground forces into South Vietnam in the spring of 1965. Over the next year and a half he supported and approved each of Westmoreland's requests for troop increases, during which time the total of combat forces in South Vietnam jumped from 20,000 to 486,000. His commitment to troop increases, however, was not without qualification. Beyond his basic expectation that American men and arms would prevail in South Vietnam, McNamara wanted tangible evidence that the United States' vast investment of military and economic resources there was yielding progress. Promises of progress by American commanders and reports of successful military operations were not enough.

McNamara's hope for victory in the ground war was substantially dampened by what he observed during a fact-finding tour of South Vietnam in October 1966. In his report to the president, he noted that although "we have by and large blunted the Communist military initiative [I see] no sign of an impending break in enemy morale." McNamara voiced his concern that the situation was approaching a stalemate, that the strategy of attrition was not working. As for pacification he asserted that it had "if anything gone backward."

McNamara's shift from confidence to pessimism about the progress of the war intensified in the spring of 1967. General Westmoreland and the Joint Chiefs of Staff, however, did not share the Defense secretary's doubts about the viability of the strategy of attrition. The differences came to a head when Westmoreland submitted to the Defense Department his optimum force request for 200,000 more troops. McNamara asked his Systems Analysis Office, headed by Assistant Secretary of Defense Alain Enthoven, to evaluate the numbers. His systems analysts had previously played only a minor role in studying the methods employed in fighting the war and evaluating their results. By 1967, however, at McNamara's direction, the Systems Analysis Office began applying its statistical techniques for determining cost effectiveness to the war in South Vietnam.

The numbers game

Westmoreland's strategy of attrition lent itself to the statistical analysis applied by Enthoven's systems analysts, because success in the war of attrition meant "good numbers" in terms of body count, reducing the ranks of the guerrillas, cutting the flow of North Vietnamese infiltrators, destroying Vietcong bases and installations, and tabulating the number of enemy weapons captured. The list of factors went on and on.

General Westmoreland never lost sight of that. In the spring of 1967 his "arithmetic report" implied to the White House that the war of attrition was grinding down the

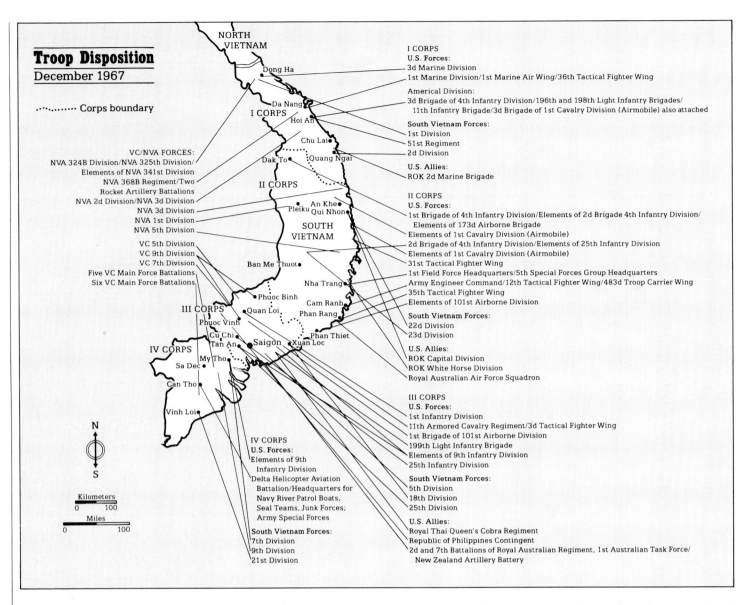

Troop Disposition
December 1967

············ Corps boundary

NORTH VIETNAM

Dong Ha

Da Nang
I CORPS
Hoi An

Chu Lai

Dak To Quang Ngai

II CORPS

An Khe
Pleiku Qui Nhon

SOUTH VIETNAM

Ban Me Thuot

Nha Trang

Phuoc Binh
III CORPS Quan Loi Cam Ranh
Phuoc Vinh Phan Rang
Cu Chi Phan Thiet
Tan An Saigon Xuan Loc
IV CORPS
My Tho
Sa Dec
Can Tho

Vinh Loi

N
S

Kilometers
0   100
Miles
0   100

VC/NVA FORCES:
NVA 324B Division/NVA 325th Division/
Elements of NVA 341st Division
NVA 368B Regiment/Two
Rocket Artillery Battalions
NVA 2d Division/NVA 3d Division
NVA 3d Division
NVA 1st Division
NVA 5th Division
VC 5th Division
VC 9th Division
VC 7th Division
Five VC Main Force Battalions
Six VC Main Force Battalions

I CORPS
U.S. Forces:
3d Marine Division
1st Marine Division/1st Marine Air Wing/36th Tactical Fighter Wing
American Division:
3d Brigade of 4th Infantry Division/196th and 198th Light Infantry Brigades/
11th Infantry Brigade/3d Brigade of 1st Cavalry Division (Airmobile) also attached
South Vietnam Forces:
1st Division
51st Regiment
2d Division
U.S. Allies:
ROK 2d Marine Brigade

II CORPS
U.S. Forces:
1st Brigade of 4th Infantry Division/Elements of 2d Brigade 4th Infantry Division/
Elements of 173d Airborne Brigade
Elements of 1st Cavalry Division (Airmobile)
2d Brigade of 4th Infantry Division/Elements of 25th Infantry Division
Elements of 1st Cavalry Division (Airmobile)
31st Tactical Fighter Wing
1st Field Force Headquarters/5th Special Forces Group Headquarters
Army Engineer Command/12th Tactical Fighter Wing/483d Troop Carrier Wing
35th Tactical Fighter Wing
Elements of 101st Airborne Division
South Vietnam Forces:
22d Division
23d Division
U.S. Allies:
ROK Capital Division
ROK White Horse Division
Royal Australian Air Force Squadron

III CORPS
U.S. Forces:
1st Infantry Division
11th Armored Cavalry Regiment/3d Tactical Fighter Wing
1st Brigade of 101st Airborne Division
199th Light Infantry Brigade
Elements of 9th Infantry Division
25th Infantry Division
South Vietnam Forces:
5th Division
18th Division
25th Division
U.S. Allies:
Royal Thai Queen's Cobra Regiment
Republic of Philippines Contingent
2d and 7th Battalions of Royal Australian Regiment, 1st Australian Task Force/
New Zealand Artillery Battery

IV CORPS
U.S. Forces:
Elements of 9th
Infantry Division
Delta Helicopter Aviation
Battalion/Headquarters for
Navy River Patrol Boats,
Seal Teams, Junk Forces;
Army Special Forces
South Vietnam Forces:
7th Division
9th Division
21st Division

enemy and setting the stage for a successful climax. He reported that the enemy death toll had doubled from the previous year to eight thousand a month, with a kill ratio of four to one in favor of the U.S. and ARVN. Moreover, by MACV's count the VC were losing about three thousand defectors and captured prisoners per month, twice the rate of 1966. Westmoreland also listed the demolition of thousands of VC bunkers, underground hospitals, food caches, ammunition dumps, and camps.

The cautious optimism created by these numbers was expressed by White House pacification adviser Robert Komer in his "Prognosis Report for 1967-68," cited in the *Pentagon Papers:* "He suspected that we had reached a point where we were killing, defecting, or otherwise attriting more VC/NVA strength than the enemy could build up—in the vernacular, the 'crossover point.'" Komer concluded: "Slow, painful, and incredibly expensive though it may be—we're beginning to 'win' the war in Vietnam."

While MACV interpreted its numbers in the context of a victory on the horizon, the Defense Department systems analysts took a markedly negative view of the future: "An

end to the conflict is not in sight and major unresolved problems remain." Those unresolved problems were directly connected to the assumptions and mechanisms behind Westmoreland's war of attrition. Instead of a continued depletion of enemy manpower and material resources approaching the crossover point, Enthoven's analysts concluded that the enemy was still able to minimize his losses so as "to fight indefinitely." And, contrary to MACV's assertions, "additional forces were unlikely to increase VC/NVA losses beyond any level intolerable to the enemy." They also opposed an increase on the grounds that more U.S. troops would put new inflationary pressures on the South Vietnamese economy. The more efficient use of forces already there, the analysts pointed out, would provide the same military output and effectiveness that MACV expected from the deployment of additional men, without added burdens to South Vietnam's economy.

The arguments raised in the critique by the Systems Analysis Office against MACV's optimum force request were criticized by Westmoreland but to no avail. McNamara wanted no troop increase at all. However,

The McNamara "Fence"

Late summer of 1966 was a particularly vexing time for Robert McNamara. A recent study by some of the nation's scientists had confirmed the Defense secretary's growing doubts about the effectiveness of the air war against North Vietnam. The elite group of scientists, working under the auspices of the Institute for Defense Analysis, expressed its findings in the "hard" numbers McNamara valued so highly. Their analysis of the intelligence data offered a gloomy prognosis: "The available evidence clearly indicates that Hanoi has been infiltrating military forces and supplies into South Vietnam at an accelerated rate during the current year. ... North Vietnam is capable of substantially increasing its support."

The evident failure of the air war made the secretary anxious for alternative solutions to unabated North Vietnamese infiltration. He turned to the same scientists who had offered blunt criticism of the Rolling Thunder bombing operation. The scientists' proposed alternative to the air war was a barrier along the DMZ. The barrier was not envisioned as a series of fortified bunkers and elaborate manned outposts. MACV simply did not have the forces to maintain such a "Maginot Line East." Instead, the suggestion was to build an electronic "fence" made of a variety of devices, especially newly developed sensors and mines, to enable American forces to monitor enemy incursions.

Among the most effective of these highly classified devices were acoustic and seismic sensors. Acoustic sensors were dropped from aircraft and drifted down by parachute to catch in trees along enemy infiltration routes and near base areas. Technicians activated them by remote control and in some cases could pick up the voices of enemy soldiers as well as movements of military vehicles. Radio signals with coded data were then relayed to surveillance planes circling overhead, which fed them to computers for analysis. If a Vietcong tried to dismantle or sabotage the sensor, a delicate crystal inside would self-destruct, rendering the device useless.

Seismic sensors were also tossed from planes and helicopters over known enemy trails. These fell freely to earth, gravity forcing a long steel spike into the ground. The jolt of landing activated an antenna camouflaged to blend with jungle foliage. The ground vibrations caused by trucks and large enemy troop movements, among others, were picked up by the sensors and radioed to American intelligence.

A simple alarm device was sometimes used in connection with acoustic sensors to amplify the sound of passing enemy troops. The alarm, a tiny, nonlethal mine, exploded when stepped on. In addition, a trip-wire system was deployed, activated by the interruption of a long, thin beam of invisible light.

The proposed system met with initial skepticism from McNamara. His doubts about the effectiveness of the barrier were overcome, however, when Pentagon researchers reported on the manpower and cost-saving potential of the new electronic devices. McNamara then embraced the scientists' description of "a dynamic 'battle of the barrier,' in which the barrier is repeatedly improved and strengthened by the introduction of new components." Technological innovation, they suggested, would keep the North Vietnamese chronically off balance in their effort to devise countermeasures.

After almost a year of further research, McNamara authorized a limited barrier. A scaled-down version of the original proposal, the barrier was to be constructed from Con Thien to the sea, less than a quarter of the length of the DMZ. In an announcement on September 6, 1967, the Defense secretary asserted that the barrier's objectives would be "consistent with those of our present air campaign against lines of communication."

Many officers unofficially viewed the barrier in a different light. They felt it symbolized McNamara's increasing frustration with the bombing and his hope of bringing it to a halt, perhaps using the barrier as an aid to a negotiated settlement. While these hopes for a bombing halt were not yet reflected in the secretary's public statements, a number of senior military officers had little doubt that the line reflected retreat from a punitive "win the war" strategy of aerial bombardment against the North.

Generals Wallace Greene and Robert Cushman of the Marine Corps and General Harold Johnson, the army chief of staff, were all on record as opposing the barrier. Westmoreland was also known to have misgivings. In the rugged highland region near the DMZ, the generals reasoned, no effective barrier could be pieced together and manned without tying down excessive numbers of men. They feared that an "end run" could easily be devised by the North Vietnamese. Said one officer, "It is like water being dammed up. If you halt the infiltration through the zone, the Communists are sure to step up their infiltration through Laos."

Criticism of the barrier's effectiveness was only one aspect of the military's opposition; another was an almost reflexive aversion to the kind of "static defense" that had characterized France's unsuccessful Indochina venture. American troops on the line would be confined to a largely defensive mission, in the commanders' view, thereby draining resources from the mobile search and destroy operations crucial to Westmoreland's strategy.

In December 1967 the Pentagon announced that at least part of the barrier was in operation. But three of the barrier's first four watchtowers were blown up after only a few days of operation, and seemingly insurmountable technical problems put the completion of the project in doubt. Like Rolling Thunder, the McNamara Line had achieved no decisive impact on infiltration when work ground to a halt in 1968. And, like so many tactical and strategic innovations advanced during the Indochina wars, it too fell by the wayside. As Major General Tran Do of the North Vietnamese Army put it: "What is the use of barbed-wire fences, when we can penetrate even Tan Son Nhut air base outside Saigon?"

confronting pressure from the Joint Chiefs not only to approve the optimum troop increase but to expand the bombing of the North, he compromised: Westmoreland would have to settle for the minimum increase, just over 47,000 men. They would raise his troop ceiling to 575,000.

While Westmoreland and the systems analysts debated the numbers, in the jungles of northern South Vietnam it was life—and death—as usual. During the first few days of May 1967, in a valley north of Khe Sanh, thirty-five thousand North Vietnamese troops were dug in on three hills, 881 North and South and 861. Hidden from air observation by thick monsoon clouds, the troops had infiltrated through Laos. When five men of a U.S. forward observer team went up Hill 861 for a look, only one returned alive. Marine commander Lieutenant General Lewis Walt then ordered two battalions into action, and a twelve-day battle ensued. It was reminiscent of the famous Pork Chop Hill assault of the Korean War. Marines moving up the slopes of 861 and 881 were blasted by a vicious crossfire from well-placed NVA bunkers. After the marines pulled back, jets and B-52s went to work, transforming the hills into a "moonscape of stumps and craters." The NVA withdrew, leaving nearly two hundred U.S. Marines dead and eight hundred wounded.

Since the beginning of the year, MACV had detected a build-up of enemy forces below the DMZ. In March coordinated attacks by NVA regulars on Con Thien and Gio Linh, both within ten miles of the DMZ, heightened fears that a Communist offensive might be in the works. Con Thien and Gio Linh "absorbed," General Westmoreland recalls, "a thousand rounds of mortar, rocket, and artillery fire . . . the next day the enemy ambushed a marine ammunition supply convoy only two miles from Gio Linh, while a few days later a marine company near Cam Lo came under sharp ground attack."

MACV had been watching for a large-scale invasion across the DMZ since Operation Hastings in July 1966. But a series of marine offensive sweeps had been effective, in Westmoreland's judgment, in keeping the NVA bottled up north of the DMZ—until now. The apparent upsurge in NVA activity disturbed Assistant Secretary of Defense John McNaughton, who played an important role in assessing enemy troop strength and North Vietnamese infiltration in 1967. McNaughton stated that the "concentration of NVA forces across the demilitarized zone and the enemy use of long-range artillery are matters of concern. There are now four NVA divisions in the DMZ area. . . . They are forcing us to transfer some forces from elsewhere in Vietnam to the I Corps area."

Giap shifts his strategy

For the North Vietnamese, especially General Giap, the build-up of American troops near the DMZ (by May of 1967 there were 35,000 marines there) was a welcome development. North Vietnam's veteran strategist comprehended the American numbers game and knew how to play it to his advantage. It was no secret in Hanoi that the war was becoming an increasingly controversial and divisive issue in the United States and that the president was feeling the pressure to hold the line on further troop increments and escalation of the American commitment.

Perceiving the prospect of a long, drawn-out struggle as politically unfeasible for Washington, Giap reverted in 1967 to a mixed strategy of guerrilla warfare punctuated by large unit attacks only when the right opportunity arose. While General Westmoreland considered the enemy's partial reversion to guerrilla tactics from its previous Main Force unit aggressiveness a sign of their having lost the initiative, Giap believed just the opposite.

Giap's attempt to seize the initiative by drawing American forces away from the defense of heavily populated coastal areas seemed to be bearing fruit. He ordered major ground operations by line divisions of the North Vietnamese Army near the seventeenth parallel. MACV reacted as expected, diverting thousands of marine reinforcements from other areas in Quang Tri. In April CINCPAC Admiral Sharp evaluated the situation in I Corps as "tight, very tight." South Vietnam's Foreign Minister Tran Van Do spoke of "the possibility of a larger-scale invasion. Our two northern provinces of Quang Tri and Thua Thien are presently under terrible pressure."

With the marines in I Corps forced to defend from 193 to 232 square miles of hills and forests they became, according to Giap, "small, scattered" contingents tied to isolated outposts and therefore vulnerable either to quick-hit, guerrilla-type strikes or Main Force assaults. Throughout the spring and summer, marine outposts in I Corps were struck by sporadic attacks both by VC guerrillas and units of NVA infiltrators. During June and July, the outpost at Con Thien (Hill of Angels) a few miles below the DMZ came under sustained attacks by NVA regulars. In the first week of July, two companies from the 1st Battalion, 9th Marines (3d Division), on a routine sweep for infiltrators, were suddenly pinned down by intense enemy mortar fire. Then NVA soldiers, perhaps a thousand of them, charged the marines from all sides.

It was a bitter encounter for the marines, who suffered 95 dead and 200 wounded. One of the companies, Bravo, was destroyed as a combat unit. First Lieutenant Gatlin Howell sent tanks in to the battlefield to retrieve American casualties. *Newsweek* reported that the "bodies of dead marines lay everywhere. . . . Two tanks were knocked out, reportedly by the enemy's RPG-7, a new Soviet antitank gun [rocket launcher]." Though NVA losses were high, 275 killed, the ambush had Giap's desired effect. As a consequence, more marine units were reassigned from the coastal areas of I Corps, opening up coastal villages to Vietcong infiltration and control.

American losses. The battle gear of U.S. Marines wounded or killed during Operation Harvest Moon in December 1965 lies in a pile near operation headquarters at Son Thanh. The marines had encountered stiff resistance trying to dislodge the Vietcong from their stronghold thirty-five miles southwest of Da Nang.

Giap's 1967 initiative was not confined to I Corps but spread throughout much of South Vietnam, particularly in the central highlands and provinces along the Cambodian border to the south. By the fall, a combination of guerrilla and Main-Force-unit warfare was menacing border provinces in the central highlands, where U.S. and ARVN forces had to defend thousands of miles of rugged terrain. All through October, South Vietnamese command posts in the central highlands were attacked by VC Main Force and guerrilla units. Giap was confident that U.S.

troops lured by such attacks to the highlands left such American strong points as Da Nang and Chu Lai along the central coast "isolated islands in the open sea of the people's war."

To the south in Binh Long Province, on October 29 the 272d and 273d Regiments of the 9th Vietcong Division slipped over from their haven in Cambodia and tried to overrun the allied base at the town of Loc Ninh, nine miles inside South Vietnam. U.S. intelligence indicated that VC and NVA units had dotted Cambodia's six-hundred-mile frontier with dozens of jungle encampments. It was believed that at least six enemy regiments and guerrilla units—for a total of twenty thousand men—were engaged in raiding and reconnoitering along the border.

At Loc Ninh, however, the VC met stiff resistance from the town's South Vietnamese defenders: three CIDG companies, a Regional Force company, and a Popular Force platoon. After several days of fighting, ARVN units and the American 1st Brigade, 1st Infantry Division arrived to reinforce the position. When the enemy broke off battle a week later, it had taken severe casualties: over eight hundred fifty killed compared to only fifty of the defenders.

Giap was not deterred by the high cost of casualties from pursuing his strategy. He had shown in the war against the French that he deemed any cost in lives bearable as long as sufficient replacements were available and a meaningful number of overall casualties could be inflicted on his enemy. As Patrick McGarvey, an authority on North Vietnamese strategy, put it, "it is by the traffic in home-bound American coffins that Giap measures his success."

Giap had plans for increasing that traffic. A North Vietnamese document captured on November 6, 1967, contained an outline of Hanoi's preparations for a 1968 offensive. The document outlined four principal objectives: "annihilate" major U.S. units forced to disperse in search of guerrillas and "disintegrate a large part of the Puppet Army"; improve combat technique; liberate areas for political struggle; and achieve unity and political-military coordination in the South.

MACV was not overly concerned. All four objectives depended to a large extent on Giap's border strategy, the results of which MACV considered negligible. In the "frontier battles of that autumn," Westmoreland affirmed, "we had soundly defeated the enemy without unduly sacrificing operations in other areas. The enemy return was nil."

"If progress continues . . ."

Westmoreland judged the military situation near the end of 1967 secure enough to take time out in November, at the request of the White House, to accompany Ambassador Ellsworth Bunker to the United States and confer with President Johnson and to "campaign" for the war effort. Westmoreland would not disappoint the administration. Even as he stepped from an air force jet in Washington he described the situation in Vietnam as "very, very encouraging . . . I have never been more encouraged in my four years in Vietnam." In addition, General Westmoreland would repeat his optimism before both the House and Senate Armed Services Committees, on television, and in his speeches.

Appearing on "Meet the Press" with Ellsworth Bunker, Westmoreland issued his most positive prediction—laced with some big ifs—regarding a timetable for victory. "If the bombing of North Vietnam continues," the general stated, "It is conceivable that within two years or less the enemy will be so weakened that . . . we will be able to phase down the level of our military effort [and] withdraw some troops." He joined Ambassador Bunker in trying "to correct" the "erroneous impressions" created by reports from Saigon, "that the war is at stalemate or that the South Vietnamese have been swallowed up in a basically American campaign." Referring to the mood of the Vietnamese people, the general stressed "an attitude of confidence and growing optimism. It prevails all over the country, and to me this is the most significant evidence I can give you that constant, real progress is being made.

Addressing the National Press Club on November 21, Westmoreland pressed his case that the war of attrition was indeed working. He said that VC and NVA troops were critically deficient in recruitment and supplies. The VC were deserting in such numbers, he said, that NVA regulars had to take their place in the South. He then reiterated that "We are making progress. We know that you want an honorable and early transition to the last phase [when U.S. units can begin to withdraw]. So do your sons and so do I. It lies within our grasp—the enemy's hopes are bankrupt. . . . We have reached an important point when the end begins to come into view."

In the *New York Times* Neil Sheehan criticized Westmoreland's vague conjectures about enemy troop strength: "Although [he] outlined steady progress in the war effort . . . he declines to give detailed evidence to support his contention that total enemy forces were declining under enemy attrition and that 45 percent of the 163 Vietcong and North Vietnamese Main Force battalions were combat ineffective, or unfit for battle."

With all the talk of winning, it must have come as a rude shock in late November when four NVA regiments surrounded the town of Dak To in the northern tip of II Corps. For twenty-two days a ferocious battle ravaged the area around Dak To. On Hill 875, the 2d Battalion, 503d Infantry, of the army's 173d Airborne Brigade, tried to dislodge enemy units entrenched in an extensive system of hilltop bunkers. As jets roared in at five hundred feet to pound the crest, one released a 500-pound bomb too soon. According to one dispatch, "It burst in the tall trees just above the battalion's command post, killing 30 U.S. paratroopers, many of them wounded, who had been pulled up to the headquarters area for safety." For the rest of the battalion there was no food or water for more than two days. After inflicting significant casualties (113 U.S. paratroopers killed and 402 wounded), the North Vietnamese abandoned the hill to the Americans. North Vietnamese casualties on Hill 875 were also heavy—322 killed.

As Christmas approached, American intelligence began to detect another North Vietnamese build-up around Khe Sanh. MACV field intelligence reports cited a "doubling of enemy truck traffic on the Ho Chi Minh Trail, a frantic enemy effort to move supplies into the DMZ and Laos." On December 20, General Westmoreland called Washington with information about what appeared to be preparations for the enemy's expected winter-spring offensive. He was confident that he had enough troops at his disposal to counter the enemy threat. MACV forces numbered 486,000 including 78,000 marines (more than half stationed in I Corps) and 320,000 army troops. In addition, U.S. ground forces were supported by 65,000 air force personnel, as well as 33,000 men in the navy and Coast Guard. ARVN had recently strengthened its ranks to a total of 343,000 regular and 300,000 irregular forces (mostly Regional and Popular Forces). The number of allied forces from Australia, South Korea, Thailand, and the Philippines had grown to 55,000.

The marines, augmented by the 24,000 men of the army's 23d Infantry (Americal) Division, which had arrived in September 1967, bore the primary defensive and tactical responsibility in I Corps. They were joined there by 8,000 Korean marines and over 20,000 ARVN soldiers and were opposed by five NVA divisions of about 40 to 50,000 men. The U.S. military was strongest in II Corps where 225,000 American troops along with 20,000 Koreans and nearly 20,000 South Vietnamese soldiers were deployed against at least three NVA divisions and smaller VC guerrilla units. In III and IV Corps the deployment was markedly different. The number of Americans, 100,000 in the former and 20,000 in the latter, was significantly exceeded by eighty-four battalions of ARVN forces, well over 200,000 men. In these same areas MACV estimated at least three VC divisions and eleven Main Force battalions were operating.

With combined forces of 1.2 million, Westmoreland felt ready to deal with any military contingency that might arise. MACV, *if* its estimates of enemy strength at 257,000 NVA and VC soldiers were correct (others estimated NVA and VC troop strength to be as high as 380,000), enjoyed a four-to-one advantage in the field. Years later MACV's figures were to come under attack as seriously misleading; but as 1967 drew to a close, the belief in Saigon and Washington was that American forces and their allies were sufficiently strong and prepared for whatever might be coming.

In his analysis of enemy options for a major offensive, General Westmoreland informed Washington that he did not anticipate attacks on cities or towns and that he had moved troops to rural sectors along the Cambodian border. A press release issued by the U.S. Mission in Vietnam on January 5, 1968, however, reported that recently captured North Vietnamese documents presaged a general offensive of "very strong military attacks in coordination with the uprisings of the local population to take over towns and cities. Troops should flood the lowlands ... move toward liberating Saigon." The release emphasized that the documents "cannot be taken as conclusive evidence that such an order has been given. Obviously it would only be given by the Central Committee of the Communist party in Hanoi, since it would stake all the human resources of the revolution upon a general attack against the strongest positions of the Government of Vietnam and its allies." Most U.S. military intelligence officers, as well as numerous American reporters covering the war, simply rejected the idea of a nationwide offensive as "fantastic" and "outlandish." Correspondent Don Oberdorfer of the *Washington Post*, then in Saigon, recalls how doubtful the Americans were of an offensive along the lines suggested by the captured documents: "The very boldness of the plan generated antibodies against belief. American officers were certain Communist forces could not seize and hold the cities ... [it] seemed implausible."

On January 2, 1968, at a listening post near Khe Sanh, six NVA officers dressed in U.S. Marine uniforms were shot as they tried to penetrate the base's barbed wire perimeter fence. MACV suspected that about six NVA regiments were lurking in that area. By the middle of January, Westmoreland and his assistant chief of staff for intelligence, Brigadier General Philip B. Davidson, were expecting a major attack on Khe Sanh and other northern regions in the vicinity of the DMZ. Westmoreland thought it "would be shortly before Tet, so that the enemy would take advantage of the Tet cease-fire and jockey his forces to exploit any gains achieved at the start." Convinced that the coming Tet offensive would be a "sizable invasion" across the DMZ, he shifted 15,000 more U.S. troops to assist the 41,000 marines already in I Corps. Westmoreland was spoiling for his long-awaited showdown with Giap's army. "I hope they try something," he said, "because we are looking for a fight." General Vo Nguyen Giap, however, had something radically different in mind, something far more momentous than "a fight."

Following page. Action near the DMZ: U.S. Marines take cover in the muddy trenches at Con Thien in September 1967 as incoming mortars zero in on their position.

Bibliography

I. Books and Articles

Albinski, Henry. *Politics and Foreign Policy in Australia.* Duke University Press, 1970.

Baral, Jaya. *The Pentagon and the Making of U.S. Foreign Policy.* Humanities Press, 1978.
Bashore, Lt. Col. Boyd T. "The Name of the Game is 'Search and Destroy.'" *Army,* February 1967.
Beecher, William. "Way-Out Weapons." *The New York Times Magazine,* March 24, 1968.
Berman, Larry. *Planning a Tragedy: The Americanization of the War in Vietnam.* W.W. Norton & Co., 1982.
Blanché, W. Wendell. *The Foreign Service of the United States.* Praeger, 1969.
Blaufarb, Douglas S. *The Counterinsurgency Era.* The Free Press, 1977.
Brandon, Henry. *Anatomy of Error.* Gambit, 1969.
Browne, Malcolm W. *The New Face of War.* Bobbs-Merrill Co., 1968.
Bundy, William P. *Memoirs.* Unpublished, no date.
Burch, Charles G. "What the U.S. is Leaving Behind." *Fortune,* October 1971.
Burchett, Wilfred G. *Vietnam: Inside Story of the Guerrilla War.* International Publishers, 1965.

Caro, Robert A. "The Years of Lyndon Johnson." *The Atlantic,* October 1981.
Carver, George A., Jr. "The Faceless Viet Cong." *Foreign Affairs,* April 1966, pp. 347–72.
Clos, Max. "The Karma of Vietnam's Buddhists." *The New York Times Magazine,* August 21, 1966.
Cohen, Warren. *Dean Rusk.* Cooper Square Publisher, 1980.
Cooper, Chester. *The Lost Crusade: America in Vietnam.* Fawcett, 1972.
Corson, William R. *The Betrayal.* W.W. Norton & Co., 1968.

Dickson, Paul, and John Rothchild. "The Electronic Battlefield: Wiring Down the War." *Washington Monthly,* May 1971.
Dinh, Tran Van. "Exercise in Deception." *Commonweal,* September 22, 1967.
Donnell, John C., and Melvin Gurtov. *North Vietnam: Left of Moscow, Right of Peking.* Rand Corporation P-3794, February 1968.

Ellsberg, Daniel. *Papers on the War.* Simon & Schuster, 1972.
_____. *The Day Loc Tien was Pacified.* Rand Corporation P-3793, 1968.

Fall, Bernard. "Viet-Nam: European Viewpoints." *The New Republic,* August 21, 1965.
_____. "Viet-Nam: The Quest for Stability." *Current History,* January 1967.
_____. "Viet-Nam's 12 Elections." *The New Republic,* May 14, 1966.
The First Air Cavalry Division in Vietnam. M.W. Lads Publishing Co., 1967.
Fulbright, J. William. "Our Responsibilities in World Affairs: The Role of the Senate." *Vital Speeches,* 1959.

Gavin, Gen. James M. "A Communication on Vietnam." *Harpers,* February 1966.
_____. *Crisis Now.* Random House, 1968.
_____. *War and Peace in the Space Age.* Harper & Brothers, 1958.

Geyelin, Philip. *Lyndon B. Johnson and the World.* Alfred A. Knopf, 1969.
Goldman, Eric. *The Tragedy of Lyndon Johnson.* Alfred A. Knopf, 1969.
Goodman, Alan. *The Lost Peace: America's Search For a Negotiated Settlement of the Vietnam War.* Hoover Institution Press, 1978.
Graff, Henry. *The Tuesday Cabinet.* Prentice-Hall, 1970.
Guzzardi, Walter. "Management of the War: A Tale of Two Capitals." *Fortune,* April 1967.

Halberstam, David. *The Best and the Brightest.* Random House, 1972.
Hamilton, Andrew. "Vietnam—Fencing in the North." *The New Republic,* July 8, 1967.
Harr, John. *The Professional Diplomat.* Princeton University Press, 1969.
Honey, P.J. *Communism in North Vietnam: Its Role in the Sino-Soviet Dispute.* MIT Press, 1963.
Hoopes, Townsend. *The Limits of Intervention.* David McKay Co., 1969.
Hsiao, Gene, ed. *The Role of External Powers in the Indochina Crisis.* Andronicus Publishing Co., 1973.

Johnson, Lyndon B. *The Vantage Point.* Holt, Rinehart & Winston, 1971.
Joiner, Charles A. *The Politics of Massacre.* Temple University Press, 1974.

Kahin, George McTurnan, and John W. Lewis. *The U.S. in Vietnam.* Dell, 1967.
Kattenburg, Paul M. *The Vietnam Trauma in American Foreign Policy, 1945–1975.* Transaction Books, 1980.
Kearns, Doris. *Lyndon Johnson and the American Dream.* Harper & Row, 1976.
Keesing's Research Reports. *South Vietnam, A Political History 1954–70.* Charles Scribner's Sons, 1970.
Kendrick, Alexander. *The Wound Within.* Little, Brown & Co., 1974.
Kinnard, Douglas. *The War Managers.* University of New England Press, 1977.
Kinnard, Lt. Gen. Harry W.O. "A Victory in the Ia Drang: The Triumph of a Concept." *Army,* September 1967.
_____. "Narrowing the Combat Intelligence Gap." *Army,* August 1969.
Kipp, Robert. "Counterinsurgency from 30,000 Feet." *Air University Review* 19 (Jan.–Feb. 1968).
Komer, Robert. *Bureaucracy Does Its Thing.* Rand Corporation R-967, 1972.
Kraslow, David, and Stuart Loory. *The Secret Search for Peace in Vietnam.* Vintage Books, 1968.

Langguth, A.J. "Our Policy-Making Men in Saigon." *The New York Times Magazine,* April 28, 1968.
Lewy, Guenter. *America in Vietnam.* Oxford University Press, 1978.
Littaur, Raphael, and Norman Uphoff, eds. *Air War in Indo China.* Beacon Press, 1972.

McClintic, Robert. "Roll Back the Night." *Army,* August 1969.
McGarvey, Patrick. *Visions of Victory: Selected Vietnamese Communist Military Writers, 1964–68.* Hoover Institution on War, Revolution, and Peace, Stanford University, 1969.
Miller, Merle. *Lyndon: An Oral Biography.* Ballantine Books, 1980.
Milstein, Jeffrey S. "The Escalation of the Vietnam War 1965–67: A Quantitative Analysis and Predictive Computer Simulation." Thesis, Stanford University, 1969–1970.
Milward, Alan S. *The German Economy at War.* University of London Athlone Press, 1965.
Mirsky, Jonathan. "The Tombs of Ben Suc." *The Nation,* October 23, 1967.
Moser, Don, and Co Rentmeester. "Battle Jump: U.S. Paratroopers in a Stepped-Up War." *Life,* March 10, 1967.

Nighswonger, William A. *Rural Pacification in Vietnam.* Praeger, 1966.
Norman, Lloyd. "McNamara's Fence: Our Eyes and Ears Along the DMZ." *Army,* August 1968.

Oberdorfer, Don. *Tet.* Doubleday, 1971.

Palmer, Lt. Col. Dave Richard. *Readings in Current Military History.* Department of Military Art and Engineering, West Point, 1969.
Palmer, Gregory. *The McNamara Strategy and the Vietnam War.* Greenwood Press, 1978.
Pike, Douglas. *The Vietcong Strategy of Terror.* U.S. Mission, South Vietnam, 1971.
_____. *Viet Cong: The Organization and Techniques of the National Liberation Front of South Vietnam.* MIT Press, 1966.
Pisor, Robert. *The End of the Line: The Siege of Khe Sanh.* W.W. Norton & Co., 1982.
Powers, Thomas. *The War at Home.* Grossman Publishers, 1973.
Pratt, Lawrence. "North Vietnam and Sino-Soviet Tension." *Behind the Headlines,* 26 (August 1967).

Radvanyi, Janos. *Illusion and Reality.* Gateway Editions, 1978.
Ridgway, Matthew B. *Soldier: The Memoirs of Matthew B. Ridgway.* Harper & Brothers, 1956.

Schell, Jonathan. *The Village of Ben Suc.* Alfred A. Knopf, 1967.
Schurmann, Franz, Peter Dale Scott, and Reginald Zelnik. *The Politics of Escalation in Vietnam.* Fawcett, 1966.
Shaplen, Robert. "A Reporter at Large." *The New Yorker,* December 17, 1966.
_____. "Letter from Saigon." *The New Yorker,* August 20, 1966.
_____. "Letter from Saigon." *The New Yorker,* June 17, 1967.
_____. "Letter from Saigon." *The New Yorker,* October 7, 1967.
Simons, Lt. Col. William E. *Coercion in Vietnam?* Rand Corporation RM-6016, 1969.
Smith, Jack P. "Death in the Ia Drang Valley." *The Saturday Evening Post,* January 28, 1967.

Spore, John. "Floating Assault Force." *Army*, February 1968.
Steinberg, Alfred. *Sam Johnson's Boy*. Macmillan, 1968.
Stevens, Robert Warren. *Vain Hopes, Grim Realities: The Economic Consequences of the Vietnam War*. New Viewpoints, 1976.
Sullivan, Marianne. *France's Vietnam Policy*. Greenwood Press, 1978.
Summers, Col. Harry G., Jr. *On Strategy: The Vietnam War in Context*. Strategic Studies Institute, U.S. Army War College, 1981.
Swarztrauber, S. "River Patrol Relearned." *U.S. Naval Institute Proceedings*, May 1970.
Swearingen, Rodger, and Rolph Hammond. *Communism in Vietnam*. American Bar Association, 1967.

Tanham, George, ed. *War Without Guns: American Civilians in Rural Vietnam*. Praeger, 1966.
Taylor, Maxwell D. *Swords and Plowshares*. W.W. Norton & Co., 1972.
Thompson, Robert. *No Exit from Vietnam*. David McKay Co., 1970.
Thompson, W. Scott, and Donaldson D. Frizzell, eds. *The Lessons of Vietnam*. Crane, Russak and Co., 1977.
Trewhitt, Henry. *McNamara*. Harper & Row, 1971.
Truong-Son. *The Winter 1966–Spring 1967 Victory*. Hanoi.

Vietnam Hearings. Vintage Books, 1966.
Vietnam War: The Illustrated History of the Conflict in Southeast Asia. Crown Publishers, Salamander Books, 1979.

Walt, Lewis W. *Strange War, Strange Strategy*. Funk & Wagnalls, 1970.
Warner, Denis. "How Much Power Does Tri Quang Want?" *The Reporter*, May 5, 1966.
_____. "South Vietnam Exists." *The Reporter*, September 21, 1967.
Weller, J. "Good and Bad Weapons for Vietnam." *Military Review*, October 1968.
Wells, W.C. "The Riverine Force in Action, 1966–1967." *Naval Review*, 1969, pp. 48–83.
Werth, Alexander. "America's Colony in Hell." *The Nation*, June 13, 1966.
West, F.J., Jr. *Area Security: The Need, the Composition, and the Commitment*. Rand Corporation P-3979, 1968.
Westmoreland, Gen. William C. *A Soldier Reports*. Doubleday, 1976.
White, Theodore. "Bell of Decision Rings Out in Vietnam." *Life*, September 1, 1967.

Zagoria, Donald S. *Vietnam Triangle: Moscow, Peking, Hanoi*. Pegasus, 1967.
Zasloff, Joseph J., and MacAlister Brown. *Communism in Indochina*. Lexington Books, 1975.

II. Government and Military Reports

Albright, John, John A. Cash, and Allan W. Sandstrum. *Seven Firefights in Vietnam*. Office of the Chief of Military History, U.S. Army, 1970.

Collins, Brig. Gen. James Lawton, Jr. *Development and Training of the South Vietnamese Army 1950–1972*. Department of the Army, 1974.
Combat After Action Report—Operation Junction City I and II, February 22, to May 14, 1967. Department of the Army.
Combat Operations After Action Report—Operation Hastings, July 15 to August 3, 1966. Headquarters, 3rd Marine Division.

Dunn, Lt. Gen. Carroll H. *Base Development in South Vietnam 1965–1970*. Department of the Army Vietnam Studies, 1972.

Fulton, Maj. Gen. William B. *Riverine Operations 1966–1969*. Department of the Army Vietnam Studies, 1973.

Gravel, Sen. Mike, ed. *The Pentagon Papers*. Beacon Press, 1971.

Heiser, Lt. Gen. Joseph M., Jr. *Logistic Support*. Department of the Army Vietnam Studies, 1974.
Hooper, Vice Adm. Edwin. *Mobility, Support, Endurance*. Naval History Division, Department of the Navy, 1972.
Larsen, Lt. Gen. Stanley. *Allied Participation in Vietnam*. Department of the Army Vietnam Studies, 1975.

Pearson, Lt. Gen. Willard. *The War in the Northern Provinces*. Department of the Army Vietnam Studies, 1975.
Pogue, Forrest C. *United States Army in World War II, the European Theater of Operations: The Supreme Command*. Office of the Chief of Military History, U.S. Department of the Army, 1954.

Report by the Joint Logistics Review Board. *Logistic Support in the Vietnam Era*. Volume II. No date.
Rogers, Bernard W. *Cedar Falls—Junction City: A Turning Point*. Department of the Army Vietnam Studies, 1974.

Sharp, Adm. U.S.G., and Gen. W.C. Westmoreland. *Report on the War in Vietnam*. U.S. Government Printing Office, 1969.
Shore, Capt. Moyers S., II. *The Battle for Khe Sanh*. Historical Branch, United States Marine Corps, 1969.
Shulimson, Jack. *U.S. Marines in Vietnam, 1966: An Expanding War*. History and Museums Division, Headquarters, U.S. Marine Corps, 1982.
Shulimson, Jack, and Charles M. Johnson. *U.S. Marines in Vietnam: The Landing and the Buildup, 1965*. History and Museums Division, Headquarters, U.S. Marine Corps, 1978.

Stolfi, Russel H. *U.S. Marine Corps Civic Action Efforts in Vietnam, March 1965–March 1966*. Historical Branch, G-3 Division, Headquarters, U.S. Marine Corps, 1968.

The BDM Corporation. *A Study of Strategic Lessons Learned in Vietnam*. National Technical Information Service, 1980.
Tregaskis, Richard. *Southeast Asia: Building the Bases: The History of Construction in Southeast Asia*. U.S. Government Printing Office, no date.

U.S. Board on Geographic Names. *South Vietnam, Official Standard Names Gazeteer*. U.S. Army Topographic Command, 1971.
U.S. Central Intelligence Agency. *Foreign Broadcast Information Service Daily Reports, 1965–1968*.
_____. *Who's Who in North Vietnam*, 1969.
U.S. Congress, U.S. Senate. Committee on Armed Services, Preparedness Investigating Subcommittee. *The Air War Against North Vietnam*. Hearings 90th Congress, First Session. U.S. Government Printing Office, 1967.
_____. Committee on Foreign Relations. *Background Information to Southeast Asia*. U.S. Government Printing Office, 1973.
_____. *Vietnam: Policy and Prospects 1970*. 91st Congress, Second Session. U.S. Government Printing Office, 1970.
_____. Proxmire, William. "Point of Personal Privilege." Congressional Record, U.S. Government Printing Office, July 13, 1970.
U.S. Department of Defense. *United States-Vietnam Relations 1945–1967 (Pentagon Papers)*. U.S. Government Printing Office, 1971.
U.S. Department of State. *Documents and Research Notes nos. 8, 23, 36-7, 40-4*. U.S. Government Printing Office, 1961–1968.
_____. "Political Development in South Vietnam." *Vietnam Information Notes*, U.S. Government Printing Office, April 1967.
_____. *The Country Team*. U.S. Government Printing Office, 1967.
_____. *Vietnam Information Notes nos. 1–16*. U.S. Government Printing Office, 1967–1970.
U.S. Marine Corps, History and Museums Division. *The Marines in Vietnam 1954–1973: An Anthology and Annotated Bibliography*. U.S. Marine Corps, 1974.
U.S. Naval Institute. *Naval Review 1968*. 1968.

III. Newspapers and Periodicals

The authors consulted the following newspapers and periodicals:
Atlas, 1965–1967.
Newsweek, 1965–1968.
The New York Times, 1965–1968.
Time, 1965–1968.

IV. Archival Sources

Lyndon Baines Johnson Library, Austin, Texas.
U.S. Army, Adjutant General's Office, Suitland, Maryland.
U.S. Marine Corps, History and Museums Division, Headquarters USMC, Washington, D.C.

V. Interviews

Ellsworth Bunker, former ambassador to South Vietnam, on January 11, 1982.
Robert Frost, former army helicopter pilot, on December 15, 1981.
Robert Komer, former presidential adviser and deputy commander, U.S. Military Assistance Command, Vietnam, for CORDS (Pacification), on January 14, 1982.
George McArthur, former AP bureau chief and *Los Angeles Times* reporter in Saigon, on January 12, 1982.
Morley Safer, CBS network news correspondent, on November 20, 1981.
Brig. Gen. E.H. Simmons, director of Marine Corps History and Museums, on January 13, 1982.

Picture Credits

Map Credits

Acknowledgments

Boston Publishing Company wishes to acknowledge the kind assistance of the following people: Major Edgar C. Doleman, Jr., U.S. Army, who helped prepare the *American Firepower* and *Small Arms* picture essays and Mr. Jack Shulimson, senior Vietnam historian, Marine Corps Historical Center, who read the manuscript. Thanks also to Charles W. Dunn, professor and chairman, Department of Celtic Languages and Literatures, Harvard University, and the staffs of the Center for Military History and the U.S. Marine Corps History and Museums Division.

Index

U.S. Military Units
(see note below)

Note: Military units are listed according to the general organizational structure of the U.S. Armed Forces. The following chart summarizes that structure for the U.S. Army. The principal difference between the army and the Marine Corps structures in Vietnam lay at the regimental level. The army eliminated the regimental command structure after World War II (although battalions retained a regimental designation for purposes of historical continuity, e.g., 1st Battalion, 7th Cavalry [Regiment]). Marine Corps battalions were organized into regiments instead of brigades except under a few unusual circumstances. The marines, however, do not use the word "regiment" to designate their units; e.g., 1st Marines refers to the 1st Marine Regiment.

U.S. Army structure
(to battalion level)

Unit	Size	Commanding officer
Division	12,000–18,000 troops or 3 brigades	Major General
Brigade	3,000 troops or 2-4 battalions	Colonel
Battalion*	600–1,000 troops or 3-5 companies	Lieutenant Colonel

* Squadron equivalent to battalion.

Names, Acronyms, Terms

ARVN—Army of the Republic of Vietnam. The army of South Vietnam.

battalion days in the field—days in which battalions were in the field patrolling. Used as a means of reporting battalions' efficiency in the war effort.

CAP—Combined Action Platoons. Pacification teams organized by U.S. Marines. Consisted of a South Vietnamese Popular Forces platoon that joined with a U.S. Marine rifle squad and a medical corpsman to form an enlarged platoon responsible for village security.

chickenplate—bulletproof breastplate.

CIA—Central Intelligence Agency.

CIDG—Civilian Irregular Defense Group. Project devised by the CIA that combined self-defense with economic and social programs designed to raise the standard of living and win the loyalty of the mountain people. Chief work of the U.S. Special Forces.

CINCPAC—Commander in Chief, Pacific Command. Commander of American forces in the Pacific region, which includes Southeast Asia.

COMUSMACV—Commander, U.S. Military Assistance Command, Vietnam.

CORDS—the Civilian Operations and Revolutionary Development Support, formerly the OCO, was established under MACV in 1967. CORDS organized all U.S. civilian agencies in Vietnam within the military chain of command. (See also OCO.)

COSVN—Central Office for South Vietnam. Arm of the North Vietnamese Communist party in South Vietnam.

DMZ—demilitarized zone. Established according to the Geneva accords of 1954, provisionally dividing North Vietnam from South Vietnam along the seventeenth parallel.

DRV—Democratic Republic of Vietnam. The government of Ho Chi Minh, established on September 2, 1945. Provisionally confined to North Vietnam by the Geneva accords of 1954.

dustoff—helicopter medical evacuation missions in Vietnam.

FMFPAC—Fleet Marine Force, Pacific Command. The U.S. Marines Pacific command.

free-fire zones—territory designated by the GVN to be completely under enemy control, thus permitting unlimited use of firepower against anyone in the zone. Such zones did not usually include densely populated areas.

GVN—government of South Vietnam. Also referred to as the Republic of Vietnam. Provisionally established by the Geneva accords of 1954.

Hop Tac—Vietnamese for "cooperation." Name of unsuccessful pacification program begun in 1964, concentrated in one seven-province area around Saigon.

JCS—Joint Chiefs of Staff. Consists of chairman, U.S. Army chief of staff, chief of naval operations, U.S. Air Force chief of staff, and marine commandant (member ex officio). Advises president, the National Security Council, and the secretary of defense. Created in 1949 within the Department of Defense.

KIA—killed in action.

limited conventional war—U.S. Department of Defense designation for conflict involving American units larger than four thousand men. Used by Pentagon to reclassify Vietnam War from a guerrilla war.

LOCs—lines of communication.

LZ—landing zone.

MACV—Military Assistance Command, Vietnam. Superseded the Military Assistance Advisory Group (MAAG), the U.S. military advisory program to South Vietnam begun in 1955 and dissolved in May 1964. First organized in 1962, MACV placed U.S. advisers in the South Vietnamese military.

MAF—Marine Amphibious Force.

MEB—Marine Expeditionary Brigade.

Mission Council—organized by U.S. Ambassador Maxwell Taylor, met weekly to coordinate activities among all U.S. agencies in Vietnam. After Henry Cabot Lodge replaced Taylor, OCO (later CORDS) oversaw Mission Council's function.

napalm—incendiary used in Vietnam by French and Americans both as a defoliant and antipersonnel weapon. Shot from a flame thrower or dropped from aircraft, the substance adheres while it burns.

NLF—National Liberation Front, officially the National Front for the Liberation of the South. Formed on December 20, 1960, it aimed to overthrow South Vietnam's government and reunite the North and the South. The NLF included Communists and non-Communists.

NSAM—National Security Action Memorandum. Presidential policy statements determining action on national security issues.

NVA—North Vietnamese Army. Also called the People's Army of Vietnam (PAVN) and Vietnam People's Army (VPA). North Vietnam's army, led by Vo Nguyen Giap.

OCO—Office of Civilian Operations. Created to have command responsibility over all civilian agencies operating in Vietnam, forming in effect a pacification high command, under jurisdiction of the U.S. Embassy. Transformed into CORDS in 1967. (See also CORDS.)

pacification—unofficial term given to various programs of the South Vietnamese and U.S. governments to destroy enemy influence in the villages and gain support of civilians for the GVN.

PFs—see RFs, PFs.

POL—petroleum, oil, and lubricants.

RD cadres—Revolutionary Development cadres. South Vietnamese who were trained to use Vietcong political tactics to carry out GVN pacification.

RFs, PFs—South Vietnamese Regional Forces and Popular Forces. Locally recruited South Vietnamese soldiers who were not a part of the regular army and remained living in their villages. Responsible for preventing guerrilla infiltration of villages after U.S. troops had conducted search and destroy operations and ARVN had conducted clearing operations. Sometimes called "ruff puffs" by U.S. troops.

slick—transport helicopter. Lacked guns, giving it a "slick" exterior.

Special Forces—U.S. soldiers, popularly known as Green Berets, trained in techniques of guerrilla warfare. In Vietnam, carried out counterinsurgency operations, many of them covert. Also trained South Vietnamese and montagnards in counterinsurgency and antiguerrilla warfare.

TAOR—tactical area of responsibility. A specific area of land where responsibility for security is assigned to the commander of the area. It is used as a measure for control of assigned forces and coordination of support.

USAID—United States Agency for International Development. Responsible for administering foreign aid in Vietnam from the early 1960s to 1972, USAID provided most of the funds to carry out the various pacification programs.

USIA—United States Information Agency. Established in 1953 with the purpose of international dissemination of information about the U.S. Overseas, the agency was referred to as the USIS (United States Information Service).

USIS—United States Information Service. See USIA.

USOM—United States Operations Mission. The name of the USAID mission in Vietnam. (See USAID.)

Vietcong—derogatory reference to a member of the NLF, a contraction of Vietnam Cong San (Vietnamese Communist). In use since 1956.

VNAF—Vietnamese Air Force (South).

war of attrition—approach to war with the goal of destroying enemy personnel and materiel faster than they can be replenished until the enemy's ability to wage war is exhausted.